THE DYNAMICS *of* BUSINESS CYCLES

THE DYNAMICS *of* BUSINESS CYCLES

A Study in Economic Fluctuations

By

JAN TINBERGEN

and

J. J. POLAK

THE UNIVERSITY OF CHICAGO PRESS

BASED ON *Economische Bewegingsleer*

BY PROFESSOR JAN TINBERGEN

FIRST PUBLISHED IN THE NETHERLANDS BY THE
NORTH HOLLAND PUBLISHING COMPANY, AMSTERDAM, 1942

THE UNIVERSITY OF CHICAGO PRESS, CHICAGO 37
Cambridge University Press, London, N.W. 1, England
W. J. Gage & Co., Limited, Toronto 2B, Canada

PREFACE

FIRST published in the Netherlands in 1942, *The Dynamics of Business Cycles*[1] was written by Professor Tinbergen on the basis of fifteen years of econometric work. This work consisted in a verification of the question whether certain observed changes in economic phenomena could be explained on the basis of economic theory. As a preliminary step to such verification, it was often necessary to give a more concrete form to existing theories. They had to be elaborated and to be put in a form in which they became susceptible of statistical verification. This book provides a systematic presentation of economic theory restated in this manner. It is distinguished from general economic textbooks primarily by the fact that attention is concentrated on the explanation of movements. Those economic laws which affect only the permanent features of the economy are not discussed. No place is given, moreover, to the exposition of actual methods of observation, such as statistical analysis, or to a description of individual business cycles in any particular country. The primary purpose of the book is to provide theory and, hence, to explain what is typical and common in economic movements.

One may query the usefulness of an explanation of past movements. In the first place, such an explanation is useful because of the possibility that past movements will repeat themselves in the future. Much more important is the knowledge acquired by such study concerning the operation of the economy. This knowledge is necessary both for a full understanding of the economy in situations different from those of the past and for the consideration of measures of economic policy.

The reader is assumed to have mastered economics; but, in

1. Professor Jan Tinbergen, *Economische Bewegingsleer* (Amsterdam: North Holland Pub. Co., 1942). The essence of this Preface is based on the Preface in the 1942 Dutch edition.

order to accommodate those economists who find it difficult to work through economics admixed with equations and symbols, this book has deliberately been so written as not to acquire any knowledge of mathematics on the part of the reader.

American economists who have wanted to inform themselves about Professor Tinbergen's numerous writings have been faced with another difficulty—many of these were not available in the English language. It is hoped that the American edition of *The Dynamics of Business Cycles*, which presents a summary of Professor Tinbergen's writings, will fill this gap.

The American edition follows very closely the original Dutch edition. In certain parts some historical material has been deleted, and chapter xi and a few sections have been entirely rewritten.

J. J. POLAK

WASHINGTON, D.C.
June 1949

TABLE OF CONTENTS

PART I. DESCRIPTION

PART III. BUSINESS-CYCLE POLICY

INDEX

PART ONE

DESCRIPTION

CHAPTER ONE

INTRODUCTION: TYPES OF MOVEMENTS

ELEMENTARY MOVEMENTS

THE objective of economic dynamics is to describe and explain the fluctuations in economic magnitudes. In this first part of our study we shall limit ourselves to description. This description can be assisted greatly by the use of diagrams in which the movements, or changes, of the various economic magnitudes are represented by certain geometric figures. For a good understanding of the various types of movements it is necessary to have a minimum general knowledge of the geometric properties of these diagrams quite apart from the economic phenomena which they represent. By way of introduction we shall start out with these geometric characteristics.

Before we can study the relationship between the movements of one magnitude and the movements of one or more other magnitudes, it will be necessary to give a description of the movements of individual economic magnitudes. It is in the nature of the object of our study that these magnitudes vary; they are "variable magnitudes," or, briefly, "variables." The movements of these variables are often complicated. There is considerable advantage in separating the movements into components of a simpler character, which we may call "elementary movements." These we shall study first.

a) Systematic and random movements

A distinction has to be made between systematic and random movements. In the case of systematic movements the numbers representing successive magnitudes of one variable follow each other according to a design. Any such design is, however, absent from the magnitudes of successive observations of random variables. Even in the very simple case in which the variable measured can have only two values (0 and 1) a distinction between systematic and random movements can be made. The following two series, for instance, represent systematic movements:

0, 0, 0, 1, 1, 1, 0, 0, 0, 1, 1, 1, 0, 0, 0, etc.
0, 0, 1, 0, 1, 0, 0, 1, 0, 1, 0, 0, 1, 0, 1, etc.

There is obviously an infinite number of systematic movements; more and more complicated systems of succession of the different values can be devised. As has been mentioned, in a random movement all design is absent in the way in which the successive values are arranged. Such a random movement will occur, for instance, when one tosses a coin and marks 1 for heads and 0 for tails. The results of an infinite repetition of this game will show random movements. A variable showing such movements is sometimes called a "random variable." A "normally distributed random variable" satisfies two conditions, namely, (1) there is no design in the succession of its values and (2) the various values satisfy the frequency distribution of the Gaussian law. The distribution under the Gaussian law, also called the law of normal distribution or of normal errors, may be expressed in a mathematical formula which is represented diagrammatically in the shape of a bell. In a normal distribution all possible values will occur—not only, as in the example just quoted, the values 0 and 1. In a normal distribution there will be a relatively large number of small deviations from the average and relatively few large deviations from the average. A normally distributed random variable will be obtained in more complicated games of chance in which the number of possible values is large, or, strictly speaking, in which the number of possible values is infinite. If, for instance, one were to toss not one coin but a hundred and were each time to count as the result of one game the number of heads that turned up, the result would approximate very closely the movement of a normally distributed random variable. In general, a variable will be a normally distributed random variable if its values are the sum of the values of a large number of random variables that are independent of each other. In nontechnical language, the variable will appear as a normally distributed random variable if its fluctuations are due to a great number of independent small causes. The larger the number of causes, the more will the series of successive values approximate the movement of a normally distributed random variable.

b) Monotonic and periodic movements

There exist a great many different types of systematic movements. Within the scope of this book there is no need for a detailed mathematical treatment of them. A variety of functions and curves is discussed by textbooks in analysis and analytical geometry. One distinction, however, is of great importance, namely, that between monotonic and periodic movements. A monotonic movement is one which never reverses its direction. It may be either monotonically increasing or monotonically decreasing. In the first case, each successive value is greater than, or in the limiting case equal to, the previous value; in the second case, each successive value is smaller than, or in a limiting case equal to, the preceding value. A periodic movement, on the other hand, repeats itself exactly after a certain lapse of time. This lapse of time is called its "period." We also include in the category of periodic movements nonmonotonic movements which repeat themselves after a certain period in an enlarged or reduced form, in a certain proportion which we may indicate by a. Such movements will be called damped and antidamped movements, respectively. The following would be an example of a purely periodic movement:

4, 8, 12, 4, 8, 12, 4, 8, 12, etc.

An example of a damped periodic movement would be the following:

4, 8, 12, 2, 4, 6, 1, 2, 3, etc.

In both cases the period is three units of time; in the second case the movement repeats itself on a reduced scale with $a = \frac{1}{2}$.

We shall have to analyze some special cases of these two types of movements in somewhat greater detail.

The simplest example of a monotonic movement is a straight

line. This line may either rise or fall, with the horizontal line as the intermediate case.

For a straight line the difference in level of two successive time units (years, quarters, or months) is always the same. This difference is called the "slope," or the "rate of increase." In accordance with mathematical usage we shall use the term "increase" also for declining lines, that is, for negative increases. A straight line has a constant rate of increase.

A second important example of monotonic movement is the exponential curve. A mathematical property of an exponential

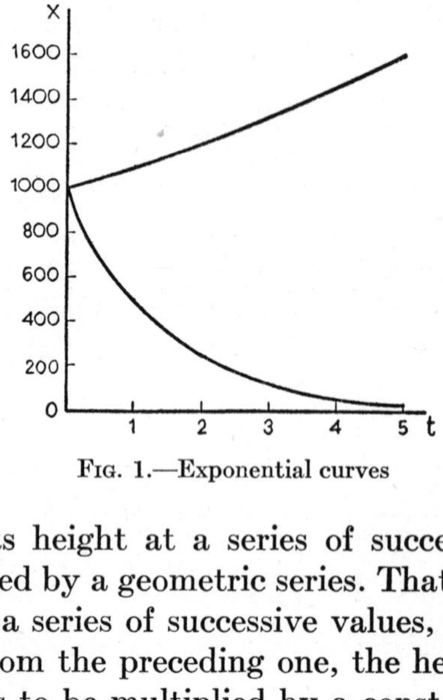

FIG. 1.—Exponential curves

curve is that its height at a series of successive equidistant points is indicated by a geometric series. That is to say that, in order to obtain a series of successive values, each at the same time distance from the preceding one, the height of the curve at each step has to be multiplied by a constant to obtain the next following step. Figure 1 shows two exponential curves. The first exponential curve is increasing. It is represented by the following figures:

Time t =	0	1	2	3	4	5	...
Height x =	1,000	1,100	1,210	1,331	1,464.1	1,610.51	...

The following series represents a declining exponential curve:

Time t =	0	1	2	3	4	5	...
Height x =	1,000	500	250	125	62.5	31.25	...

It will be noted that the slope, or rate of increase, of the exponential curve is not constant. It is proportional to the height attained by the curve. This may also be expressed by saying that the relative rate of increase is constant.

There are a number of other important monotonic movements. They cannot be treated without mathematical formulas. We mention here the parabolas of different degrees, represented by formulas of the form $x = at^n$, where n is the degree. These

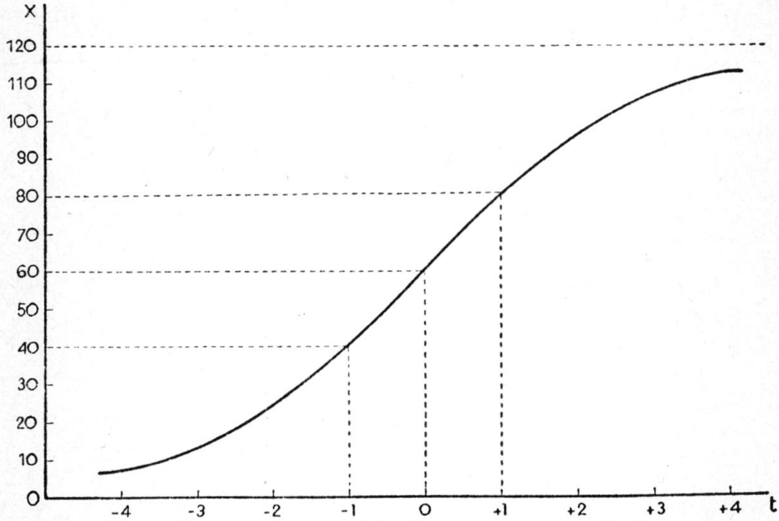

FIG. 2.—Logistic or growth curve ($a = 1$, $b = 2$, $k = 120$)

curves are monotonic for all positive values of t. Another monotonic curve of great importance is the logistic, or growth, curve: $x = k/(a + b^{-t})$. An example of the logistic curve is shown in Figure 2. A logistic curve will be described, for example, by the movement of a population, whose rate of growth per unit of time is proportional to (a) the size of the population already attained and (b) the size of the population for which, in addition to the population already present, means of subsistence are still available. The total means of subsistence are assumed to be such that a population of constant size can be maintained.

We count among the monotonic movements also certain movements that cannot be defined by one mathematical curve for the entire period of time but that are defined, for instance, first, by a rising straight line and, after a certain period, by a horizontal straight line.

A very simple type of periodic movement is the sine curve shown in Figure 3. As this diagram shows, the sine curve may be described as the distance from the horizontal axis of a point which moves at constant speed around the circumference of a circle. This distance is measured vertically while time is measured horizontally. The distance *AB* is called the period; the distances *CD* and *EF* are also equal to the period. Half the distance *AG* is called the "amplitude."

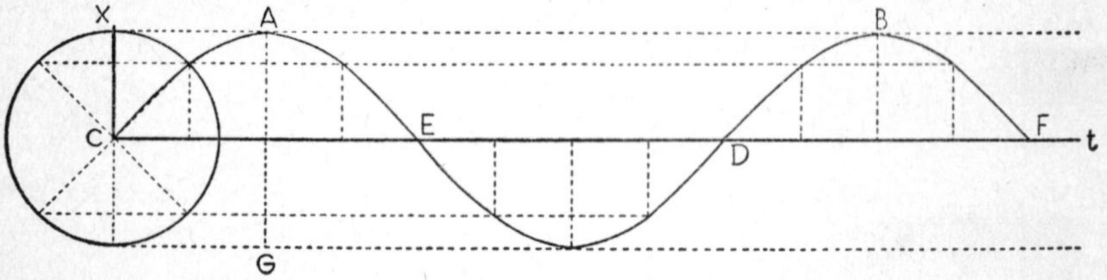

FIG. 3.—Sine curve (*C, A, E, D, B, F* . . .) indicating the distance from the horizontal axis of a point which moves around a circle with constant speed.

We shall often meet movements that are not exactly but approximately periodic in character. Such movements will show fluctuations repeating themselves approximately after roughly the same period. We shall sometimes refer to such movements as "fluctuating movements," or "fluctuations," or "waves." We may also call them "quasi-periodic movements." It should be noted here that random movements are also quasi-periodic. It may be proved that the quasi-period of these movements is three units of time, that is to say, that, on the average, one of every three values of such a series will be a peak and one a trough. The unit of time of such a series must be taken to be the distance between two successive independent observations.

c) Damped, undamped, and antidamped movements

As mentioned above, we include among the periodic movements those nonmonotonic movements that repeat themselves on an increasing or decreasing scale. We call periodic movements "damped" if each successive fluctuation is on a smaller scale than the preceding one, that is to say, if the factor a mentioned earlier is smaller than 1. The rate of damping is indicated by the fraction $1/a$. Movements which show antidamping are sometimes called "explosive movements." The purely periodic movement is undamped.

The same distinction can be made for exponential movements. If in an exponential movement the ratio between two successive values is smaller than 1, the movement is called damped; if the ratio is greater than 1, the movement is called antidamped, or explosive.

THE COMPONENTS OF COMPOSITE MOVEMENTS

The movements shown by most economic phenomena are much more complicated than any one of the simple movements we have discussed. First, any actual series will at most be an approximation of any one of the elementary movements considered above. Purely periodic movements, for instance, are rarely met in reality; in successive periods the shape of the movements repeats itself only approximately; often the period which one can distinguish is by no means constant. Second, actual series often represent combinations of elementary movements. We are using the mathematically rather vague expression "combinations" to cover not only the sum of elementary movements but also their product and in some instances even more complicated combinations. Whatever the mathematical nature of these combinations, all have in common the attribute that the actual movement can be constructed out of elementary movements.

Statisticians have adopted very generally the practice of separating the movements of economic variables into various elementary components before studying these components in further detail. In many respects this is a useful procedure; but a number of objections, to which we will refer below, can be made against it.

Normally, a series is decomposed into four components, as follows: (*a*) the trend component, which indicates the general tendency of the movement, and which usually is represented by a monotonic movement; (*b*) the cyclical component, consisting of fluctuations with a period of between three and eleven years; (*c*) the seasonal component, consisting of fluctuations with a period of one year, attributable to fluctuations of the natural and conventional seasons during the year; and (*d*) the random component, which covers both nonrecurrent changes, such as sudden changes in the level due to a "trend break," and fluctuations due to a large number of random causes, these latter fluctuations being usually of very short duration, e.g., those with a quasi-period of three months.

It is not advisable to apply this procedure mechanically, since there are many exceptions to the rule that these four components can be found in every economic series. We shall first mention a number of these exceptions and then treat the whole subject in a systematic manner.

Some fluctuations have a period in excess of eleven years. Among these should be counted the so-called "long cycles" and the fluctuations in certain individual markets. Depending on the subject and the period under consideration, such movements are classed under (*a*) or under (*b*); hence, a movement of type (*a*) cannot always be represented by a monotonic movement. There are, further, certain fluctuations which by their nature are equivalent to seasonal fluctuations but which have a shorter period, for instance, three months, a month, a week, or a day. On the other hand, random movements sometimes show quasi-periods that are considerably longer than three months. The fluctuations in crops, which must certainly to a large extent be considered as random, have a time interval of a year between two successive independent observations and hence may produce quasi-periods of three years. For these reasons it is often difficult to isolate components (*c*) and (*d*), or even (*b*) and (*d*), at all accurately.

On closer scrutiny, a variety of objectives may be discerned in the standard procedure. The first and clearest objective is to isolate movements with different periods. As a rule, all fluctuations with a period in excess of eleven years are comprised in the trend component. The monotonic movements of the trend component may be considered as parts of very long cycles or even of movements with an infinitely long period. All movements with a period of between one and eleven years are considered to be part of the cyclical component; those with a period of one year represent the seasonal component; and those with a period of less than one year, the random component. As mentioned above, however, it is sometimes difficult to classify the actual movements in accordance with this scheme.

A second objective in the standard procedure is the separation of systematic and random movements, discussed earlier.

The third objective would appear to be to obtain a classification according to the causes of the movements. The separation of seasonal movements and trend movements would reflect this objective. The trend movement, for instance, may often be ascribed to the very slow movements of such data as the size of the population, technical knowledge, etc.

A fully satisfactory decomposition of an economic variable into its various elements can be achieved only on the basis of a complete theory of economic movements. At this stage in our analysis, therefore, we can consider this decomposition only as a provisional tool. After having dealt with economic theory in the second part of this study, we shall in certain simple cases be able to give very definite directions with respect to the separation of the various elements (see chap. xvi). It will be shown that the systematic and random components are often combined in a very intricate fashion which renders it logically impossible to separate them in any simple way.

Here, as in the case of the separation of movements according to causes, a clear distinction between direct and indirect causes will have to be made. An example may make this clear. If fluctuations in the quantity demanded of a particular commodity are due to (*a*) changes in income and (*b*) changes in price, while the changes in price are due to (*c*) changes in the price of raw materials, then we call (*c*) an indirect cause of changes in the quantity demanded. On the other hand, (*a*) and (*b*) are considered direct causes.

It is often useful to isolate the components on the basis of the various direct causes; in such cases, however, indirect causes should be kept clearly separated from direct causes. The separation according to causes may not at all agree with the separation according to periods: one direct cause may be the origin of movements of different periods; one and the same period can occur in movements of different direct causes. In some instances the separation by causes and by periods may coincide. This will often be the case for seasonal movements that have both a special cause and a special period which does not coincide with the periods of movements due to other causes.

THE RELATIONSHIP BETWEEN THE MOVEMENTS OF TWO SERIES

Having discussed the various types of movements and the combination of these types of movements into one series, we shall now deal with the relationship that may exist between the movements of two series. These movements may be simple or composite.

We refer purposely to the relationship that *may* exist between the movements of two series. There need not be any relationship between them. The movements may be entirely independent. In reality there would usually be a certain degree of relationship. The examples treated below are the ideal case of a perfect relationship which can only be approximated in reality. Two series of figures show an exact relationship (or, in mathematical language, a functional relationship) if for any given value of the one series there is always a precisely defined value of the other series. Often no such precise relationship is present, but instead any given value of the one series is always found to be accompanied by approximately the same value of the other series. In statistics such a relationship is called a "stochastic relationship." In the following pages we shall discuss some of the most common functional relationships.

To indicate these relationships, we may make use of two types of diagrams: one shows the movement of the two series in time, preferably using the same time scale for both series; the other shows both series on a "scatter diagram." Such a diagram consists of a number of points in a rectangular system of co-ordinates. Each point has two co-ordinates, of which one, the x-co-ordinate, represents a value of the one series; and the other, the y-co-ordinate, the corresponding value of the other series. In such a diagram there are, therefore, as many points as there are values in each series. The time sequence of points cannot be traced in the diagram unless each point is labeled according to the time period to which it refers.

The simplest relationship between two series is that of equality. In that case the time diagrams of the two series cover each other in every point, if one adopts the same vertical scale for both series. In the scatter diagram, all points will lie on a straight line running through the origin at an angle of 45 degrees to both axes.

The next simplest relationship between two series is that of proportionality. In this case the time diagrams do not coincide, if the same vertical scale is used for both series. They can, however, be made to coincide by a special choice of the units for the vertical scale. If all figures of series Y are five times as large as those of series X, then the choice of the unit for Y at one-fifth of the unit for X will make the two series coincide. The scatter diagram still shows points on a straight line through the origin, but the slope of this line is now different. In this particular case the slope will be equal to a ratio of 5:1 (See Fig. 4).

One stage more complicated is the general linear relationship. In this relationship there is proportionality between the changes of the series but not between the absolute values of them; as a consequence, the ratio of the changes in the series is different from the ratio of their averages. The following two series give an example of this relationship:

X : 10, 12, 11, 14, 12, 13 (average 12), and
Y : 20, 22, 21, 24, 22, 23 (average 22).

Here the changes of the two series are equal, but the ratio of the averages is $\frac{12}{22}$, not $= 1$.

A second example is shown in Figure 5. The figure used in this diagram are as follows:

X : 10, 12, 11, 14, 12, 13 (average 12), and
Y : 20, 26, 23, 32, 26, 29 (average 26),

in which each change in Y is three times as large as the corresponding change in X, whereas the ratio of the averages of the

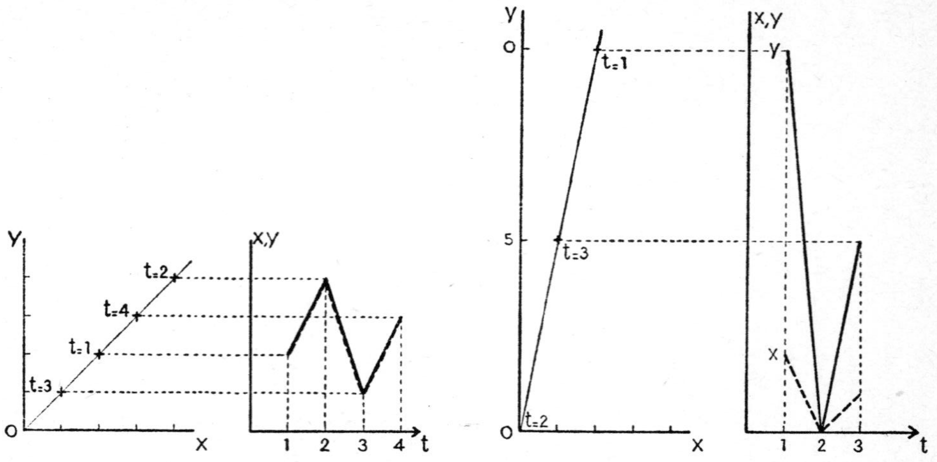

Fig. 4.—Equality (1st and 2d diagrams) and proportionality (3d and 4th diagrams) between X and Y. The first and third diagrams are scatter diagrams; the other two are time series.

two series is $26 \div 12$, obviously different from 3. If one wanted to make the graphs of these two time series coincide, it would not be sufficient to select different scales for them; it would also be necessary to draw the lines at different levels. In our first example it would be necessary to set the zero point for the Y series at the point -10 on the scale for X; in the second example it would be necessary to make the scale for Y one-third as great as the scale for X and, in addition, to set the zero point of the Y scale at the point $3\frac{1}{3}$ on the X scale.

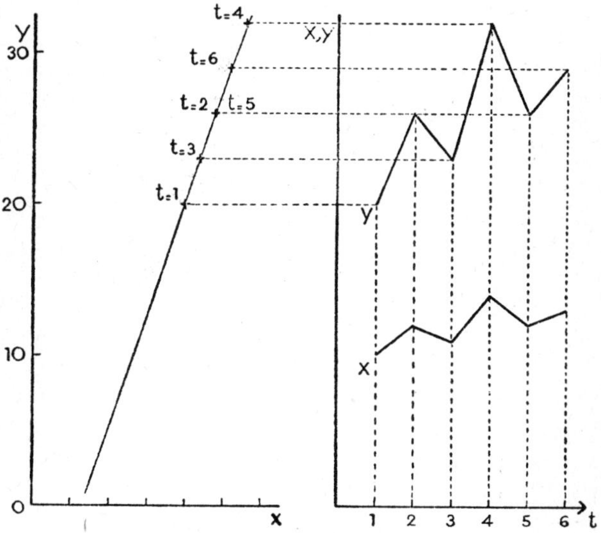

FIG. 5.—General linear relationship between X and Y

If two variables are related by a general linear relationship, it is sometimes said that their movement is parallel and also that there is a linear correlation between them. To distinguish this case from the one in which the relationship is only approximate in the stochastic sense, it is said that the correlation is perfect.

It will readily be realized that, depending on the absolute magnitudes of the fluctuations of the series and on their averages, one series may have larger absolute fluctuations while the other has larger relative fluctuations.

Equality, proportionality, and a general linear relationship may occur with a negative sign. In such instances the movements of the two series are in opposite directions.

The three forms of functional relationship discussed can all be represented by a straight line in a scatter diagram. We have discussed them in some detail because it will be found that they occur very frequently. There is, further, an infinite number of curvilinear functions that can be represented by other than straight lines in a scatter diagram. Curvilinear relationships can have many different shapes, depending on the nature of the relationship between the two variables. One example is given in Figure 6, which shows the relationship between the price, p, of a

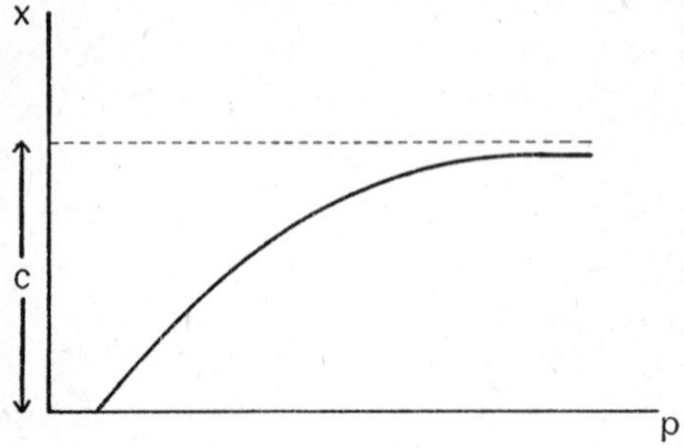

FIG. 6.—Example of a curvilinear relationship between two variables as represented by the supply curve (p = price, x = quantity supplied, and c = productive capacity).

commodity and the quantity supplied, x, on the assumption that there is a certain given productive capacity, c, and that no stocks are available. Starting from a relatively low price, every increase in price will initially produce a considerable increase in the quantity supplied. As the total capacity is approached, however, every further increase in the price by a constant amount will produce a smaller and smaller increase in the quantity supplied. The quantity supplied cannot exceed productive capacity and will approach this magnitude asymptotically; the horizontal line drawn at the distance c from the origin is called the "asymptote." In a time graph a curvilinear relationship of this nature will be recognized by the fact that the two series, though increasing and decreasing at the same time, show a pronounced difference in shape; the peaks in the p series will be much more pronounced and sharper than those in the x series. It will not be possible to make these series coincide by an appropriate adjustment of the scales. This phenomenon will, in particular, be encountered with respect to the prices and production of mineral raw materials in some periods of boom, when production bottlenecks occur.

We have so far discussed only the case in which the corresponding values of the two series referred to the same moment of time for the two economic magnitudes. If, however, there is a causal relationship between the two variables and if the process of causation which links Y to X takes a certain time, T, there would be good reason to compare the value of X at a given moment with the value of Y at a moment T later than the corresponding value of X; hence one would compare the value of X at time t with the value of Y at time $t + T$. If the two variables are plotted against time in the normal manner, the fluctuations of Y will be shown to be lagging behind those of X; by shifting the diagram of Y to the left over a distance T, the two series can be made to coincide again, provided that appropriate scales have been chosen for X and Y. Similarly, in the scatter diagram the co-ordinates should be chosen in such a way that the value of X at time t is combined with the value of Y at time $t + T$, in order to obtain points which lie on a straight line. In such instances we say that Y shows a lag with respect to X, or that the relationship between Y and X is a lagged relationship (Fig. 7).

In the case of two series with irregular movements, the presence of a lag can readily be observed empirically. If, however, the two series have monotonic movements, the lag is almost impossible to establish. If the movement is purely periodic, it is not possible to establish from the data the direction of the lag, that is, whether Y lags behind X or X lags behind Y, unless one has separate information concerning the order of magnitude of the lag.

Besides lagged relationships, many other relationships are possible between two variables in which time plays a role. A very common relationship in economic analysis is that of cumulation. Series Y represents the cumulation of series X, if the nth value for Y is equal to the sum of all values from 1 to n

for X. Hence, the first value for Y (Y_1) is equal to the first value for X (X_1); the second value, Y_2, equals $X_1 + X_2$; Y_3 equals $X_1 + X_2 + X_3$; Y_4 equals $X_1 + X_2 + X_3 + X_4$, etc. This relationship will occur, for instance, if Y represents the stock of a certain commodity, while X represents the excess of production over consumption for each time period. If X is gold production, then Y represents the total gold stock (assuming

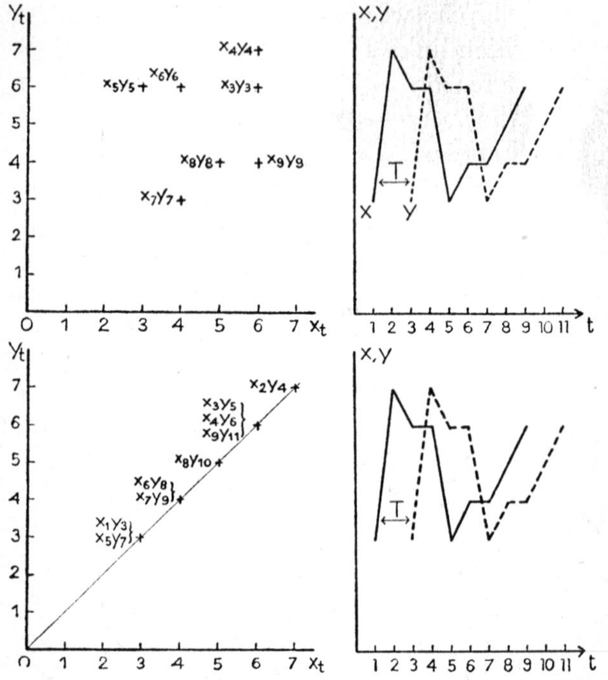

FIG. 7.—Example of a lag between two series X and Y. The top scatter diagram shows simultaneous value of X and Y; the bottom scatter diagram combines X_1 and Y_3, X_2 and Y_4, etc.

that the consumption of gold may be neglected); if X is the net increase of the number of houses during the year, then Y is the total stock of houses.

If X fluctuates, Y will fluctuate too. Normally, the fluctuations of Y will contain a trend component, unless the average value of X equals zero. If the series X is a sine curve with zero average, the Y curve will also be represented by a sine curve.

This may be proved mathematically and can also be seen from the following example computed on the basis of approximate values (compare Fig. 8):

t =	0	1	2	3	4	5	6	7	8	
X =	0,	0.7,	1,	0.7,	0,	−0.7,	−1,	−0.7,	0,	etc.
Y =	0,	0.7,	1.7,	2.4,	2.4,	1.7,	0.7,	0,	0,	etc.

Although Y also shows a sine curve, it is lagged in comparison to X; the peaks of Y are approximately one-fourth of the period of fluctuation behind those of X. Any numerical experiment will show that the cumulation of an irregular series will not reproduce a series of the same shape.

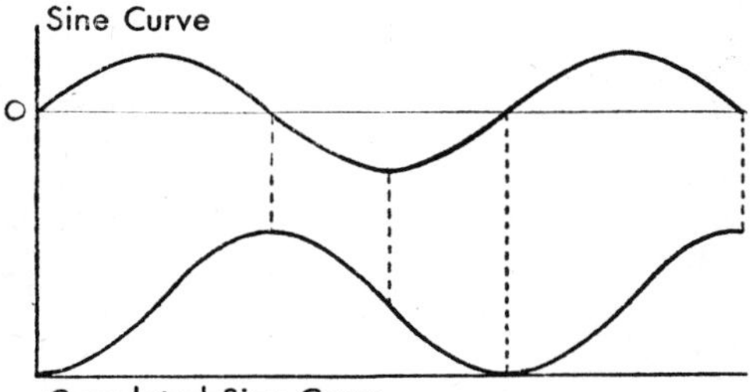

FIG. 8.—Sine curve and cumulation of sine curve

A purely empirical inspection of Figure 8 might lead one to believe that the relationship between X and Y was a lagged one, whereas in reality it is a cumulative relationship. Only theoretical knowledge of the real relationship between variables can prevent erroneous inductions of the type just mentioned.

THE RELATIONSHIP AMONG MOVEMENTS OF THREE OR MORE SERIES

In the preceding section we discussed the relationship between the movements of two series. The changes in two series will be exactly parallel when the changes in the one are caused by changes in the other and by nothing else. In the case of economic phenomena, however, fluctuations in one variable are usually due to fluctuations in more than one other variable. On this account it will normally not be possible to find a relationship between one of these causes and the variable in whose causation one is interested. Instead of the relationship between two variables, we will now have to have recourse to more complicated relationships. The simplest of these occurs when the values of one variable are equal to the sum of the simultaneous values of two other variables. The numerical example shown in Example I may make this clear; in each year the value of

EXAMPLE I

Year	1	2	3	4	5	6	7	8	9
Series *A*	0	+2	0	0	−2	−1	−1	+2	0
Series *B*	0	+2	0	+1	0	0	0	−3	0
Series *C*	0	0	0	−1	−2	−1	−1	+5	0

series *A* is equal to the sum of the values of series *B* and *C*. A relationship of this nature can graphically best be represented by time graphs. Figure 9 shows this for Example I. It will be noted that certain of the characteristics of series *B* and certain of those of series *C* can be found in series *A*. Thus, the first peak in year 2 can be traced back to series *B* and the second peak in year 8 to series *C*. The second peak is less pronounced in *A* than it is in *C* because it is in part offset by a trough in series *B*. The irregular depression in series *A* in years 5–7 is also found in series *C*. In short, series *A* shows the joint effects of series *B* and *C*. Neither series *B* nor series *C* can by itself explain series *A;* only their sum can explain it.

The relationship between series *A* which we want to explain and the explanatory series *B* and *C* can be much more complicated in many respects. To take a relatively simple case, it may be that series *B* and *C* require to be multiplied each by a certain coefficient before they are added up. An example of this is worked out below and is also shown in Figure 9, in which series A' equals $2\ B + \frac{1}{2}\ C$.

EXAMPLE II

Year	1	2	3	4	5	6	7	8	9
Series A'	0	+4	0	+1.5	−1	−0.5	−0.5	−3.5	0
2×series *B*	0	+4	0	+2	0	0	0	−6	0
½×series *C*	0	0	0	−0.5	−1	−0.5	−0.5	+2.5	0

It will be seen that the values of B are multiplied by 2 and those of C by $\frac{1}{2}$ in order to yield A' by addition. Graphically, the depression of A' in the years 5–7 can again be found in series C, and the peak in year 2 is now more pronounced in series B. A', however, has a peak in year 4 which A did not have and which is due to B; in the first example this peak was offset by a trough in C. In year 8 the greater influence of series B now dominates the peak in C; hence, there is a trough in A', whereas in our first example there was a peak in A.

It would be possible to cite many more complicated cases. In the examples given so far the relationships were additive, that

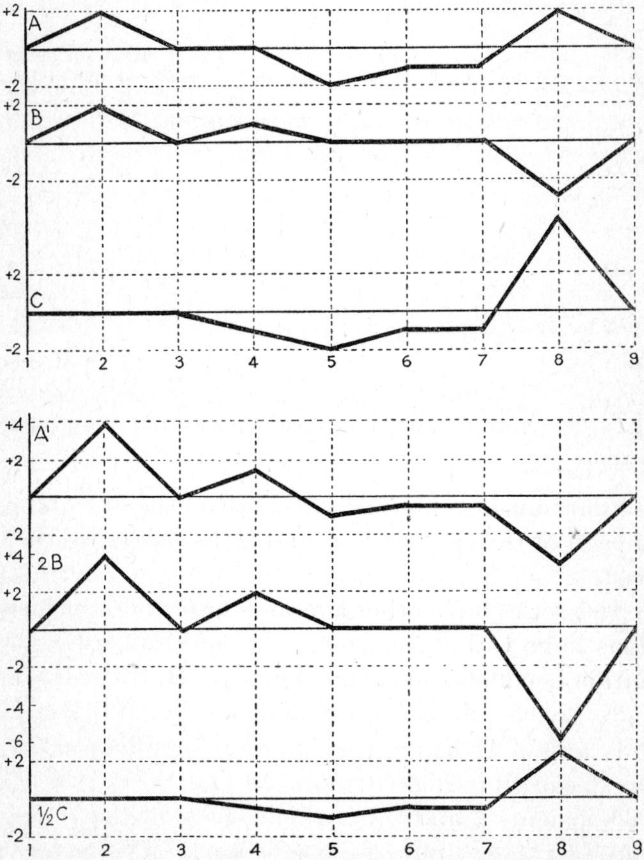

FIG. 9.—Examples of multiple correlation; $A = B + C$; $A' = 2\,B + \frac{1}{2}C$

is to say, A was obtained by the addition of B and C, A' by the addition of $2\ B$ and $\frac{1}{2}\ C$. Sometimes more complicated mathematical relationships (multiplicative, exponential, etc.) may prevail. It may, however, be proved that, for fluctuations that are relatively small in proportion to the average of the series, the more complicated operations will yield results only slightly different from the results of appropriate additions. Thus, for instance, the multiplication of two index numbers that deviate only slightly from 1, as shown in Table 1, may, with a high degree

TABLE 1

MULTIPLICATION OF TWO INDEX NUMBERS

Year	1	2	3	4	5	6	7	8	9
Series P	1.02	1.04	0.99	1.00	0.98	0.97	1.02	1.00	0.98
Series Q	1.01	0.99	.98	1.02	1.00	1.01	1.02	0.97	1.00
$P \times Q$	1.0302	1.0296	0.9702	1.0200	0.9800	0.9797	1.0404	0.9700	0.9800

TABLE 2

APPROXIMATION OF PRODUCT BY SUM

Year	1	2	3	4	5	6	7	8	9
Deviations:									
P	0.02	0.04	−0.01	0.00	−0.02	−0.03	0.02	0.00	−0.02
Q	.01	− .01	− .02	.02	.00	− .01	.02	− .03	.00
Sum	0.03	0.03	−0.03	0.02	−0.02	−0.02	0.04	−0.03	−0.02

of approximation, be replaced by adding to 1 the sum of the deviations of each of the two series P and Q, as shown by the figures in Table 2.

If the two series have other averages or if other mathematical operations have to be performed, the addition used as an approximation becomes somewhat different. But it will always be possible to give a suitable approximation by addition. For this reason, Example II has a very general significance. We shall therefore discuss it in slightly more detail.

The coefficients 2 and $\frac{1}{2}$ by which series B and C are multiplied may be called "influence coefficients." The series $2\ B$ and $\frac{1}{2}\ C$, given on the last two lines of Example II, are called the influence of B on A' and the influence of C on A'. If we desire to represent these influences by one single number, by which we may want to indicate whether the influence of B on A' is large or small, we can use for this number the average deviation of the standard deviation of $2\,B$ or $\frac{1}{2}\,C$, respectively, as is known from theoretical statistics. The theory of mathematical statistics provides an answer to the question of how to select the influence coefficients of the two series B and C in order to obtain as good an approximation as possible to any given series A''. This is of particular importance if we want to verify and give quantitative precision to a certain economic theory which would state that the movements of the variable A'' result from the movements of B and C but which does not indicate how large the relative influences are. This is the usual situation in economic theory, namely, that it can give qualitative but not quantitative indications about certain relationships. The coefficients found by the methods developed in theoretical statistics are usually called "regression coefficients." If A'' is exactly equal to the sum of a certain number times B and a certain number times C or, as we shall say, to the weighted sum of B and C (as is the case in Example I for series A and in Example II for series A'), then a perfect multiple correlation between A'', on the one hand, and B and C, on the other hand, is said to exist; if A'' is not exactly equal to the weighted sum of B and C for all periods of time, there is a certain degree of multiple correlation which may be expressed by the multiple-correlation coefficient. Reference is made to the textbooks on statistics for the conditions which have to be satisfied in order to estimate, with a stated degree of precision, regression coefficients on the basis of series of figures for A'', B, and C.

Example II, as shown in Figure 9, will be considered as the prototype of a multiple relationship among more than two variables. The number of explanatory variables need, however, not be limited to two; indeed, there may be any number. But, whatever their number, the explanatory series will always have to satisfy the condition that they must provide the explanation for the peaks and troughs in the series to be explained. Thus, not all the explanatory series can be straight lines. Applied to economic fluctuations, this would mean, for example, that it would not be possible to explain cyclical fluctuations on the basis of series which themselves show only a trend movement. This statement would not seem to be redundant since, for example, in certain theories the recovery phase of the business cycle has been attributed to an increase in the population. Yet this series shows almost exclusively a trend movement. Similarly, changes in labor productivity cannot provide an explanation for cyclical fluctuations, since for the economy as a whole labor productivity normally shows a straight line or only a very slightly curved line.

CHAPTER TWO

LONG-RUN DEVELOPMENTS

IN THE descriptive part of this book we shall, on the whole, follow the conventional decomposition of time series into their components, referred to in chapter i.[1] We start, therefore, with a description of the broad outlines of the development, that is, with the trend movement, and in this chapter describe the long-run economic development since the beginning of the nineteenth century.

POPULATION

The rapid economic growth during the nineteenth century may be shown first by reference to population figures. In the

TABLE 3

GROWTH OF POPULATION IN FOUR INDUSTRIAL COUNTRIES, 1800–1930

	Around 1800	1930
France (1930 territory)	28	42
Germany (1930 territory)	22	66
England and Wales	9	40
United States*	5	123

* The rapid increase was due partly to immigration.

course of the nineteenth century the population of the world increased very rapidly, mainly as a consequence of reduced mortality rates. The figures in millions in Table 3 give a clear indication of this movement.

Toward the latter part of the nineteenth century the rate of increase slowed down as a consequence of birth control. Al-

1. Cf. p. 9, *supra*.

though the curve of a population, calculated on the basis of its marriage rate, fertility rate, and mortality rate for different ages and changing with time, is by no means a simple curve, it can for most countries be represented with a very high degree of approximation by a growth curve and for the early part of the period by an exponential curve. For certain countries, such as Germany, however, this approximation does not yield satisfactory results. In Germany the rate of increase of the population has shown a notable upward change after 1870 and after 1933.

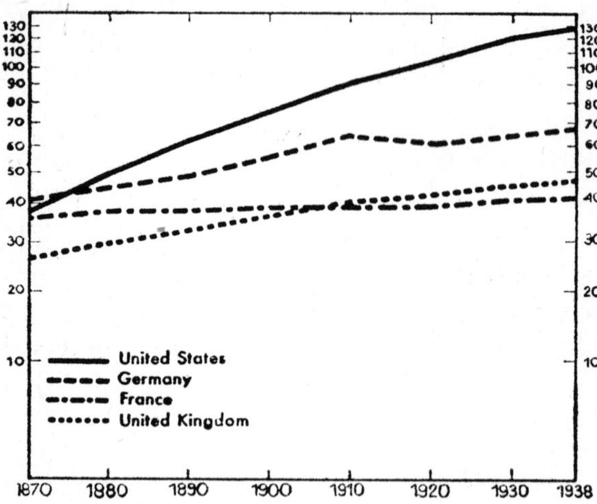

FIG. 10.—Population growth in the four largest industrial countries since 1870 (in millions).

Generally, however, the curves that indicate the growth of population are very smooth, as will be seen from Figure 10.

LAND

The availability of natural resources also increased in the nineteenth and, though in lesser degree, in the twentieth centuries. Most important in this respect was the opening-up of the natural riches of the United States. But in Europe, too, the area under cultivation, the capacity of mines, etc., increased. The same is true for other continents. A few of the available figures are shown in Figure 11.

PRODUCTIVITY

Running parallel with the increase of this factor of production, nature, and not always easily distinguishable from it, is the great increase in technical knowledge. This increase in technical knowledge showed itself not only qualitatively in the production of many new products. It also made itself felt quantitatively in that the same quantity of output was obtained by the use of smaller quantities of the factors of production. The fact of technical progress can easily be established if there is a reduction in the use of each of the factors of production;

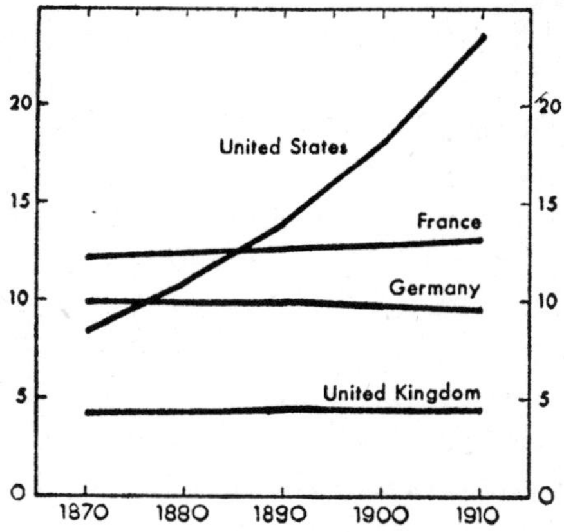

FIG. 11.—Growth of the quantity of arable land in the four largest industrial countries. (Value at prices of 1890 in billions of dollars.)

sometimes, however, a decrease in the quantity of labor may be accompanied by an increase in the quantity of capital used. If the increase in capital represents less sacrifice as measured by current prices than the decrease in the quantity of labor, there is a net reduction in sacrifice. It must be realized, nevertheless, that at a given state of technical knowledge, different production processes are always possible—different combinations of the factors of production which, at a given level of prices for the various factors of production, involve different costs. In the simplest case in which there are only two factors of production, labor and capital, all these combinations may be represented by points on a curve; the co-ordinates of each point indicate the quantities of labor and capital used per unit of product. All these points lie on one and the same "curve of technical possibilities." A switch from one of these possibilities to another may mean a reduction in total cost; yet it does not indicate technical progress. An exact definition of technical progress can therefore be given only as follows: Technical progress occurs when new combinations become possible that are cheaper than the cheapest combination possible before, at the given level of prices. One might also say that technical progress represents a change in the curve of technical possibilities, as a result of which a smaller quantity of one factor of production is necessary for any given quantities of the other factors of production.

There is no doubt that the quantity of labor per unit of product has on the whole gradually declined. In other words, the volume of output per unit of labor, or the statistical labor productivity, has increased. Between 1870 and 1914 this increase amounted roughly to the following percentages per annum: for Germany 1.8, for England 0.5, for France 1.1, and for the United States 1.1.

Very few figures, and on the whole rather defective ones, are available with respect to the quantity of capital and of natural resources used per unit of product and with respect to the development of these quantities over time. It would seem probable that the quantity of natural resources per unit of product, like the quantity of labor, has decreased and that the quantity of capital per unit of product has increased. It is possible, therefore, as Professor Douglas[2] believes, that there has been no real technical progress in the theoretical sense of the word. According to him the changes we observe are simply the forms in which labor and nature are replaced by capital; these are the previously unknown parts of the same "curve of technical possibilities." The mechanization of production (replacement of labor and nature by capital) would, according to Douglas, have taken place as a result of changes in relative prices: capital has become more abundant and thereby cheaper in relation to the other factors of production. Although this explanation is possible, it would seem to us more probable that actual technical progress has taken place.

2. Paul H. Douglas, *The Theory of Wages* (New York, 1924), pp. 209 ff.

The presence of capital in the form of capital goods with a long life-span leads to fixed costs that are practically independent of the volume of output. It is generally believed that the share of fixed costs in total costs has gradually increased. It is not easy, however, to find a statistical verification of this belief for production as a whole, and a recent study would rather tend to indicate that the reverse is true.[3]

THE STOCK OF CAPITAL

Population, natural resources of a country, and technical knowledge can generally be considered as data; but, for the quantity of capital goods available, this treatment is proper only in the short run. In the somewhat longer run the quantity of capital goods is dependent on economic activity itself and is therefore a variable to be explained by economic science. In the period under consideration the increase in the quantity of capital has been quite rapid. Before we give figures on this subject, we will have to dwell for a moment on the difficulties involved in the concept of "the quantity of capital goods." We consider as capital goods all commodities that have been produced and are to be used in further production. The stock of capital goods may be measured in different ways. A somewhat primitive way would consist in the counting of numbers and the weighing of physical quantities, for instance, counting the number of locomotives, ships, houses, and weighing the quantities of iron, stone, and timber incorporated in them. Such methods have great disadvantages. Some houses may be much larger than others. In weighing the quantities of raw materials used in their production, some allowance is made for this, but no account is taken of the fact that "one ton of iron" may represent commodities of quite different quality, such as iron bars or machines.

A less primitive method consists in measuring some aspect of

3. P. J. Verdoorn, *De Verstarring der Productiekosten* ("Increasing Rigidity of Cost of Production") (Rotterdam: Netherlands Economic Institute, 1943). Roughly speaking, this finding would be due to the fact that, although the quantity of capital per unit has increased and the quantity of labor (constituting chiefly variable-cost items) has decreased, their money values have moved proportionally because of the divergent price movements of the two factors.

the productive capacity of capital goods. Thus, one can measure the horsepower of a locomotive, the capacity of a ship, the number of rooms of a house. Obviously, this form of measuring is also not quite satisfactory. An old house and a new house with the same number of rooms do not have the same value. Moreover, this yardstick indicates only one aspect of the capital goods, whereas in reality more than one characteristic determines the importance of the capital goods for productive purposes. These measures fail in particular to reflect the depreciation which each capital good undergoes in the course of time.

All the various aspects of the significance of capital goods are reflected in their money value, as indicated either by the market price (for capital goods that have a current market) or by the book value. This measure also has its disadvantages, however. The value of money is not constant, and book values are often subject to peculiar considerations. The ideal method would be to distinguish a very large number of capital goods (one-year-old locomotives of type A, two-year-old locomotives A, three-year-old A's, etc.; locomotives B of all ages, etc.), evaluating them at the prices they have at some moment t and changing these valuations by means of the chain-index method. So far, however, insufficient data are available to apply this method.

The series in Table 4, computed by the Netherlands Central Bureau of Statistics, have therefore been based on a combination of the first and second methods of measurement, that is, measurement by number, size, or capacity.

The stock of capital goods of the categories indicated increased by more than 2.5 per cent per year for each of the countries shown, considerably faster than the increase in the population. This rapid increase was made possible by intensive saving. It may be assumed that in these countries over the period under consideration approximately 15 per cent of the national income was saved.

THE VOLUME OF OUTPUT

We shall now give some indication of the growth of some characteristic economic variables, starting with those of a physical nature. Within this group a distinction may be made between "flow" magnitudes and "stock" magnitude. Among the former we count such variables as production per year and consumption per year; among the latter, the stocks available at a certain moment of time. The most important general flow variable which would indicate the position of the economy as a whole is the total volume of production. A second very important variable is the total volume of labor performed, sometimes roughly indicated by the term "employment." Both variables have increased rapidly during the nineteenth century, the

TABLE 4*

AVERAGE INCREASE PER YEAR (IN PER CENT) OF CERTAIN CATEGORIES OF CAPITAL GOODS AND OF THE POPULATION, IN SIX COUNTRIES 1870–1910

	Germany	France	United Kingdom	Netherlands	United States	Sweden
1. Livestock	1.0	0.4	0.4	0.8	1.6	1.0
2. Industry	6.2	6.2	4.5	5.0	5.8	9.7
3 Railroads	2.9	2.5	1.5	1.9	3.2	5.3
4. Commercial fleet	4.8	2.0	3.5	3.5	2.5	3.7
5. Houses	0.6	0.4	1.5	1.2	2.5	0.9
6. Weighted average†	3.7	3.1	2.8	2.6	3.8	4.6
7. Population	1.1	0.1	0.9	1.2	2.1	0.7

* Netherlands Central Bureau of Statistics, *Maandschrift*, 1942, p. 113.

† Weighted in accordance with the importance of the five series in the national wealth around 1910 of the countries concerned.

former more rapidly than the latter on account of the increase in labor productivity. Employment would show a greater rate of increase if it were expressed in the number of days worked rather than in the number of hours worked, as the average working day has been considerably reduced. Even the number of hours worked has increased considerably. It should be noted that neither of the two measurements takes into account any possible changes in the intensity of labor. This magnitude, however, would be very difficult to define and even more difficult to measure, and opinions differ greatly as to its changes over time.

In the four main industrial countries the annual rate of increase of production between 1870 and 1914 was as shown in Table 5.

The rate of increase has not been constant. Thus, for British industrial production (excluding building) the average rate of increase over different periods has been estimated to have been as shown in Table 6. The development of a few index numbers of activity is shown graphically in Figure 12.

An important distinction in the series for total production is that between consumers' goods and investment goods. As shown by the figures in Table 7 for the United Kingdom over the last

TABLE 5

ANNUAL RATE OF INCREASE OF PRODUCTION IN FOUR INDUSTRIAL COUNTRIES, 1870–1914

	Per Cent
United States	4.1
Germany	3.4
England	1.6
France	1.5

TABLE 6*

ANNUAL RATE OF INCREASE OF INDUSTRIAL PRODUCTION IN THE UNITED KINGDOM, BY PERIODS

	Per Cent per Annum
1700–1780	0.9
1781–1913	2.8
1819–1913	2.6
1855–1913	2.0
1923–35	1.9

* W. Hoffmann, *Wachstum und Wachstumsformen der englischen Industriewirtschaft von 1700 bis zur Gegenwart* (Jena, 1940), p. 28.

two centuries, the latter series has increased at a faster rate than the former. These figures reflect the fact that capital per unit of product has increased. Since the production of investment goods is not of direct consequence for the satisfaction of human needs, the series of the production of consumers' goods is a better indicator of the development of human well-being than is the series of total production. A simple and useful indicator of the movement in the physical basis of human well-being is found in the volume of production of consumers' goods per capita per year. All available figures indicate that this series

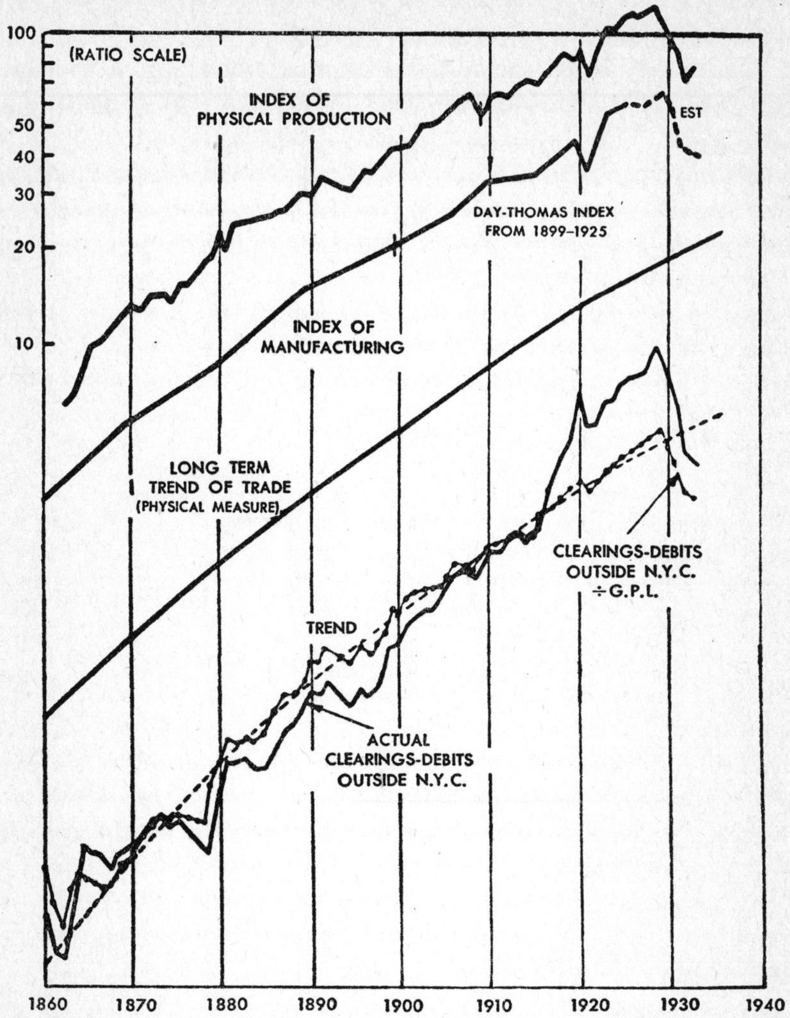

FIG. 12.—Rate of growth of production and activity in the United States. Source: Carl Snyder, "Commodity Prices versus the General Price Level," *American Economic Review*, XXIV (September, 1934), 394. (The three lower curves show [*a*] the dollar value of bank clearings and, for later years, bank debits outside New York City; [*b*] the same series deflated by an index of the general price level; and [*c*] a trend fitted to the deflated series.)

has also increased, although obviously at a slower rate than has the total production of consumers' goods.

Side by side with the series of production, those of the foreign trade of the various countries deserve attention. Until the first World War the development of international trade was somewhat more rapid than the development of production. This would reflect a tendency toward increasing international division of labor. Since World War I there has been a reaction to this development.

On the whole, less is known concerning the stock variables than concerning the variables indicating flows. We have already given some indications concerning the development of the

TABLE 7*

NET VALUE OF PRODUCTION OF INVESTMENT-GOODS INDUSTRIES IN PER CENT OF THAT OF TOTAL INDUSTRY IN THE UNITED KINGDOM, 1740–1924

1740	16	1881	47
1783	29	1907	58
1812	31	1924	53†
1851	40		

* W. Hoffmann, *Wachstum und Wachstumsformen der englischen Industriewirtschaft von 1700 bis zur Gegenwart* (Jena, 1940).

† On the basis of later data it can be ascertained that this reduction was only temporary.

stock of capital goods. Some information is available further, concerning the stocks of raw materials. Generally speaking, these stocks have increased less rapidly than the corresponding figures on production; this would indicate a certain rationalization in the use of inventories, made possible in part by more rapid means of communication and in part by improvements in the technique of production.

PRICES

After the physical magnitudes, we consider prices. Over the last century and a half, nominal or money prices do not show any pronounced general trend, but their movement shows very characteristically the so-called "long waves." If one considers prices over much longer periods than those we study here, a pronounced upward movement can be clearly observed from available fragmentary data on prices in past centuries.

In the nineteenth and twentieth centuries, however, no such tendency can be spotted; in fact, there are some indications of a falling long-run trend for prices of finished industrial products; but the validity of any price comparison of industrial goods over long periods of time is greatly affected by the qualitative improvement of many commodities. Long waves in prices are shown clearly by the fact that most price series show

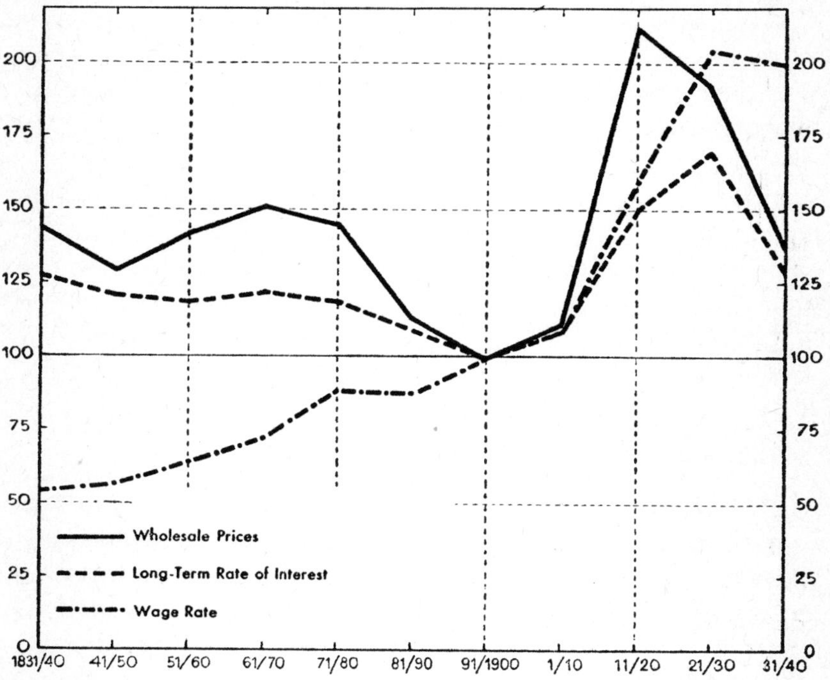

FIG. 13.—Long-run development of certain price series for the United Kingdom (1891–1900 = 100).

a peak around 1810, another one around 1873, and one around 1920; and troughs in 1850, 1896, and 1933 (see Fig. 13). The first peak comes shortly after the period of the Napoleonic Wars, the second one after the Franco-German War and the American Civil War, and the third one after the first World War. The first and the last one of these peaks were no doubt in part caused by the inflation associated with these war periods; for the peak of 1873 this is not so certain.

If, however, no definite trend can be discerned in the movement of nominal prices, a pronounced trend can be seen in relative prices. In particular, the ratio of the wage rate to the general price level has increased almost without interruption, if one abstracts from cyclical fluctuations. The real wage rate, in other words, has increased considerably. There is no pronounced tendency in the ratio between the rate of interest and the general price level. The long waves also show up in the movements of the rate of interest, in particular in the long-term rate.

FINANCIAL DEVELOPMENT

We may refer, further, to the developments of certain money amounts which are characteristic of the economy. We start with money flows and deal subsequently with money stocks. Important flow series are the value of national income and the shares of it accruing to the various factors of production. For practically all countries both total national income and its various components—income from labor, from capital, and from land—show a very pronounced tendency to increase. Even after allowance is made for changes in the general level of prices and for the increase of population, the series still show an ascending tendency, indicating a tendency for real income per head to increase. It is remarkable that the proportion of income going to the various factors of production has changed very little. The figures given for these proportions depend to some extent on the definitions and the methods of calculation chosen, and these are not the same for all countries; for the two countries, however, for which the most impressive amount of information is available—the United Kingdom and the United States—the percentage of income that goes to labor is remarkably similar and, at least in the United Kingdom, appears to have remained at nearly the same level for over a century (Table 8).

Among the stock variables in terms of money, national wealth and money and banking figures may be mentioned in particular. Here again all figures indicate a very pronounced upward trend. The figures shown in Table 9 refer to the period 1870–1910 which, although representing only a fraction of the total period from 1800 to the present, is in many respects the most characteristic period of an undisturbed process of growth. More statistical data are available for this period than for earlier years, and certain comparisons are therefore possible which cannot be given for longer periods.

During this period national wealth apparently increased at approximately the same rate as national income, but for both

TABLE 8

NATIONAL INCOME AND ITS DISTRIBUTION

UNITED KINGDOM
(Billions of £)

	1843	1913	1938	1946
1. Total national income	0.52	2.17	4.67	7.97
2. Labor income	0.33	1.36	2 92	5.22
3. (2) as per cent of (1)	*63*	*62.5*	*62.5*	*65.5*

UNITED STATES
(Billions of $)

	1850	1910	1938	1946
4. Total national income	2.21	30.5	67.4	178.2
5. Labor income	1.76	22.5	44.7	116.8
6. (5) as per cent of (4)	*80*	*74*	*66.5*	*65.5*

TABLE 9

FINANCIAL DATA CONCERNING THE FOUR LARGEST INDUSTRIAL COUNTRIES IN 1910
(Index Numbers, 1870=100)

	Germany	France	United Kingdom	United States
National income	....	182	194	454
National wealth	....	154	183	572
Gold stock of central bank	235	378	177	....
Total gold stock in country	....	....	160	1185
Note circulation	273	257	121	386
Total money supply	....	....	190	865
Foreign investments	710	306	271	*

* No figure shown, as in 1870 the United States was still a debtor country.

series the differences between countries were pronounced, the rate of increase being fastest in the United States and slowest in France. The development of the various components of national wealth was also quite divergent. The value of land in the national wealth of England decreased, whereas in Germany and France it remained approximately the same. On the other hand, the value of foreign investments increased greatly, well in excess of the increase in total wealth; but wealth in the form of domestic capital goods also showed a considerable increase during the period.

TABLE 10

DEVELOPMENT AND COMPOSITION OF MONEY SUPPLY IN THE UNITED STATES, 1860–1940*

	In Billions of Dollars			In Per Cent of Total		
	1860	1900	1940	1860	1900	1940
Gold coin	0.21	0.61	0.00	31	8	0
Other currency	0.23	1.47	7.85	33	21	14
Total currency	0.44	2.08	7.85	64	29	14
Demand deposits	0.25	5.11	33.17	36	71	58
Time deposits			15.80			28
Total	0.69	7.19	56.82	100	100	100

* Currency in circulation outside Treasury and Federal Reserve banks; deposits of all banks, excluding mutual savings banks. Deposit figures do not include interbank and U.S. government deposits.

The figures relating to monetary and banking statistics also show great increases. They show, further, important shifts among the various components with differences among countries which are much more pronounced than those in the field of production.

Most complete data are available for the United Kingdom. In this country the gold stock at the central bank increased much more rapidly than that of the country as a whole, indicating a concentration of gold in the central bank. The note circulation increased less than either of the two gold series and also less than total money supply, clearly indicating a substitution of deposit money for currency. This same tendency is also clearly shown by the figures for the United States in Table 10.

Whereas in the United Kingdom the money supply increased at approximately the same rate as the national income, it increased much faster than the national income in the United States, indicating apparently a relative extension of the money economy during the period.

In France, as in the United Kingdom, the note circulation decreased relative to the gold stock, whereas in Germany it increased.

In addition to banking statistics, it would be of great interest to have figures concerning the entire money and capital markets, including, for instance, the total value of bonds outstanding at various periods. With the exception of public debt data, however, this information is not available for most countries.

TABLE 11

TOTAL PUBLIC DEBT IN BILLIONS OF NATIONAL CURRENCY

	1870	1910	1930
Germany	0.4	5.0	10.4
France	12.3	32.8	480
United Kingdom	0.80	0.76	7.6
United States	2.44	1.15	16.2

Public debt figures show very clear differences between periods of peace and periods of war. As shown by the figures in Table 11, the total public debt was much larger in Germany and France in 1910 than it had been in 1870, whereas it declined during that period in the United Kingdom and the United States. From 1910 to 1930, however, the figures show an increase for all four countries.

CHANGES IN TREND AFTER WORLD WAR I

Public debt figures are not the only ones that show a different development since the first World War. In many other respects there was a change in trends. But the many disturbances to which the economies of most countries were subjected in the postwar years make it particularly difficult exactly to discern the new trends. It would seem that the previous tendencies to grow continued but became less regular and less intensive, in any case with respect to the older industrial countries. On the other hand, in the U.S.S.R., in Latin America, in Japan, and in a number of other countries the development was rapid. The links between the various countries became on the whole somewhat looser, and as a consequence the general picture became less homogeneous. Economic nationalism put many obstacles in the way of increasing world trade, and tendencies in this direction were reinforced by the great depression. International trade declined somewhat in proportion to world production. Similarly, the significance of foreign investments declined. As a consequence of the many disturbances in the economies of various countries, the cyclical and incidental movements tended to dominate the long-run tendencies of growth which were so clearly visible in the period from 1870 to 1910. In a description of the interwar period, cyclical and incidental movements are of much more significance than the long-run trend; it is for this reason that we have confined ourselves in this chapter mainly to the period before World War I.

CHAPTER THREE

INTERRUPTIONS AND SUDDEN CHANGES IN STRUCTURE

FROM time to time interruptions occur in the relatively regular pattern of growth described in the preceding chapter. Particularly important interruptions are caused by periods of war and inflation, while nation-wide strikes, floods, or earthquakes cause interruptions that are usually relatively less important. We use the term "interruptions" purposely, because normally after the termination of the period of an interruption the tendencies of the preceding period are resumed. The old structure, however, is never fully restored; there are always some lasting consequences of an interruption.

Certain other events have as their main consequence not a temporary but a lasting change in the economy. Here we do not refer to the gradual changes that occur continuously and the most important of which have been described in the preceding chapter; we refer, in particular, to the rather sudden changes in the structure of the economy which occur from time to time, the more revolutionary changes which take place in a relatively short time, usually after a time of great internal tension—war, inflation, crisis. We shall indicate the economic aspects of such changes by the term "sudden changes in economic structure."

PERIODS OF WAR AND INFLATION

The most important periods of war in the nineteenth and twentieth centuries which have interrupted the regular process of economic growth were the period of the Napoleonic Wars (with the inflation of the assignats), the American Civil War (1861–65), during which the inflation of the greenbacks occurred, and the first and second world wars, both of which were accompanied by world-wide inflation. The Franco-German War (1870–71), which occurred shortly after the Civil War, as well as most of the other numerous wars which occurred during this long period, may be considered as of more local importance in duration and intensity. Wars themselves cannot be attributed fully to economic causes; on the other hand, a certain connection between wars and economic causes cannot be denied. Some authors have seen a link between the frequency of the occurrence of wars and the phase of the long waves, with wars more frequent in the ascending phase of a long wave and culminating in a large conflict at the crest of the long wave. It would seem at least doubtful whether the occurrence of World War II fits this theory.

Although, as has been said, the tendencies prevailing before a war will to a large extent be resumed after it has ended, each war has a number of lasting consequences. The increase in the public debt will lead, at least for a considerable time, to increased expenditure of interest and amortization. Expenditure for veterans, war widows, etc., will also continue for a long time. One of the lasting effects of World War I was the loss of foreign investments suffered by France in particular as a consequence of the annulment of all Russian debts. The loss of foreign investments and the increase of indebtedness of the main European creditor countries in World War II are more important examples of the same tendency. Wartime increases in the price level usually persist to a considerable extent after the war. Thus after World War I and up to 1929 the cost of living and the wage rate in terms of gold remained in most countries at approximately 60 per cent in excess of the prewar level. In countries where prices in national currency had increased much more than that, there were also permanent adjustments of the rate of exchange. The French franc depreciated to approximately 20 per cent of its prewar value after World War I, and the value of the German mark declined practically to nil. Sterling and the currencies of a number of neutral countries, however, returned to their prewar par value. Some of the shifts in income distribution, in particular the reduction in the share of those who were hit by severe inflation, also tended to remain after the end of the war.

Besides these more or less permanent changes brought about by World War I, there were many and important ones that proved only temporary. The abnormal state of public finance was overcome, even though with difficulty; rationing and cost-of-living subsidies disappeared; the backlog of residential construction was worked off, slowly in one country, faster in another; international trade was resumed to a large extent; and markets lost during the war were recovered. Even though absolute prices did not return to their prewar level, most relative prices did, and rates of real income approached their prewar level.

THE PERIODS OF INFLATION AFTER 1914 IN GERMANY AND FRANCE

The preceding remarks referred in particular to the periods of war. The periods of inflation, of which those of Germany and France after World War I may be quoted as an example, are of sufficient importance to be treated here in somewhat more detail. The period of active inflation in Germany started only after the end of the war. During the war the money supply and the price level had risen considerably but not excessively, considering the general situation. The rate of exchange of the mark in foreign markets had approximately been maintained. After the end of the war, however, a process of inflation started for which history knows no precedent.[1]

Despite the end of the war, government expenditure in Germany continued at a high level, due in part to the desire to subsidize the first necessities of life, in part to the reparations obligations of the Treaty of Versailles, and in part to extensive new social provisions which had been promised and without which a stable political situation appeared impossible. Finally, in 1923 the occupation of the Ruhr by France caused a wave of new large expenditures, among them indemnity payments to enterprises in the Ruhr area. In order to finance this level of

1. The inflations in Greece in 1944 and in Hungary in 1945–46 were of the same order of intensity.

expenditure, recourse was had to the banknote press to a very large extent.[2]

As a consequence of the inflationary pressure, the level of prices rose and so did the rate of exchange for the dollar; at some stages the first, at some stages the latter, was the higher. With certain interruptions this process of inflation lasted until November, 1923; by that time the increase both in prices and in the rate of the dollar was of the order of magnitude of one trillion (10^{12}). With the increase in prices, wage rates and share prices increased, although not fully proportionately. For a considerable time the prices of domestic commodities increased less than the rate of exchange and the prices of foreign commodities, although toward the end of the period of hyperinflation opposite tendencies made themselves felt, and the mark tended actually to become overvalued when it fell most rapidly. Share prices rose considerably less than commodity prices.

TABLE 12

THE GERMAN PRICE STRUCTURE IN HYPERINFLATION
PRICES IN TERMS OF GOLD, SEPTEMBER, 1923
(1913=100)

World:	
Wholesale prices	150
Germany:	
Wholesale prices	100
Cost of living	75
Real-wage rate	75
Share prices	20

* C. Bresciani-Turroni, *The Economics of Inflation* (London: Allen & Unwin, 1937), p. 41.

The figures in Table 12, expressed in gold, indicate the approximate position in September, 1923. The money supply increased but not in proportion to the price of gold; hence the gold value of the circulation decreased considerably. Since incomes in terms of gold declined by a moderate amount, the velocity of circulation of money increased very considerably. By the end of the inflation period, this velocity had risen to

2. In the period from 1914 to October, 1923, receipts from taxes were twenty-one billion gold marks, from loans fifty-three billion gold marks, and from the issue of Treasury paper (reflecting, on the whole, credit creation by the central bank) fifty-nine billion gold marks. There was futher large-scale credit creation by the private banking system.

ten to seventeen times the prewar figure. Toward the end of the period the fear of a further depreciation of money was so great that income was spent almost as soon as it was received.

In the period 1914–18 (the war period), as well as in the period 1920–21 when the government also issued large amounts of floating debt, the increase in the circulation was the leading factor in the inflation. In the periods 1918–20 and 1921–23, on the other hand, the depreciation of the mark, caused in part by speculation against it, was the dominating phenomenon.

Different periods may indeed be distinguished, with one phenomenon increasing more rapidly in one period and another in another period. If we indicate the money supply by M, the price level by p, and the rate of exchange of the dollar by r, the

TABLE 13

LEADING FACTORS IN GERMAN INFLATION, 1914–23

	Most Rapid	Intermediate	Least Rapid
1914–18	M	p	r
1918–July, 1919	r	M	p
July, 1919–February, 1920	r	p	M
February, 1920–May, 1921	M	p	r
May, 1921–December, 1923	r	p	M

order of the rate of increase may be indicated as shown in Table 13.

The extreme changes in the monetary sphere also produced certain consequences in the commodity sphere. Through the end of 1922 employment rose to the absolute maximum; by the middle of 1922 unemployment amounted to only 0.6 per cent, an extremely low figure. After that an increase occurred, and by 1923 the unusually high figure, for that time, of 6 per cent was reached. Compared to 1913, production was at no time unusually high, since labor productivity was affected unfavorably by the low consumption level of the workers and by political tension; the large backlogs of orders, however, indicated that production was practically at capacity.

The production of investment goods in particular was stimulated; shipbuilding may be mentioned as one of a number of examples in this connection. Entrepreneurs, who made large profits and were afraid of the loss of value of money, invested heavily in capital goods. Many of these investments turned out to be useless after the end of the inflation period. Hyperinflation compressed the demand for consumption goods, and there was an important transfer of labor from the consumption goods industries to the investment goods industries.

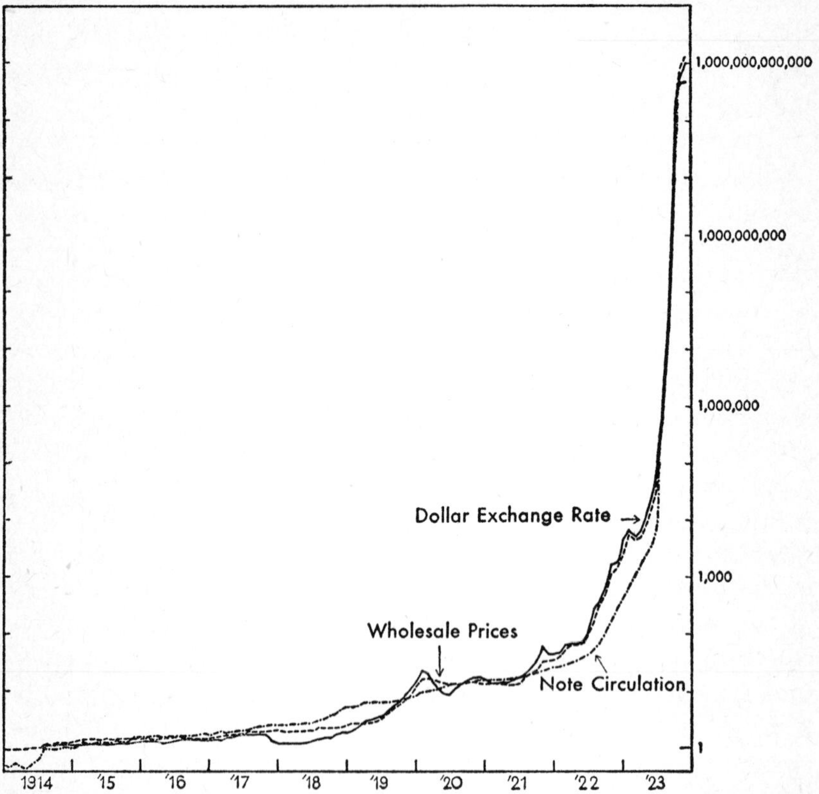

FIG. 14.—Curves showing the course of inflation in Germany, 1914–23. Logarithmic scale, August, 1914 = 1.

The quality of the commodities produced declined also. According to an index computed by the *Frankfurter Zeitung*, the quality of production had fallen to 64 per cent of the April, 1921, figure by October, 1923; after the stabilization of the mark, in April, 1924, it reached 124 per cent of the 1921 value.

Figure 14 shows a few salient series of the German inflation process. Clearly, this was a unilateral process which did not in itself lead to a reversal. The process was reversed from the outside as the social intolerability of inflation produced forces, by no means only economic forces, that terminated it. The attempts to stabilize the currency by the end of 1923 were not in advance certain of success. They were entirely experimental. The experiment succeeded; the mark was stabilized at one-trillionth of its original gold value, and a new currency unit, the Reichsmark, was introduced with a gold parity equal to that of the mark.

The postwar inflation in France was in intensity not comparable to that in Germany, but by normal standards of strong financial countries it was doubtless quite serious: the final stabilization in 1928 reduced the French franc to 20 per cent of the 1914 parity. As one of the victors of the war, France was in a somewhat better position than Germany; but the financial and economic problems she had to face were also very difficult. A considerable part of the country had been invaded during the war; heavy expenditures were made both during the war and afterward in connection with the service of the public debt, pensions, and social policies. There was much uncertainty concerning the economic future and in particular concerning the ultimate fate of the franc. In the process of inflation in France, as in Germany and in many other European countries, various factors were leading at various times.[3] A first impression of this is given by Figure 15, which indicates the index number of prices in terms of francs, the money supply, world prices in terms of dollars, and the rate of exchange of the French franc against the dollar. The comparison is easier for France than for Germany because the movements reverse themselves, and differences between the curves may easily be distinguished. During the war, when France was to some extent isolated from other countries and the French balance of payments was supported by English and American credits, the rate of exchange of the dollar did not change greatly, and the movement of prices was determined mainly by the money supply and tended to be proportional to it. After the war there was a short period during

3. A. Aftalion, *Monnaie, prix et change* (Paris: Recueil Sirey, 1927).

which price movements in those countries that remained on the gold standard or had relatively little depreciation were so strong that they also dominated French prices. This was the period of the strong price increase in 1919–20, followed by the sharp fall in 1920–21. In this period the typical cyclical phenomena dominated. The money supply did not determine but followed the fluctuations in prices, though less than proportionately, with

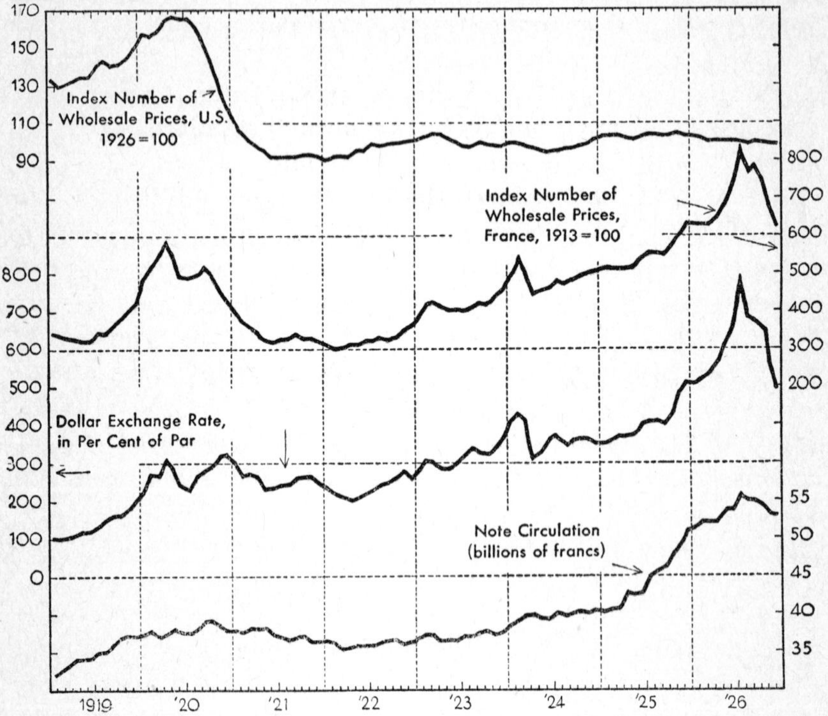

FIG. 15.—Curves showing the course of inflation in France, 1919–26

an increase of the velocity of circulation during the recovery period and a fall during the crisis and depression.

The disproportionality between the price level and the money supply continued in the period 1922–24, as fluctuations in the circulation lagged behind the fluctuations of prices by about five months in 1920–21 and by about one month in 1922–24. The latter period shows a high correlation between the price of the dollar and the price level of commodities. To obtain a good correlation for the entire period 1920–24, account must also be taken of the changes of prices in the United States. A comparison has then to be made between prices in France, on the one hand, and the product of the cost of the dollar in terms of francs and prices in the United States, on the other hand. The latter series fluctuated more strongly than the French price level since prices of French commodities showed a certain tendency to remain constant in terms of francs as long as the fluctuations in the exchange rate were not too great.

In the fifth period, 1925–26, the money circulation provided, again, an independent explanatory factor in the movement of prices, in addition to changes in the rate of exchange of the dollar.

MINOR INTERRUPTIONS

As examples of minor interruptions we may cite the periods of relatively minor wars such as the Franco-German War of 1870–71, the Boer War of 1899–1902, etc. Because of its quite interesting consequences, we select as our first example the effect of the American Civil War on the English economy. The main effect on England of the Civil War was the complete interruption of the supplies of cotton. As a consequence, the raw material of one of England's most important branches of industry became extremely scarce. We want to study the consequences of this scarcity in more detail. In contrast to the major part of this book we will now have to pay particular attention to one individual branch of industry.

Some of the relevant statistical series bearing on this period are shown in Figure 16. They lead to the following observations. As a result of the small supplies, the price of cotton rose very considerably in 1862; the increase continued in 1863 and led to a price level more than double that of normal. This level was again exceeded in 1864 and declined rapidly after 1865. In 1867 a new equilibrium was reached. During the same period the general level of wholesale prices showed practically no movement.

Because of the lack of supplies, imports declined sharply from 1861 to 1862. In contrast to what happened to prices, the lowest level of imports was reached in the first year. The movements shown by import statistics are also shown by data on the consumption of raw cotton, the production of yarns and cotton goods, the export of yarns and cotton goods, and the domestic consumption of cotton goods. Practically all these series show their lowest point in 1862. The continued rise of prices after that year should probably be explained by the fact that, as the scarcity lasted longer, demand became more intensive because the supplies of cotton goods in the hands of consumers were being used up.

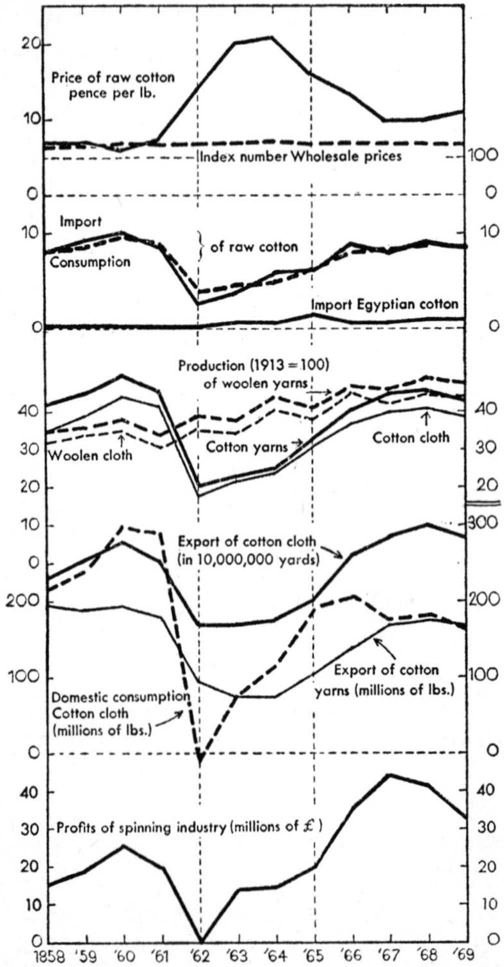

FIG. 16.—The "cotton famine" in England

An interesting detail is that the consumption of raw cotton in 1862 was somewhat higher than imports since stocks could be drawn upon; it is to be noted, however, that the margin available for use in this way was apparently not very great. To verify our assumption that the decline of 1862 and the low level lasting from 1863 to 1865 were caused by the scarcity of cotton and not, for instance, by a cyclical depression, certain figures concerning the production of woolen yarns and woolen goods are also shown in the diagram; they indicate a very regular development, with two-year cycles of very little intensity and no trace whatsoever of the sharp declines of the cotton figures.

The two main consequences of the cotton scarcity discussed so far, namely, the increase of prices and the decline in production, might have been expected; it would be difficult, however, to make any a priori statement about the effect of the scarcity on the profits of the cotton industry. These profits were affected by two opposing forces, namely, the increase in prices and the reduced turnover, and without further knowledge of the structural data it would not be possible to say which of these tendencies would be dominating. The curve of profits in cotton spinneries shows that the profits were unfavorably affected by the cotton famine.

We may, finally, point to one important secondary consequence of the Civil War, namely, the competing import of cotton from Egypt. This import was not very great in absolute amount, but its movement is of interest for two reasons. As might have been expected, it increased sharply in the years of the scarcity of cotton, without, however, making any considerable dent in that scarcity. And it remained on a higher level because cotton-growing, once started, remained an industry in Egypt.

A second interesting example of a minor interruption is provided by the period of the large coal strike in England from May to December, 1926. The relevant statistics are shown in Figure 17. From May to November, 1926, coal production ceased almost completely. One immediate consequence was that the export of coal declined practically to zero, although with a

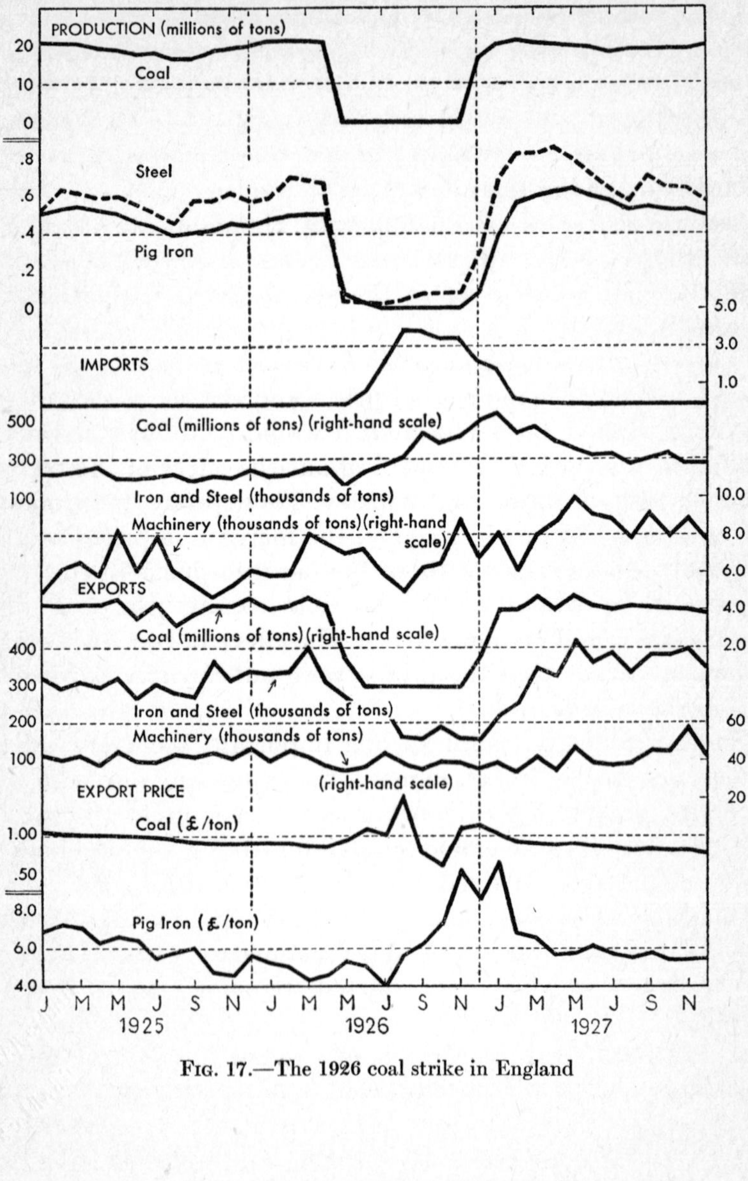

FIG. 17.—The 1926 coal strike in England

small lag; the recovery of exports showed the same lag. Partial compensation was provided by imports of coal; but it took until August, fully three months, before the imports curve flattened out, and as late as January, 1927, a rather considerable import of coal still occurred. The price of coal showed certain irregular fluctuations but did not, on the whole, show any pronounced increase, probably on account of the very active international competition in coal.

A further important consequence of the cessation of coal production was the interruption of the production of pig iron and steel that followed almost immediately. After the termination of the conflict, however, it took somewhat longer before the old level of production in these industries had again been reached. Then, it was immediately exceeded; there was a compensating increase in production which lasted until about the middle of 1927. The reduction in the production of iron was reflected also in changes in imports and exports of iron; imports increased and exports declined. The import and export statistics shown in the diagram refer not only to pig iron and steel but also to semimanufactured products of iron and steel. Owing to the greater degree of fabrication, the lag shown is somewhat longer than in the case of coal. Very little movement is to be seen in the import and export of machines, at one remove further from the source of the disturbance. Only a trace of a decline can be discerned in the export figures for machinery; random movements are much more pronounced. In contrast to the coal price, finally, the pig-iron price shows a pronounced increase, again with a lag of a number of months.

In summary we see that the disturbances in the different branches of industry are of smaller amplitude and occur with greater lag, the further the industry is away from the initial source of disturbance. In one case only, in the production of iron and steel, is a compensating movement shown by our statistics.

SUDDEN CHANGES IN ECONOMIC STRUCTURE

In the nature of things, it is impossible to make a sharp distinction between gradual and sudden changes in the economic structure. Certain changes may take place so rapidly that there is no room for doubt. Other changes, even if they take place over a very short period of time, will nevertheless require a considerable time to make themselves fully felt. Certain legal measures affecting the organization of industry may, for instance, take a considerable time to become fully operative. We shall nevertheless consider such changes as sudden changes, in particular if they are of considerable quantitative influence.

Two of the most important changes in structure of the inter-war period may be referred to in more detail. They refer to the sets of measures introduced in Germany and the United States in 1933 and succeeding years. In both countries the changes in structure were to a considerable extent due to the long and profound crisis that affected the world economy from 1929 to 1932. The problems facing the two countries were the same in many respects: large-scale unemployment, great losses in industry, low agricultural prices, the difficult situation in public finance. The measures taken to overcome these problems were in part the same, but to a considerable extent they were different. Important differences were bound to occur in view of the important differences between the two countries in natural resources, international position, and public opinion.

In the structural changes that took place in Germany one of the main objectives initially was the reduction of unemployment. Some measures in this direction had been taken already by the governments which preceded the National Socialist regime; they were intensified thereafter. Among the recovery measures taken we may mention the execution of large public works, the provision of cheap credit through a system of rediscountable tax certificates, tax exemption for reinvested profits, compulsory labor service, etc. The public works program was followed by a rearmament program that, in the economic field, had the same effect. The amounts spent on it (ninety billion marks) were enormous.

As a result of these measures employment increased considerably. Production increased particularly in the metal industries and the building industries; initially, the production of consumption goods was also allowed to increase in order to satisfy increased incomes and to prevent a rise in prices.

Prices, however, were kept down, mainly by a system of price control which was continually extended. As a result of price control the reamament boom shows a pattern quite different from that of a normal recovery in that the normal parallelism between quantities and prices did not occur. The recovery was entirely in terms of quantities (compare Fig. 18).

The "multiplier" of the public works, that is to say, the ratio between total and primary employment created (the latter de-

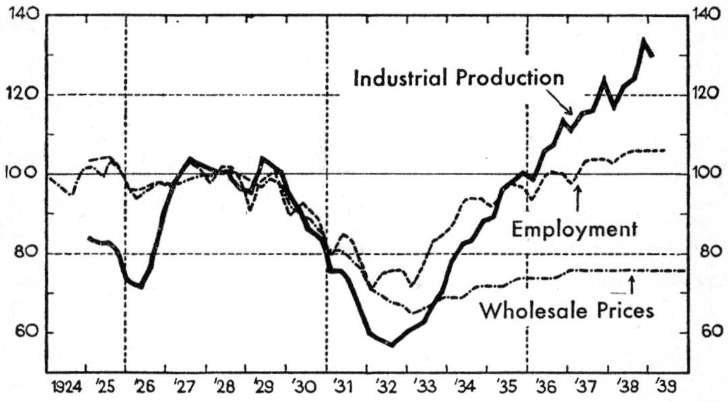

FIG. 18.—Certain business-cycle indicators for Germany, 1924–39 (index numbers, 1928 = 100).

fined as the increase in employment in the public works themselves and in the industries that produced the raw materials and the means of production for these public works), was quite low. This was due to the fact that a large part of the works were executed at very low wages in compulsory labor service; it was due, further, to the fact that a considerable part of the increased incomes was used to repay debts and, finally, to the weak reaction of private investment as a consequence, in part, of the existing investment controls.

The measures to combat unemployment were complemented by financial and commercial measures which were to protect the recovery policy from domestic and foreign financial difficulties. The charter of the Reichsbank was completely modernized in 1933; at that time open-market policy was officially recognized as an instrument of economic policy.

The service of foreign loans was reduced or stopped altogether. Imports were regulated by exchange control and, at a later stage, by an import-licensing system. Exports were promoted by export premiums. A number of different marks were created for special purposes, each with a limited usability of its own; there were security marks, travel marks, etc. The quotations for these special marks in foreign markets fell well below the official rate of the mark; the latter, however, was maintained in the calculation of import and export prices, partly in view of the strong popular feeling against devaluation after the experience of 1923. With practically no gold reserve, Germany kept its balance of payments in equilibrium by its exchange policy and managed to keep the official rate at par and also to stabilize the domestic price level. The isolation from world markets was so complete that the depression of 1937–38 hardly touched the German economy.

We may now discuss briefly the structural changes that occurred in the United States during the depression, in particular those under the "New Deal." In the early period after the assumption of power by President Roosevelt, many recovery measures had increased prices as their objective or as their consequence. The depreciation of the dollar, the agricultural restriction policies, the NRA codes and corresponding wage increases—all tended to raise prices and were intended to do so. It was hoped that by such measures purchasing power would be increased and recovery promoted.

These policies, however, did not prove particularly successful in stimulating recovery. After an initial increase, production declined rather sharply, partly as a reaction to undue optimism of the first few months of the New Deal, partly because high wages were considered as impairing profitability. Toward the fall of 1933 the emphasis was put on a different set of policies which were calculated to increase purchasing power directly by large-scale public works. In addition, large amounts were spent on unemployment relief and, at a later stage, on veterans' bonuses. The amounts spent for these purposes, in addition to those spent for agricultural relief, amounted to the sums shown in Table 14. The major portion of these sums was obtained by borrowing.

These direct injections of purchasing power helped to overcome the recession in 1933 and led to a recovery which was first hesitant, then pronounced (see Fig. 19). Partly as a consequence of the high level of expenditure in 1936 and the decline of expenditure from 1936 to 1937, there was a rather considerable depression in 1937. This recession, however, was of much shorter duration than that of 1929. The government resumed rather quickly its policy of compensating government expenditure, and possibly in part due to this policy the depression lasted for a brief period only.

TABLE 14

RELIEF-TYPE EXPENDITURE IN THE UNITED STATES, 1933–37

Calendar Year	Amounts (In Billions of Dollars)
1933	1.3
1934	3.1
1935	2.7
1936	4.5
1937	2.3

It would appear that the initial recovery policies were too uncertain and also tended to some extent to antagonize employers. As a result the recovery was not so rapid as it might have been if a clear policy had been followed from the start.

In addition to recovery measures, the government adopted another set of policies, the purpose of which was to change the economic structure of the country.[4] The distinction is by no means a sharp one. The fact that the government accepted the responsibility for the level of economic activity and took measures in consequence of this responsibility was itself a structural change of greater importance than many of the individual reconstruction measures. Among the latter we may mention, first, the introduction of social security, particularly un-

4. For a further discussion of the concept of economic structure the reader is referred to Part II.

employment insurance and old age insurance. Both measures were patterned approximately on European examples.

Of particular importance were measures in the financial sphere. By heavy taxation of capital gains an attempt was made, apparently with some success, to limit the extent of stock-exchange speculation and thereby the influence of fluctuations in share prices upon the economy as a whole. Since this speculation, as we shall see, contributed considerably to the

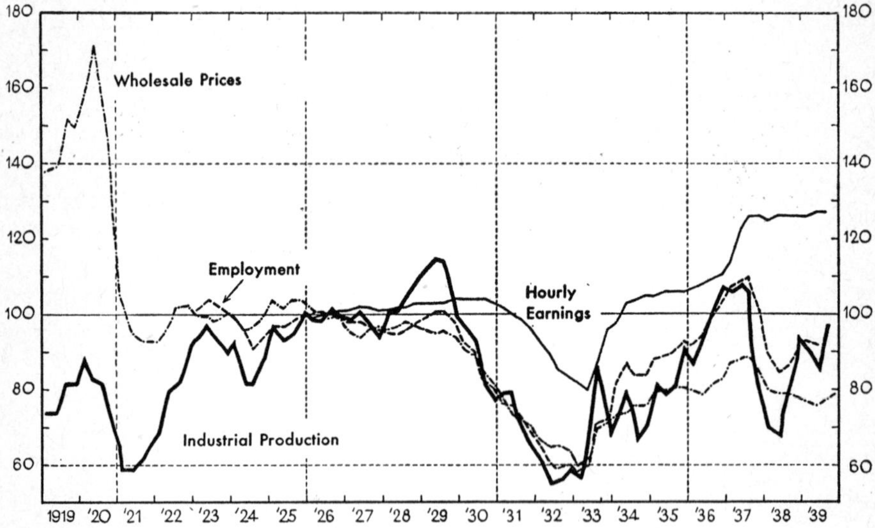

FIG. 19.—Certain business-cycle indicators for the United States, 1919–39 (index numbers, 1926 = 100).

crisis of 1929, these measures should be considered as of great importance.

Not so certain is the effect of the tax on undistributed profits. It may or may not have had favorable consequences for the stability of the economy. There is no question that the tax led to higher dividends in the years following 1936. In the depression years 1931–33 corporations had paid considerable dividends from surpluses accumulated during the preceding boom. It is doubtful whether this will be possible again in a later depression if additions to surplus are much smaller during boom periods.

In the period under consideration the reserve percentages of banks were changed a number of times; in particular, they were raised considerably in the beginning. Owing to the great liquidity, these increases had very little influence on the economy. However, the principle of the regulation by means of changes in reserve percentages is important and may be considered as a structural change of consequence.

Another important structural change was the regulation of agriculture by a system of premiums, fines for excess production, government purchases, etc.

CHAPTER FOUR

CYCLICAL MOVEMENTS

CYCLICAL movements are movements of a periodic character, superimposed on the general long-run tendencies of the economy. We shall now proceed to a more detailed analysis of such movements. To begin with, a distinction should be made between general cycles and specific cycles. General cycles refer to movements of the entire economy of a country or even of the world as a whole; specific cycles refer to individual markets or commodities. We shall give examples of the latter in chapter viii. In this chapter we shall deal only with general cyclical movements.

PERIOD

One very important characteristic of general cyclical movements is that they are periodic or at least quasi-periodic. As Figures 20 and 21 show, they are far from regular. It is possible, therefore, to question their periodic character, and one might maintain that the figures show nothing but an accidental succession of increases and decreases. We shall refer to this question later. To the extent that a periodic movement can be observed, the length of the period shows great differences. Distinctions have been made on the following basis: (*a*) long cyclical waves with a period of about forty years, (*b*) the normal wave with a period of from seven to eleven years, and (*c*) the short American cycle with a period of from three to four years.

These various cycles have not always been uniformly named. Cycles under (*b*), in particular, have sometimes been called short cycles to distinguish them from those under (*a*) and sometimes long cycles to distinguish them from those under (*c*). To end this confusion, Schumpeter[1] has proposed to name the three

1. *Business Cycles* (New York: McGraw-Hill Book Co., 1939).

types of waves after their discoverers, viz., (*a*) Kondratieffs,[2] (*b*) Juglars, and (*c*) Kitchins.

The best-known long cycles, in particular the long cycle in prices, do indeed show a period of about forty years, at least between the troughs in 1850, 1896, and 1933; the peaks around 1810, 1873, and 1920 are further apart (Fig. 20). But Professor Wagemann, who has made further studies in this field, has also discovered long waves with a period of about twenty years and a few with a much longer period of perhaps a hundred years or more. The latter type of wave could be observed, with any

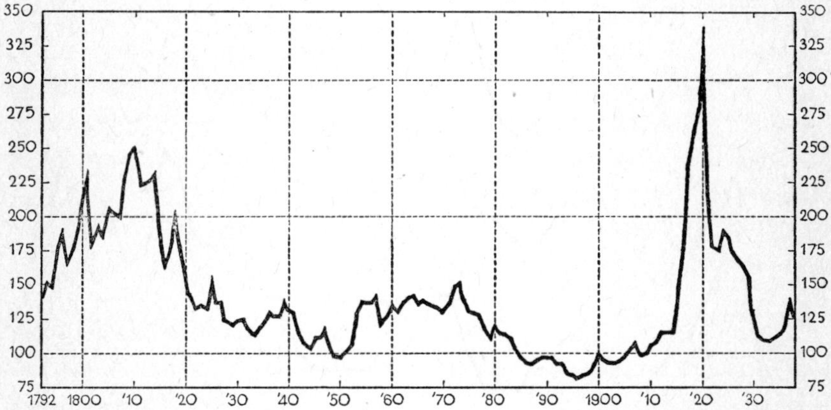

FIG. 20.—Movement of wholesale prices in the United Kingdom (index numbers, 1901–10 = 100).

degree of certainty, on only very few phenomena. Therefore we shall not concern ourselves with them.

A further difficulty in distinguishing between cycles of different periods is due to the fact that their length is often not easy to determine on account of the irregularity of the movements (see, for instance, Fig. 21). The numbers of seven and eleven years, therefore, are not at all intended to mean the extremes for the periods of individual cycles in individual time series but

2. The Dutch may perhaps put in some reservations with respect to the name given by Schumpeter to the long waves; these waves were described by two Dutch authors (Van Gelderen and De Wolff) before they were discovered by the Russian economist Kondratieff.

rather the extremes for the average periods that can be observed in a large number of series.

The shortest cycles occur especially in the United States. In some series, however, particularly in the rate of interest for short-term credits, such cycles can also be observed in European countries.

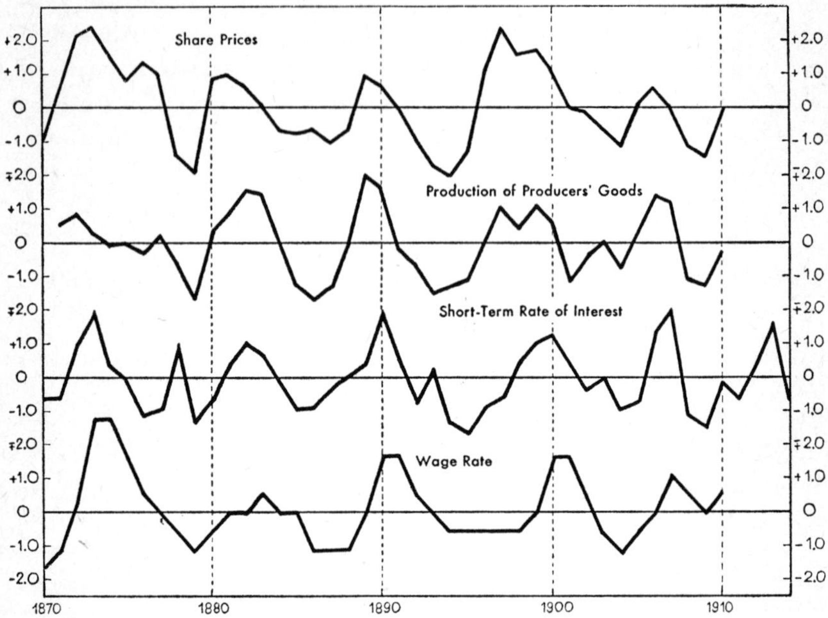

FIG. 21.—Cyclical components of various economic series for the United Kingdom. The curves represent deviations from nine-year moving averages expressed in units of their own standard deviation.

DAMPING

Since most cycles are irregular, it is difficult to measure their degree of damping. Since, roughly speaking, cycles repeat themselves with approximately the same amplitude, no "gross" damping can be observed, that is to say, there is no damping in the observed cycles. It is very well possible, however, that the cycles do have a natural tendency toward damping but are continually kept going by new disturbing factors. Again, it is difficult to state with certainty that the amplitude has remained approximately the same. The crisis of 1929 showed a very large amplitude, and from it a certain tendency toward antidamping might be inferred. Against this, however, it should be borne in mind that sharp and less pronounced crises have alternated over the past century.

TIMING

Cycles in the most important economic series are on the whole if not exactly at least approximately simultaneous. This applies in particular to cycles in the general level of prices and in the general level of activity. In this connection, the price level may refer to the prices of commodities at different stages of production, such as raw materials, semimanufactured products, finished products, either at wholesale or retail, and also to the wage rate and the rate of interest. Activity may be measured either as the volume of production in the broadest sense of the word or as the volume of employment. The simultaneous movement of prices and quantities implies that their product, the value of production in terms of money, must also move approximately simultaneously. Among the value series of importance in this connection are the total value of output and the total value of labor, that is to say, total national income and total labor income (with certain qualifications which are not of great consequence in this connection).

It is always possible by mathematical operations to devise certain other series whose cyclical movements are not simultaneous with those of the series mentioned. Thus, the increase from year to year of any of the above series will usually lead the cycle by about one-quarter of its period; any series which by its nature indicates the opposite of some of the series mentioned, such as an unemployment series, may be considered as one that either leads or lags by half a period; but these are self-evident and entirely artificial statements. It is much more important to see whether there are certain series that have an economic significance of their own and show a cyclical movement with a pronounced lag from that of most other series. Some of these can be found. Thus it will be found that productive capacity will normally lag by about one-quarter of a period, compared to the standard business-cycle series. This is due to the fact that capacity is by its nature a cumulation of series of net investments, the latter being net additions per unit of time to that capacity. As said above,[3] a series resulting from the cumulation of another series normally shows a lag of about one-quarter of a period compared to that series (Fig. 22).

Although most of the important economic series show cyclical movements approximately simultaneously, certain minor differ-

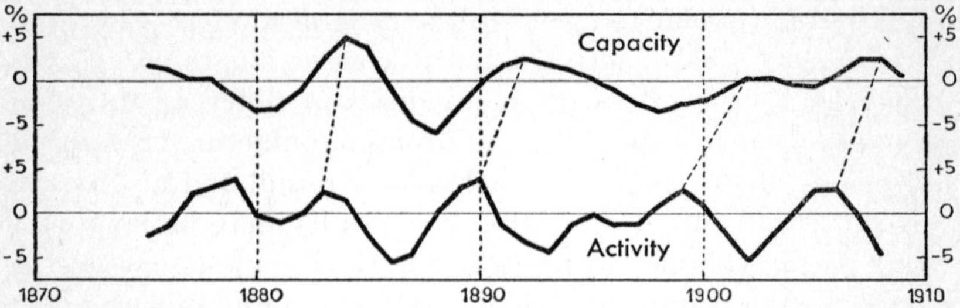

FIG. 22.—Cyclical movements in productive capacity and activity as shown for shipping. The capacity series represents the tonnage of the commercial fleets of the most important countries. The activity series is a transportation index for the most important commodities. Both series are shown as three-year moving averages (in order to eliminate random fluctuations) of deviations from nine-year moving averages.

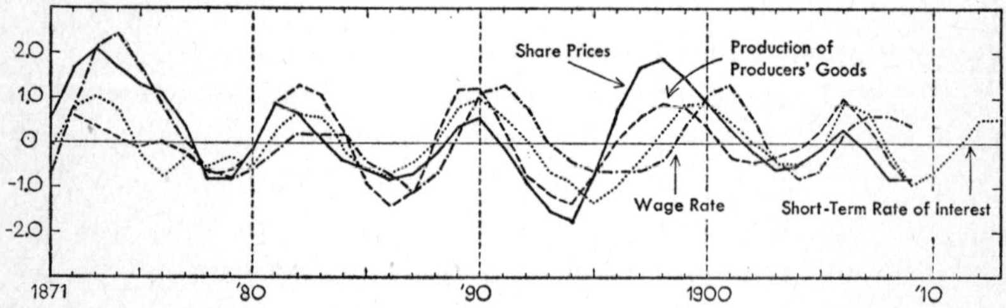

FIG. 23.—Lags between the cyclical component of certain important economic series for the United Kingdom. Deviations from nine-year moving averages expressed in units of their own standard deviation.

ences in timing may, nonetheless, be observed. These differences are not always systematic, but sometimes they are. Figure 23 indicates some of them. Normally, share prices slightly lead the series of production and the general price level; and these, in turn, slightly lead the wage rate and the rate of interest. There are also small differences in phase be-

3. Cf. p. 19, *supra*.

tween the prices of commodities at different stages of production. Prices of raw materials subject to active competition show cycles on the whole somewhat earlier than prices of other commodities. Retail prices lag somewhat behind wholesale prices.

It is often not easy to determine the lag between two series each of which has its own irregular movements. A more reliable way to determine lags or leads is to construct one series on the basis of one or more others with which it is causally connected, along the lines indicated in chapter i. It is obviously easier to determine lags for series for which monthly data are available than for those for which only annual data exist. Except for the United States, unfortunately, only annual figures are available for those economic variables that are most important to business-cycle analysis, such as national income, total consumption expenditure, and total investment; even these annual figures embrace only a relatively short period.

Some of the empirical statements that have sometimes been made about lags and leads have, on closer analysis, only a very limited validity and do not indicate any fundamental economic relationship. On the basis of purely empirical material it is impossible to determine whether any observed regularity indicates a permanent relationship between the variables involved. In anticipation of our theoretical analysis we may at this stage refer to one example. It has often been held that residential construction shows a cyclical movement having a systematic connection with the general business cycle. This relation has been made the basis for observations concerning the significance of the building cycle for the general business cycle and for business-cycle policy. It appears, however, that the various authors on this subject insist on quite different relations between the two cycles. Some hold that the building cycle runs counter to the cycle of the general economy, others that the building cycle leads, and still others, again, that it lags behind the general cycle. This in itself throws some doubt on the existence of any clear and simple relation. Analysis of the data for the United States shows that building has a cycle of its own with a period entirely different from that of the general business cycle. In the case of Germany, too, a building cycle following its own immanent development can be observed at least for certain periods; during these periods, therefore, no regular relationship between residential construction and the general business cycle can be observed. In all countries residential construction appears to be strongly influenced by abrupt changes in confidence; this is a further reason why its fluctuations may show a pattern quite different from that of the general business cycle.

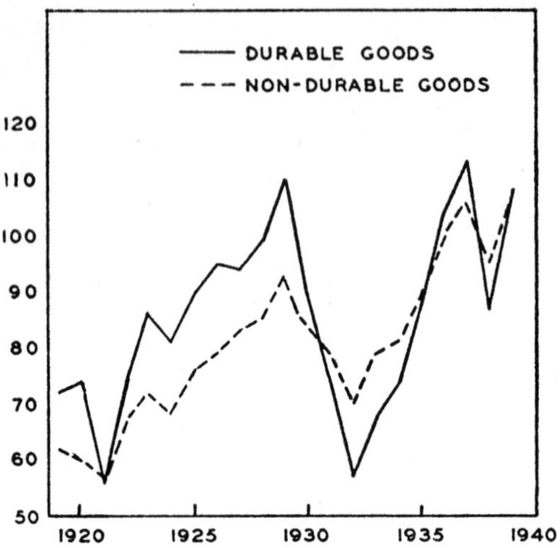

FIG. 24.—Production series with different relative amplitudes in the United States. Durable goods and nondurable goods (index numbers, 1935–39 = 100).

AMPLITUDE

The regularities of business cycles appear clearest in their amplitude, particularly in the ratio of the amplitudes of different phenomena. The relative amplitude of various series, that is to say, the ratio of their amplitudes to their average height, varies considerably. To mention only a few of the most important economic series, the production of durable goods has a much larger relative amplitude than has the production of nondurable goods (see Fig. 24). The relative amplitude of the production of raw materials, also, is somewhat larger than that of finished products, and the relative amplitude of the production of luxury commodities is larger than that of commodities of first necessity.

The differences in amplitude of the production series are matched by corresponding differences in amplitude of the employment series in different branches of industry, but each employment series tends to show a slightly smaller relative amplitude than the corresponding production series.

Among the price series, raw materials show the greatest relative amplitude, and the cost-of-living index and the wage rate

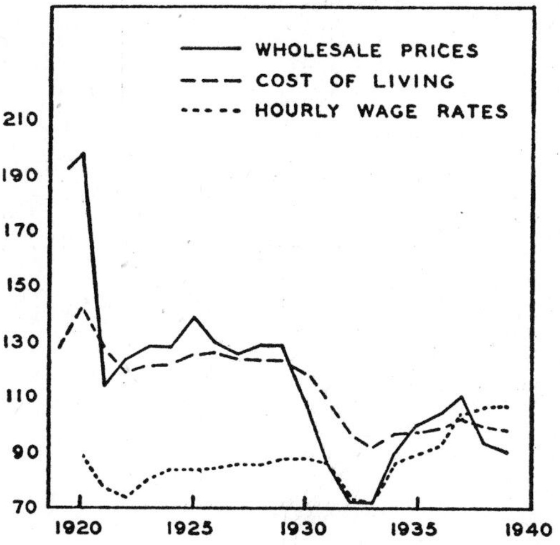

Fig. 25.—Price series with different amplitudes in the United States (index numbers, 1935–39 = 100).

the smallest (Fig. 25). There is also a pronounced difference between corresponding or nearly corresponding prices for contracts of different terms, the longer contracts showing a much smaller relative amplitude. One of the clearest examples of this is in the rate of interest. The rate for short-term credits shows a sharp relative amplitude, whereas that for long-term credits, for instance, yield on irredeemable bonds, shows a very moderate relative amplitude.

Figure 26 indicates that among the income series in the United States the greatest relative amplitude is shown by the figures for profits and the smallest for interest-and-rent income and salaries, whereas wages occupy an intermediate position. It has been found, for the Netherlands at least, that,

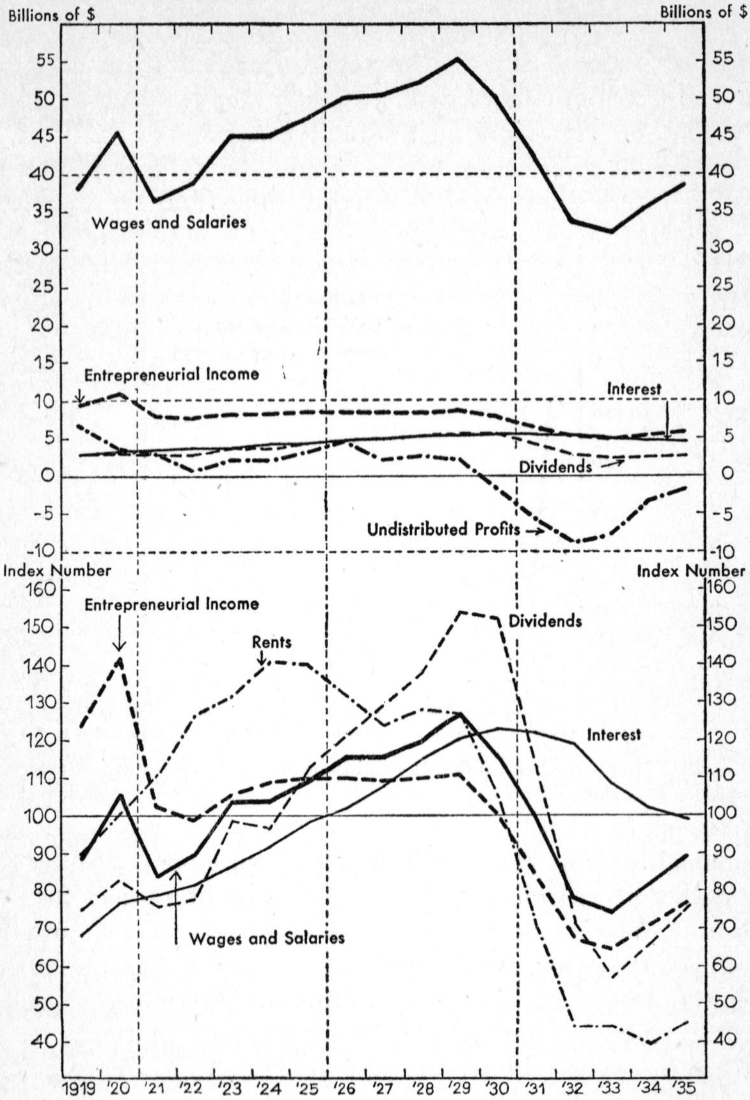

FIG. 26.—Income series with various amplitudes in the United States. *Upper half*, series in billions of dollars; *lower half*, series as index numbers based on average for period (1919–35 = 100).

if incomes are arranged according to size, the highest and lowest incomes fluctuate more strongly than those in the middle of the scale.

SHAPE

As has been indicated, the shape of the fluctuations is often quite irregular. Random influences produce sometimes an acceleration, sometimes a retardation, of the movement. Random fluctuations are particularly important in series that are directly or indirectly connected with agriculture, since all these series are at least partially determined by crop fluctuations which, from an economic point of view, have an almost en-

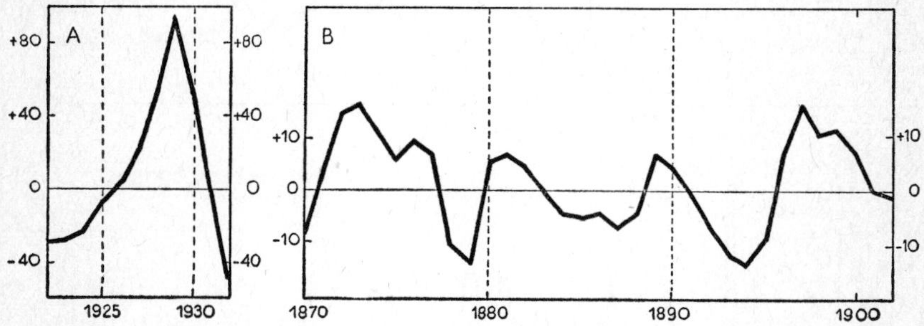

FIG. 27.—Examples of asymmetrical business-cycle components. *Left:* Slow increase and rapid decline as shown by share prices in the United States, 1919–32 (index numbers, 1926 = 100; deviations from average). *Right:* Rapid increase and slow decline as shown by share prices in the United Kingdom, 1870–1905 (index numbers, June, 1890 = 100; deviations from nine-year moving average).

tirely random pattern. Even freight rates that are partially affected by grain shipments show the indirect effect of crop fluctuations.

Other irregularities are of a more systematic character. Thus, there appears to be a tendency to a certain asymmetry in cycles, in the sense that they increase slowly and decline rapidly, particularly when the decline takes the form of a crisis leading into a severe depression. This tendency, however, is much less general than is sometimes believed. There are some clear examples of the opposite tendency; the prices of shares in the United Kingdom during the period from 1870 to 1914 tended to increase rather rapidly during short recovery periods and then to decline slowly during the longer depression periods (see Fig. 27). De Wolff has ascribed these asymmetries to the influence of long waves on the business cycle; in the downswing of the long waves there would, according to him, be short recoveries and long depressions; and in the upswing of a long wave, long recoveries and short depressions. With respect to series such as the price level, which show clearly the influence of long waves, this statement might be proved generally if one might assume an entirely symmetrical normal business cycle.

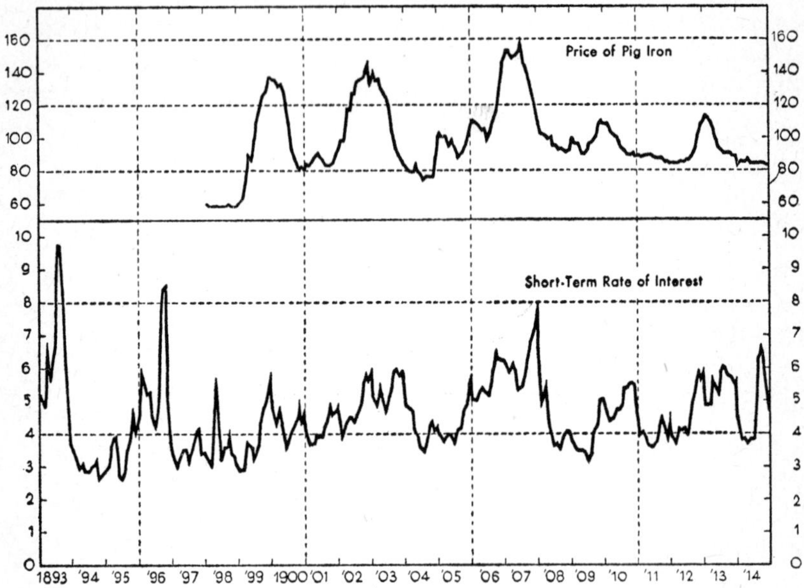

FIG. 28.—Example of cyclical movements with sharp peaks. Pig-iron price and short-term rate of interest in the United States.

In the downswing of the long wave the total movement of such a series would then be represented by the sum of a falling line and a symmetrical wave movement, in the upswing by the sum of an ascending line and a symmetrical wave movement. For most types of symmetrical waves this sum would yield relatively long depressions and relatively short recoveries during the downswing of the long wave and rather shorter depressions and longer recoveries during the upswing. This, however, would not be the case for all symmetrical movements. It would, for instance, not hold for a zigzag movement, which is characterized by very sudden changes of direction. Most cyclical series, though, do not show such sudden reversals.

There are a number of other asymmetries. Somes series show sharp peaks and flat troughs; other series show flat peaks and sharp troughs. A flat peak or a flat bottom will occur in the case of phenomena which have an upper or lower limit. Thus, employment cannot increase above the total labor supply. Owing to this upper limit, this series will normally show flat peaks. The rate of interest, on the other hand, cannot fall below 0; this series will therefore show flat bottoms. Sharp increases and sharp decreases will be found for series which are particularly sensitive. Before the first World War the rate of discount of the central bank used to respond quite sharply to reductions in the gold stock. In boom periods with tight credit the discount rate showed quite sharp peaks (see Fig. 28).

Similar peaks can be observed for the prices of mineral raw materials. In some boom periods the demand for these materials increased tremendously, while the limited capacity of production did not permit any great increase in the quantity supplied. Prices (if they were free, as they usually were at the time) increased rapidly under such conditions and fell again rapidly as soon as the tension eased. The sharp price peaks indicated certain spots in the economy, certain bottlenecks, where the tension between demand and supply was most pronounced. Sometimes these spots are of decisive influence for the amplitude of the cycle in the entire economy, since they provide a brake to further expansion. Not every cycle, however, shows bottlenecks. Various upper turning points show rather flat tops for the prices of investment goods.

CHAPTER FIVE

SEASONAL FLUCTUATIONS

SEASONAL fluctuations, that is, fluctuations caused by the changes of the natural or conventional seasons, are the most important of the shorter rhythmic fluctuations. In this connection, "season" should be taken in the broadest sense of the word, to refer to all fluctuations that are connected with periodic astronomic changes of the calendar. It would include changes of day and night, of great importance for the load of the electric and gas companies and for transportation, and changes in habits connected with various days of the week, month, and year, affecting, e.g., retail sales.

The term "seasonal component" is used in two different senses. The term is used most often to indicate the average or normal seasonal movement, that is to say, a regular movement that represents some sort of average of the actual movements taken over a number of successive periods. In the simplest and most common case these movements are purely periodic, either additive or multiplicative. In the former case a certain sum is added, for instance, for each January month to the sum of all other components; in the latter case this sum is multiplied by a certain factor for each January month. The regularity may, however, be more complicated. Thus the amplitude of the season may show a gradual change, or the season itself may move according to a certain pattern (e.g., the date of Easter).

In the second sense the term "seasonal component" is used to indicate the exact influence of the particular natural or conventional factors. If the particular natural factor that affects the phenomenon under consideration is the temperature, then the seasonal component in the second sense of the word is the actual change in the phenomenon due to changes in temperature. As a matter of fact, the fluctuations in temperature, although roughly periodical, are not exactly periodical. There are cold and mild winters. If, in a particularly cold winter, shipping shows very low figures, then the strong negative component caused by the temperature will be considered entirely as a seasonal component. Under the former definition of the seasonal component, however, only the normal decline of shipping in winter would be considered seasonal, and the additional decline would be considered as a random influence.

We shall now give a brief enumeration of the most important seasonal fluctuations in the economy. Some are indicated graphically in Figure 29.

The influence of the natural season is felt most strongly in economic activities carried on in direct contact with nature. Agriculture is the clearest example. Production in agriculture, agricultural employment, consumption of fertilizer, etc., are strongly seasonal. Construction activity also is still greatly affected by temperature and precipitation. A third industry heavily affected by the weather is shipping, in particular lake and river shipping. The seasonal pattern of these industries affects again those other industries that use their products, such as agricultural industries, and the trade in products whose transportation is interrupted by the freezing of rivers, like the lumber trade. In these industries it is the supply that is seasonal.

In other industries, such as the clothing, heating, and hotel industries, demand is affected by seasons. We have already referred to the important changes, in the course of the day, in the demand for electricity and gas. In a sense, of course, every industry has its fluctuations during the day; but in the case of electricity where inventories cannot be accumulated, the influence of the "seasonal" fluctuation during the day is of particular importance.

The conventional season makes itself felt particularly in retail sales, due to fluctuations during the day (rush hours), the week (if wages are paid toward the end of the week), and the month (salary payments). Retail trade is further affected by

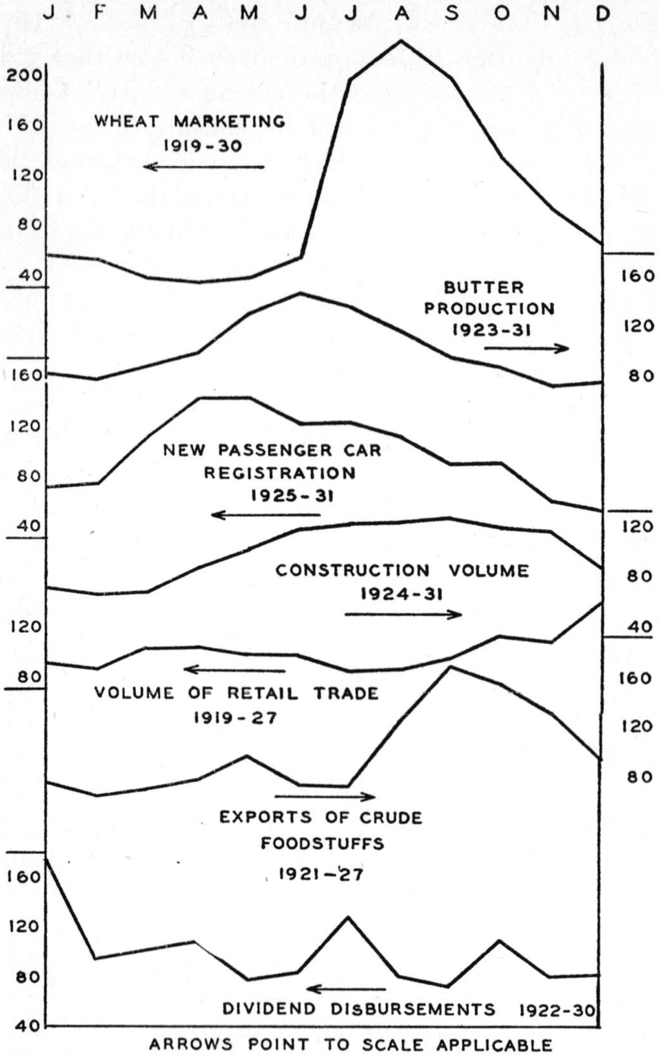

FIG. 29.—Seasonal components in a number of economic series. Source: S. Kuznets, *Seasonal Variations in Industry and Trade* (New York, 1933).

seasons in the narrow sense of the word, of which the December peak associated with Christmas trade is particularly pronounced.

The financial sphere also has conventional seasons; this is due to the habitual seasonal pattern in payments. The weekly payments of wages, the monthly payments of rents, and quarterly dividend payments produce certain regular seasonal peaks in banking activity, which affect to some extent the money market and the short-term rate of interest.

CHAPTER SIX

RANDOM MOVEMENTS

In CHAPTER I we mentioned two types of random movements, those which are distributed normally and those which are not. Both have in common an absence of system in the succession of values of the variable in question. This may be further explained as follows. From all the values wich a certain variable x assumes, we take all instances in which x has one particular value, for example, 2. We then take all values which follow immediately upon this value 2. These may be very different; in general, they will represent all values which the series x can assume. We now make a frequency distribution of all these "immediately succeeding" values: so many times 0, so many times 1, so many times 2, etc. We may make a similar frequency distribution for all values following immediately upon another value, for example, 1. If we have a sufficient number of observations, we should, with any desired degree of approximation, find the same frequency distribution. This is the essential character of a random movement. This property of a random movement may also be expressed by stating that its successive values are independent. Given a certain first value of any two values of the series, one cannot determine the second one. The frequency distribution to which we referred is the frequency distribution of the series.

A random variable may be normally distributed, in which case its frequency will, for a long succession of values, approximate a normal or Gaussian distribution. If a random variable may be considered to be the sum of a large number (in principle, an infinite number) of components, each small and independent of the others, it will tend to be distributed normally.

In economic analysis one usually deals with normally distributed random variables, since the number of forces which affects one economic variable is usually very large.

Whether any particular economic variable should be considered as random will depend on the nature of the analysis. Two examples will make this clear.

a) First, successive values may or may not be independent, according to the period of observation. Thus, a series may be random in its annual figures but not in its monthly figures. The monthly figures may show a certain inertia: they may change only little from one month to the next. In such a series a high value for one month is likely to be followed by a high value for the next month, and a low value is likely to be followed by another low value. Yet the sum of twelve monthly figures, represented by an annual figure, may very well satisfy the criterion of independence. Thus it depends on the period used whether a series should be considered as a random variable or not.

Many series of prices and production of agricultural products provide good examples of this. During one crop year with a large crop, prices will be low in every month. There may still be some variation at the beginning of the crop year, when the size of the crop is not yet exactly known; similarly, the prices at the end of the crop year will be affected by expectations concerning the new crop. But generally prices will tend to be low. Prices in successive months are not independent of one another. On the other hand, average prices for successive crop years will be practically independent of each other. Here, the year is the natural unit of time. Successive annual figures may be considered as independent and therefore as random.

b) Second, the random character of a component depends on how far our analysis is pushed. Assume that the movement of a certain economic variable may be considered as consisting of the sum of a number of elementary movements, each of which is due to the influence of one particular other variable. Usually, a few of these elementary movements will be very important; their amplitude will be great, whereas the amplitude of any one of the other elementary movements will be relatively small. Normally, the important components will be due to factors that are known: they are most readily observed or are due to factors that are easily identified or at least they will be made the subject of the most intensive research. There will therefore be a tendency to consider these most important components as the systematic components and to consider the sum of all other influences as the random component.

This random component will then combine the minor influences of all other factors. In view of the complicated nature of the economy, the number of these other factors is usually very large, and their influences may be considered as approximately independent of one another; they often represent factors originating in very different parts of the economy. The distribution of the random component may therefore be approximately normal. The arbitrary nature of the distinction between systematic and random components is clear, as the border line between important and unimportant factors may be drawn differently and a different random component found accordingly. To some extent this may depend on the state of economic science. Only known influences will be called systematic; as the influence of more factors becomes understood, there will be a tendency to shift the border line, although it need not always coincide with the demarcation line between known and unknown influences.

Although an economic variable may have a random distribution through time, this does not mean that one may not choose to explain it further. The values which such a variable assumes through time may be explained as the result of values assumed by other random variables through time. Thus, an economically systematic explanation has been given for a mathematically random variable. The size of the crop, for instance, will normally be considered as systematic in the economic sense, although it is a random variable in the mathematical sense of the word.

Among the most important concrete examples of random fluctuations in the economy are the economic series related to agriculture. Crop yields per acre fluctuate from year to year, and these series show a random pattern. The explanation of this pattern does not fall within the scope of economics; it belongs to biology. It has been found that many factors affect yield, but a few among them are most important, such as the amount of sunshine in a certain critical period, the amount of rain in another critical period, etc. Since both the amount of sunshine and the amount of rain (their explanation lies in the field of meteorology) depend on a very large number of factors, the random character of yield fluctuations is attributable to this large number of factors.

The random character of crop yields does not imply that certain related series, such as the total crop or the price of agricultural products, are also random. These latter series depend on systematic factors as well. The total crop represents the product of the yield per acre and the number of acres under cultivation. This latter series is affected to some extent by prices and in this way indirectly by the yields of previous years. Often, however, this influence is relatively unimportant in comparison with the fluctuations of yields. Even if we abstract from this and consider the entire crop as a random variable, it would still not be permissible to consider prices as entirely due to chance. In the simplest case the price is determined by the total supply available during a certain crop year. This supply is equal to the sum of the current crop and the carry-over from previous years. The larger the crop was in the preceding year, the larger the carry-over will be. Thus the price in any one year will reflect not only the current but also the past crop; since last year's crop also affected last year's price, the prices in the two successive years will not be independent of each other. Hence, the price cannot be considered to be entirely a random variable.

Other examples of random movements in the economic sense are provided by certain series that are in many respects analogous to those of agriculture, such as the catch of fish. Fluctuations in catch are also in part due to fluctuations in temperature. Here again the unit of time necessary to obtain a random pattern of the series is one year.

Most other examples of random fluctuations are relatively of less importance; usually the appropriate time unit is less than a year. Short random fluctuations occur in almost all economic series. They are very pronounced in series that refer to a small number of subjects, such as the series of capital issues. Economically speaking, the month in which a certain issue is floated is largely a matter of chance. One issue of a large corporation that happens to take place in a particular month will make the figures of capital issues for that month accidentally high. In the trade figures of relatively smaller countries, the random entry of one large ship in a particular month (rather than in the preceding or the following month) may also play some role. Another example of a somewhat different character is given by the international movements of short-term capital. They may show large random fluctuations in disturbed periods. A certain rumor, a measure of economic policy that happens to be announced in a particular month, may produce sharp movements that should be considered as random compared with the general cyclical pattern.

CHAPTER SEVEN

DIFFERENCES AMONG INDIVIDUAL COUNTRIES

WE HAVE observed previously that economic fluctuations, in particular cyclical movements, are not very regular. In this connection it would seem worth while to analyze the differences among fluctuations occurring in different surroundings, particularly the differences among the movements in different countries. To these differences this chapter is devoted. We may deal first with systematic differences.

TRENDS

Some references to differences in trend have been made before in chapter ii. It was noted there that the rate of population increase and the rate of capital formation differ among countries. Mainly as a consequence of these factors, the trends in production and in the position of the various countries in international competition show great differences. Thus, in the United Kingdom and France the rate of development after the middle of the nineteenth century was relatively slow, whereas in Germany and the United States it was quite rapid. After the first World War, the rate of development in Japan and the U.S.S.R. was much faster than in other countries.

CYCLES

Differences in cyclical patterns may exist in various respects. We have already mentioned that the period of the cycle in the United States is usually only half that in European countries. Even if the natural period of the United States short cycle were not exactly one-half the European cycle, the various links between economic phenomena in different countries would have tended to synchronize important declines in Europe with declines in the United States. The tendency toward synchronization of cycles would lead to simple numerical relations among the period in one country and those in other countries.

There are some systematic differences among countries in the amplitude also. In general, countries with a strong trend also show a tendency to a large relative amplitude. But within one country the period of the greatest relative amplitude is not associated with the period of the sharpest upward trend. More nearly the contrary is true. The sharpest cyclical fluctuations have been observed in the period from 1919 to 1939, when the general development showed rather a period of stagnation. In the years before 1914, business cycles were very moderate in countries such as France and the Netherlands, where the upward trend was relatively weak. In the commodity sphere practically no cyclical movements could be observed in the Netherlands. Only a slight influence of cycles was found in the financial sphere and in certain series strongly related to foreign countries, such as shipping, while a weak effect could also be observed in investment. The influence of the directly affected industries on all other industries was small, however, partially because investment goods were imported to a large extent.

Differences among various countries in the degrees of damping can hardly be observed (with one or two exceptions to which reference is made below). As long as economic events in the various countries are closely interrelated, a pronounced difference in the rate of damping would hardly be conceivable. If such a difference existed, the cyclical movements in various countries would have to show an ever increasing ratio in their amplitudes. If this ratio assumed proportions of any consequence, it would imply either that the cyclical movement in some of the countries would almost completely disappear or that in other countries it would assume an intolerable magnitude. In a period of active international competition such a situation is hardly conceivable.

Certain countries that isolated themselves from the rest of the world and adopted a policy toward cyclical stabilization did, however, succeed in remaining untouched by crises occurring in other countries and even by world crises. Thus the U.S.S.R. was hardly affected by the depression of 1929–32 and Japan only to a minor extent; similarly, the crisis of 1937–38 hardly touched Germany.

Phase differences in the cycles in various countries have been quite common; often the cycle in one country preceded that in another one. At different times different countries acted as the origin of cyclical movements and particularly of crises. It is apparent from the description of crises of the past that at some times the origin was to be found in the United States, at other times in the United Kingdom, and sometimes in Germany. Also, the origin of a certain crisis was often situated in some peripheric country or in more than one country at the same time; obviously, countries with very active economic life provided the origin of a crisis more often than did other countries. The very important crisis of 1929 originated in the United States, with the Stock Exchange crash initiating the downward movement. But there were very many other weak spots, for instance, in agricultural countries and in Germany. France and also the Netherlands were affected by this crisis only very much later.

SEASONAL PATTERNS

Various countries have also considerable differences in their seasonal patterns, due in particular to differences in climatic conditions. It is understandable, for instance, that the seasonal movement in unemployment in the building industry is much greater in Sweden than in Australia (see Fig. 30). Differences in the dividend payments between the United States and Europe provide an interesting example of differences in the conventional seasonal pattern. In Europe, dividends are normally paid once a year, as against quarterly payments in the United States.

RANDOM MOVEMENTS

Differences in random movements are due mainly to the different significance of agriculture, compared to the entire economy, in the various countries. In a country like the United Kingdom, this significance is quite limited; in India it is preponderant. It is understandable, therefore, that the economic series for the latter country show many more irregular movements than those for the United Kingdom. Individual deviations in the behavior of large enterprises or of individual markets will, further, produce random movements of much greater relative importance in a small country than in a large country. A large order for ships or for railroad rolling stock or the flotation of a loan by a large corporation will have a considerable influence on the economy or the capital market of a country of the size of the Netherlands, whereas in the United States its relative influence will be much smaller.

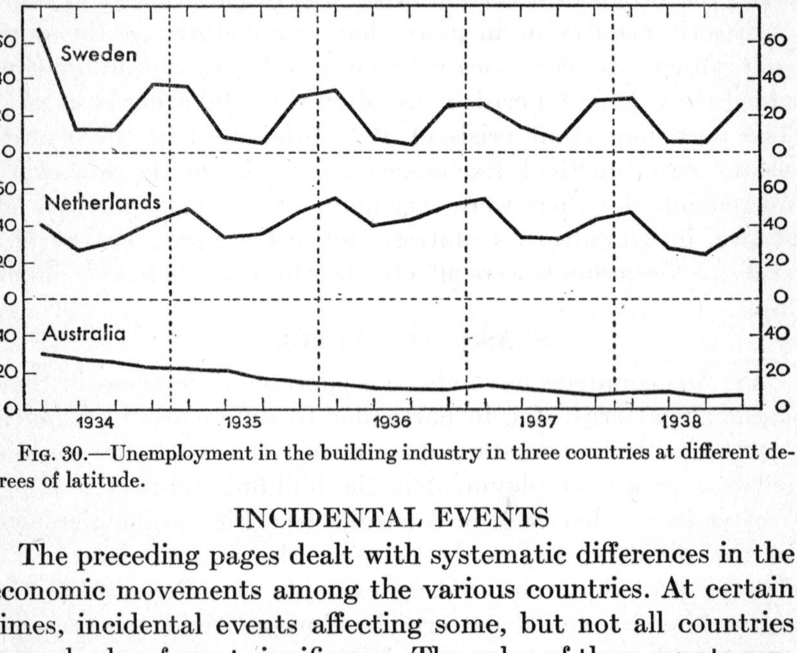

FIG. 30.—Unemployment in the building industry in three countries at different degrees of latitude.

INCIDENTAL EVENTS

The preceding pages dealt with systematic differences in the economic movements among the various countries. At certain times, incidental events affecting some, but not all countries may also be of great significance. The value of these events consists in that they occasionally provide the student with the equivalent of an experiment, so rare in the social sciences.

It is not our intention to attempt anything like a complete catalogue of incidental differences in the economic movements in various countries. Much interesting material on this subject will be found in national periodic economic reviews and in various monographs. However, we do want to mention certain striking divergences in economic development that lead to certain important generalizations. Instances of this character are possible particularly when the origin of the divergence is not too complicated, e.g., when only one or a few factors are different between the two countries compared. Such situations have occurred a number of times in the period between the two wars, as various countries followed different exchange-rate policies. One of the least complicated of these cases is provided by a comparison of Norway and Denmark in the years 1923–29 either with the other western European countries or, if one prefers, with the other Scandinavian countries. Both Norway and Denmark appreciated their currency considerably in the years 1924–26, bringing them back to par by 1926, from 50 and 60 per cent of par, respectively. This policy implied for these countries an unusually severe process of deflation: prices of imported materials fell heavily in terms of crowns and dragged all other prices along. The comparison of the curve of industrial production in the two countries with that of other countries is particularly interesting. While the world cycle developed rather smoothly during this period, production in Norway and Denmark showed a sharp decline and continued at a considerably lower level for a number of years. Figure 31 gives an impression of the influence of the exchange-rate policy on activity in Norway and Denmark.

Similar comparisons may be made for the period after 1931, when many countries successively depreciated their currencies with respect to gold, either by abandoning the gold standard or by choosing a new lower parity. The first major country to depreciate was the United Kingdom in 1931, followed immediately by a number of the dominions and by the Scandinavian countries. In 1933 the United States followed, in 1934 Czechoslovakia, in 1935 Belgium, and finally in 1936 the still remaining members of the so-called "gold bloc," France, Switzerland, and the Netherlands. Comparisons concerning economic developments in this period must be made with great caution. The period was in many respects disturbed, and a great variety of measures of economic policy was superimposed on the more "normal" economic forces. It is sometimes pos-

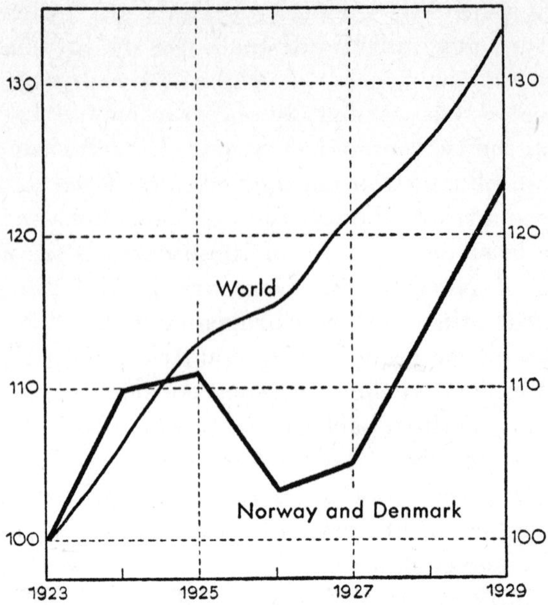

FIG. 31.—Industrial production in Norway and Denmark, compared with industrial production of the world as a whole in the period after the appreciation of the Norwegian and Danish crowns.

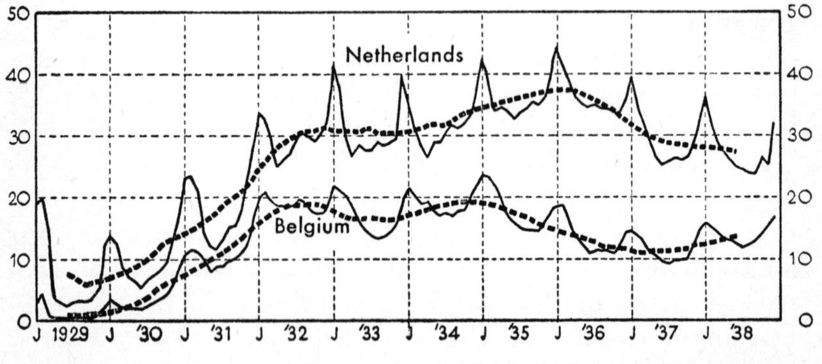

FIG. 32.—Unemployment (in per cent) in the Netherlands and Belgium during the great depression (1929–36). (March, 1935: devaluation of the Belgian franc. October, 1936: devaluation of the Netherlands guilder. *Solid line:* monthly figures; *dotted line:* twelve months' moving average.)

sible to eliminate the influence of these various measures by comparing data for a number of countries in a similar position.[1] At this stage we deal only with the descriptive part of the movements; therefore, we give without further comment a diagram indicating the unemployment figures for the Netherlands and Belgium (Fig. 32), with an indication of the dates at which the exchange-rate policy was changed.

Figure 33 also shows a remarkable divergency for the same period in a comparison of Sweden and Finland. For both countries two indices of production are shown, one relating to industries operating primarily for the home market, the other

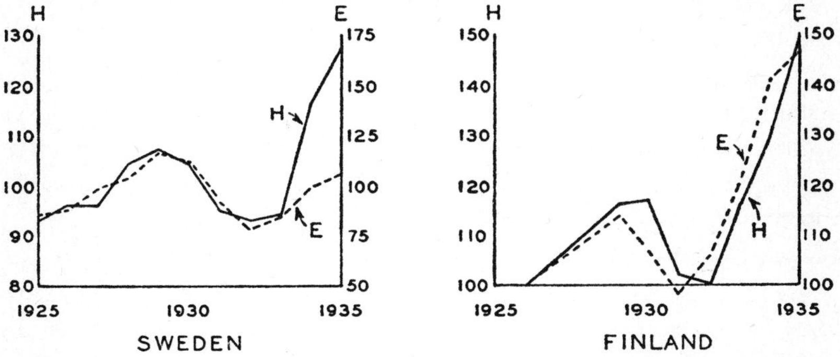

FIG. 33.—Indices of the production for the home market (*H*) and for export (*E*) in Sweden and Finland. Scales have been selected so that the two curves *H* and *E* coincide as closely as possible in the period 1925–32 (bases of indices: Sweden, 1925–30 = 100; Finland, 1926 = 100).

to industries producing primarily for export. The scales of the two curves have been chosen in such a way that they coincide as closely as possible for the period 1925–32, when there was no business-cycle policy of any consequence. It will be seen from the diagram that on this basis in Sweden production for the home market increased much more after 1933 than production for exports. This should probably be attributed to the measures taken by the Swedish government to stimulate activity such as public works and measures to raise the purchasing power of the farmers. No such difference in development can be seen in Finland, where much less was done in the nature of public works and where, on the contrary, the increase in exports was the cause of the general improvement after 1933.

1. Cf. Fig. 53, *infra.*

CHAPTER EIGHT

FLUCTUATIONS IN INDIVIDUAL MARKETS

IN THE preceding chapters we have dealt only with fluctuations of very general economic series, such as total production, production of all consumption goods, general price level, general wage level, etc. We shall now devote some attention to the pattern of fluctuations in individual markets. We use the broad term "movements [or: fluctuations] in a market" to refer at the same time to prices and quantities. Normally, the fluctuations of prices and of quantities sold in the same market are closely related. In cases where there is no such relation between the movements of prices and quantities sold in the same market, we shall have to specify to which of the two we want to refer when speaking of the fluctuations in a market.

Fluctuations in a particular market can show divergencies from the general business cycle in two respects. In the first place, there may be a difference in the proportion of the various components (trend, cycle, etc.) compared to those of the general series. In the second place, the components may show a different development from those of the general series. We shall discuss in this chapter a number of examples of such divergent movements, the most important of which refer to the cyclical component. Certain markets have a special cycle of their own, with a period different from that of the general business cycle. This phenomenon has induced Professors Warren and Pearson to believe that the general cyclical movement might be understood as the sum of such different cyclical movements in individual markets. Warren and Pearson[1] show that the addition of a number of purely periodic curves of different periods will

1. G. F. Warren and F. A. Pearson, *World Prices and the Building Industry* (New York: John Wiley & Sons, Inc., 1937).

yield new curves that are again periodic but much less regular than the original curves, a proposition well known from mathematics. In our view, their proposition is of no great value in the explanation of the general business cycle. It is, of course, true that all general business-cycle series are either sums or averages of corresponding series of individual markets. But for the theory of Warren and Pearson to be of any value as an explanation of business cycles, it would be necessary that each market had a life of its own, that is to say, that it could fluctuate entirely under the impetus of data which are independent of other markets. There are in fact only a few markets that have such an independent character. We shall refer to them later. Most markets, however, strongly influence one another, and the fluctuations in each of them depend to a large extent on the same data. Most individual markets are very strongly under the influence of the general business cycle. For this and other reasons, the fluctuations in these markets are by no means more elementary in character than those of the general business cycle. A reduction of the latter to the movements in individual markets is therefore no real explanation, no reduction to simpler concepts.

We may start out with some examples of the first type of divergency mentioned, in which individual markets have an entirely different proportion of the various components from that of the corresponding general series. The most striking examples of this are cases in which one component dominates the three others. There are markets, for instance, in which the trend movement is entirely dominant. This is particularly the case for the markets of new commodities. The production of rayon, for instance, shows an almost uninterrupted tendency to increase, its price an almost uninterrupted tendency to decline. The business-cycle position has little effect on either. Of course, it is not likely that this will continue. When a new product has obtained its place in the economy, its trend component will automatically become less pronounced and, by the same token, its business-cycle component will become more pronounced, both as to the volume of output and as to price. Also, very little cyclical effect is to be observed in the production of the most essential foodstuffs and in such series as the number and the nominal value of all bonds and shares. The price of foodstuffs and the quotations of bonds showed only very small cyclical fluctuations before 1914,[1] but their fluctuations have increased since World War I. Share prices, on the other hand, have at all times been very responsive to the general business cycle.

In some markets the cyclical component, that is to say, the general cyclical component, dominates. This will be the case particularly where the trend is of relatively minor importance.

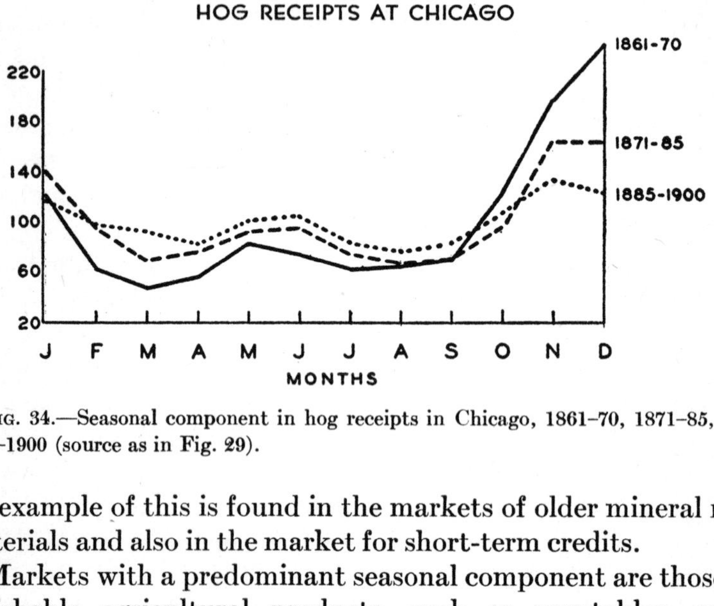

FIG. 34.—Seasonal component in hog receipts in Chicago, 1861–70, 1871–85, and 1885–1900 (source as in Fig. 29).

An example of this is found in the markets of older mineral raw materials and also in the market for short-term credits.

Markets with a predominant seasonal component are those of perishable agricultural products, such as vegetables, some fruits, and, to a lesser extent, dairy products and eggs. The further extension of preservation techniques (canning, drying, deep-freezing) has a continuing tendency to reduce the importance of this type of market. A clear example of the gradual reduction of the seasonal component in an agricultural series is shown by the figures of hog receipts in Chicago up to 1900 (see Fig. 34).

As we have mentioned, the markets in which the random components dominate are those of agricultural products.

We shall now deal with the second type of divergency, in which the components of the movements in individual markets show a character of their own. With respect to the trend and the random component, this is not possible. In a sense all trend movements are of the same character. They are monotonic movements, and the only difference that can be observed is one of direction, positive or negative. A difference in slope may be considered as a difference in intensity and would therefore be of the nature of the differences discussed in the preceding paragraphs. A difference in direction may in fact also be considered as a difference in intensity. Thus the products which are gradually disappearing from the market because of the competition of new products show a trend of direction opposite to that of production in general. The construction of sailing ships, for instance, shows a declining trend since 1870. The same negative trend will be found for minerals, deposits of which become gradually exhausted. The production of copper in England, for example, has been steadily declining since 1892.

A finer distinction may, however, be made in the shape of the trend curve. One may distinguish between trends which, over a period of a number of decades, show clearly the form of a growth curve and trends which cannot be distinguished from a straight line or an exponential curve. If this distinction is made, it will be found that the growth curve is the trend for a large number of individual markets, whereas for the more general series a straight line or an exponential curve is the appropriate trend. The trend of these general series represents the sum of the growth curves shows a much more regular pattern than each of point of most rapid increase at a different time. The sum of the growth curves shows a much more regular pattern than each of the component curves, as one after the other of the growth curves passes through its period of maximum rate of increase.

Random movements too, it may be said, are all of the same character. A distinction might be made according to their natural time unit. We have seen that this time unit is different for crop figures from that of most other types of random components.

Relatively little needs to be said in this connection concerning the seasonal components, for their most important characteristic is their common period, the year. An infinite variety of seasonal patterns and seasonal intensity may be distinguished. Examples were given in chapter v. Of importance in this connection is the possibility of seasonal compensation, that is to say, the heavy season in one market may coincide with a quiet season in another market. As a consequence of such compensation, seasonal fluctuations in general activity are considerably less pronounced than those in individual branches of industry; the same applies with respect to prices. Individual enterprises often follow the policy of compensating the seasonal fluctua-

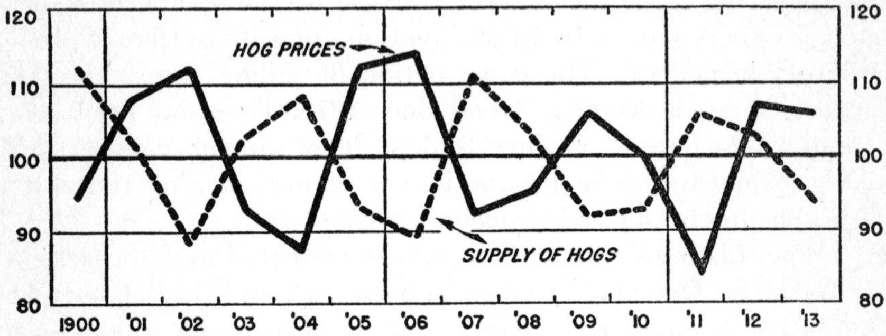

FIG. 35.—Supply and prices of hogs in Germany. Both series in per cent deviation from their trend. Source: A. Hanau, "Die Prognose der Schweinepreise," *Vierteljahreshefte zur Konjunkturforschung*, Sonderheft 2, 1927.

tions of one article by selecting other articles with opposite, or at least divergent, seasonal patterns.

Most important for our discussion here are the cyclical movements. A study of cyclical patterns in individual markets will show unmistakable differences in periods and may give us a clue to entirely new problems (see chap. xiv); in this chapter only a brief description of cycles in various individual markets is presented.

HOG CYCLE

The tendency toward individual cycles is most pronounced in certain branches of livestock production. The well-known hog cycle is one example. Both prices and quantities sold in the hog market have a very clear period of from three to four years, observed for many countries and over long periods (see Fig. 35).

The maxima and minima of these series sometimes coincide with the general business cycle; sometimes they do not. The maxima in the quantities coincide with the minima in the prices and vice versa. In this respect, the hog cycle is entirely different from the general business cycle, where quantities and prices tend to fluctuate jointly.

OTHER AGRICULTURAL CYCLES

Similar cycles have been observed also in the cattle market, though less regular and apparently much more disturbed by fluctuations in other markets. The period found for the Nether-

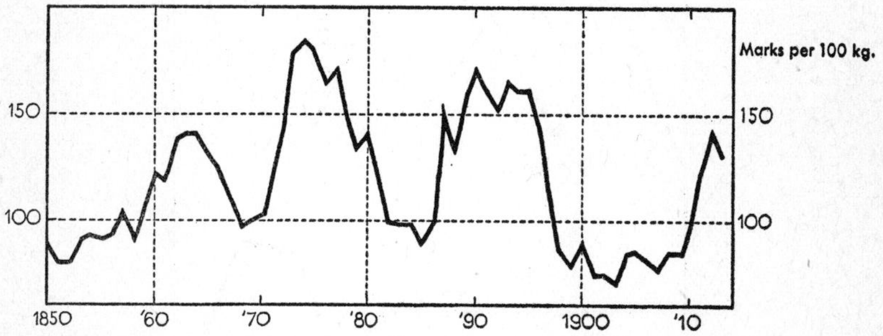

FIG. 36.—Cycles in coffee prices. Source: *Nederlandsche Conjunctuur*, June, 1930, p. 26

lands cattle market is entirely different from that for the American cattle market. In the Netherlands the period observed was approximately five years, whereas in the United States it was seventeen years.

A number of markets of vegetable products also show cycles of their own. The clearest example of this is the coffee market (Fig. 36). The period of this cycle is approximately sixteen years. In this market an opposite movement of prices and quantities may be observed.

A different type of cycle, which can be observed for almost all agricultural products but which is much less regular, is the two-year cycle. An example of it for cotton is shown in Figure 37. As we shall show later, there is some room for doubt whether this is a true cycle.

BUILDING CYCLES

Figure 38 shows the individual cycle of residential construction in the United States. This cycle, again, has a period of approximately sixteen years. The statistical material for a study of this market is rather incomplete. Of the relevant series, only that of construction is known over a considerable period, and even the material for this series is quite defective for a good

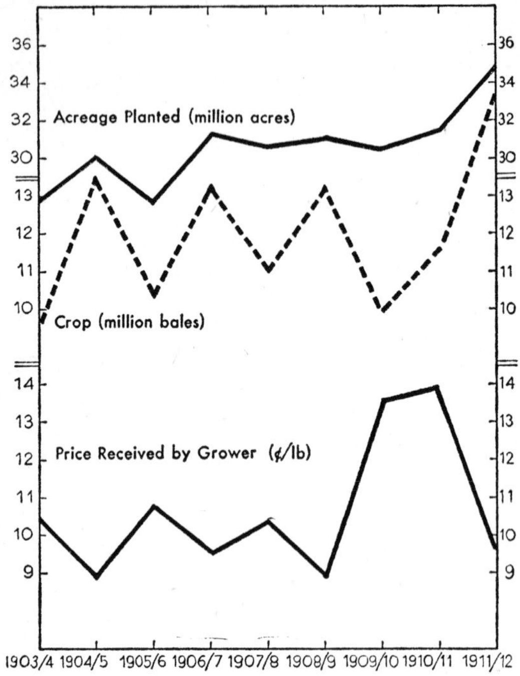

FIG. 37.—Example of the two-year cycle in agriculture: cotton in the United States.

part of the period. The series of rents, which would be of great importance in this connection, is known only for a much shorter period: really representative figures are available only recently, while figures for earlier years are available only for one or two towns. A third series of great importance in connection with this market, on which, unfortunately, only very inadequate information is available, is that of the total stock of houses. As houses are durable commodities, the total supply of dwelling services available for sale has but little connection with current building activity; this in contrast to the supply of nondurable commodities. Almost nothing is known of a fourth series that would be of importance, namely, the selling price of houses.

Whatever little statistical material is available would lead to the conclusion that, in the market of dwelling services, prices, i.e., rents, do not show a pattern precisely opposite to that of the quantity of production or the quantity of the total supply available. Closer analysis shows, further, that, although there is a clearly recognizable cycle, there are many disturbances, as might indeed have been expected theoretically.

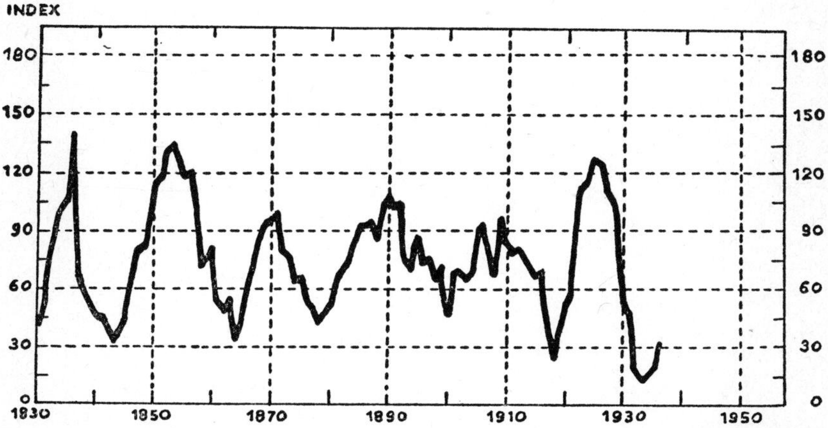

FIG. 38.—Long cycles in residential construction in the United States. Source: G. F. Warren and F. A. Pearson, *World Prices and the Building Industry* (New York, 1937).

Evidence of the existence of a cycle in residential building is limited almost exclusively to the United States. In other countries, too, there is great difficulty in obtaining in suitable form data concerning residential construction for earlier decades. Only a few series are available for long periods, in particular for a number of large cities (Amsterdam, Hamburg, London, Glasgow). Apparently, some traces of a long building cycle could be observed in the nineteenth century; toward the end of that century and in the twentieth century, moreover, other tendencies connected with the general industrial cycle dominated the housing market. As mentioned before, however, the relation between the general cycle and the building cycle is quite complicated; residential construction is strongly affected also by abrupt changes in confidence.

It is possible that tendencies toward an individual cycle exist also in shipbuilding.

Finally, a few tendencies toward a cyclical movement may be observed in markets with a speculative character. As a first example we may mention the import of raw materials. Comparison of import figures with the corresponding figures of consumption of raw materials will show a difference of a

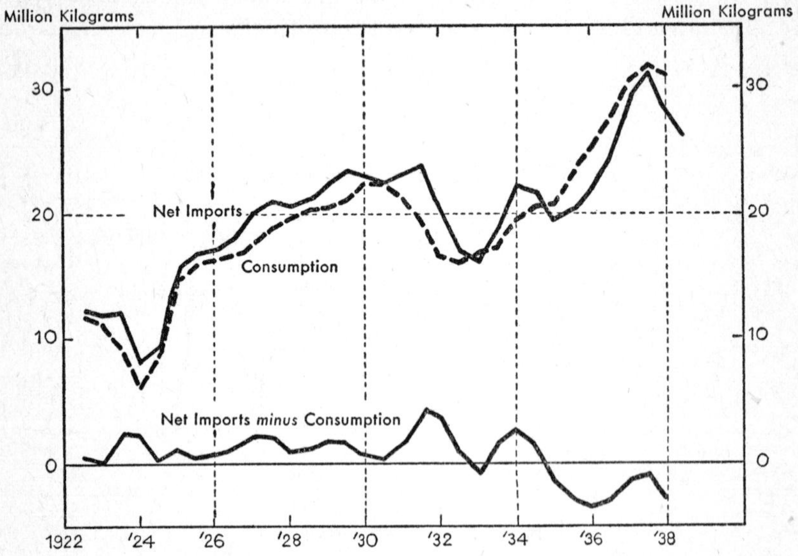

Fig. 39.—Consumption and import of raw cotton in the Netherlands. The difference between the two series, at the bottom of the diagram, shows a tendency toward a two-year cycle.

cyclical nature; the imports, which in the long run must be approximately equal to consumption, show sometimes excesses, sometimes deficiencies, compared to consumption (Fig. 39). There may be an indication here of a separate cyclical movement. However this may be, the cycle is in any case strongly disturbed by other factors. A second example is provided by the fluctuations in the share market, to which we shall refer in greater detail below.[2]

2. Cf. chap. xiii, *infra*.

PART TWO

THE EXPLANATION OF ECONOMIC FLUCTUATIONS

CHAPTER NINE

ECONOMIC STATICS AND ECONOMIC DYNAMICS

DATA AND VARIABLES

IN CHAPTERS II–VIII we have given a description of the fluctuations of economic variables. Our second task, to which Part II is devoted, will be to give an explanation of these fluctuations. We enter therefore into the field of economic science. Before we devote our attention to the concrete problems presented by the observation of economic fluctuations, we must, in this introductory chapter, make some general remarks concerning economic science itself.

The subject matter of economic science is the process of satisfaction of human needs. This process takes place within the framework of natural, technical, and institutional conditions that may be considered as given. Among them we may count the size and composition of the human population, the psychic characteristics of the people, the natural resources of the countries in which they live, the technical means they use, the legal structure—free competition or a more controlled economy—etc. From these data follow certain phenomena and magnitudes, with respect to the satisfaction of needs, which we call "economic phenomena" or "economic magnitudes." Examples are the quantities of various commodities and services produced and traded, prices, incomes, and expenditures of individuals. The magnitudes of these variables are the unknowns in the quantitative problem that economic science has to solve.

It will be noted that the definition of the purpose of economic science has been stated rather loosely and, in particular, that the division between those magnitudes which are given and those which must be considered as unknown has been indicated by examples only. This looseness of definition, which may be thought unsatisfactory by some, is due to the fact that within the entire field of economics a great variety of problems is conceivable and admissible, and the border line between given magnitudes and magnitudes to be determined varies according to the problem under consideration. Certain economic problems may be posed in such a general fashion that even parts of the legal structure of the country may be considered as unknown. On the other hand, it will often be suitable even for problems of a very high degree of abstraction to assume as given the stock of capital goods available to a certain population; in still more general problems, however, this variable will no doubt have to be considered as an unknown. In the more limited problems, with which economics has been most productive, it will often be possible to assume as given all magnitudes outside one particular market.

In each economic problem there are, therefore, certain given variables which may also be called "data," or "exogenous variables." Those data, which must be considered as given even in the most general economic problems, will be called the "fundamental economic data." Among such data we may distinguish between those that are constant and those that are variable. The size of the population, the stock of capital goods, the main outlines of the legal organization and of technical knowledge, are normally assumed to be constant or nearly constant; on the other hand, annual crops and certain parts of the legal organization, tariffs for example, are considered as variable data. The more constant data describe the characteristics of the economy under consideration or of a certain portion of it; these data are often referred to by the term "economic structure."[1]

The results of economic science are often put in the following form. From the given values of the economic data, certain

1. It follows from this definition of economic structure that one cannot count as part of the structure the ratio between agricultural and industrial production and similar magnitudes which are often considered as elements of the economic structure. The volume of production is an economic magnitude, not a datum. We prefer, therefore, not to consider this ratio as an element in the economic structure but to reserve this term for the more fundamental magnitudes of natural and technical character that lie behind this ratio, such as the quality of the arable land, the size of the population, and per-

values follow for the economic variables; for instance, with respect to an individual market: Given productive capacity and costs as data on the supply side and incomes and preference scales of potential buyers as data on the demand side, the quantity sold and the price are determined (leaving aside many details, for purposes of simplification). Another example for an economy of a very simplified structure would be the following: Given the size of the population, the stock of capital goods, the preference scales of the individual persons, and the production function (that is to say, the technical coefficients), the volume of production, the real wage, and the real rate of interest may be determined.

The values for the economic variables determined in this way are thought to "correspond to" the given values of the data; in accordance with the type of reasoning given, they are equilibrium values. In other words, the theory implies the additional assumption that the situation is stationary; and the question is put this way: How large should the volume of production be, how high should the price level be, in order that the situation remain stationary? The question as to what would happen if the situation were not stationary falls outside the scope of this line of reasoning. When the data change, the preceding values of the economic magnitudes cannot be maintained. A process of movement will occur. But the type of theory to which we refer does not describe this process. It describes only a position which would continue to exist once it has come into existence. The theory does not concern itself with the question whether this situation will actually come into existence. This would require that (*a*) the data remain unchanged after an initial change and (*b*) the movement of the economic system is in the direction of adaptation, or, in the terminology introduced earlier, represents a damped process. If the process following upon a change of data were of a different character, particularly if it were undamped or antidamped, the new equilibrium position would

---

haps the stock of capital goods. To the extent that these more fundamental magnitudes determine approximately the ratio indicated—with little effect of other economic variables—it may be said that the ratio reflects approximately an element of the economic structure.

never be reached. Nor would it be reached if the data were changed again before a damped process had led to the attainment of the new equilibrium values.

STATICS AND DYNAMICS

The economic theory which is based on the assumption of a stationary position may be called "economic statics." It may be said that this theory is applicable only to long-run tendencies, provided always that the movements set into motion by the changes in data are damped and that the data themselves do not change again in the meantime. It would also be applicable if these movements were damped and took place very rapidly, in other words, if the economic magnitudes adapted themselves immediately to the data. This latter assumption is often made tacitly, sometimes with more justification, sometimes with less.

If this assumption is satisfied, movements in the economic variables can occur only as a consequence of movements in the data. Many attempts have been made to explain economic movements on this basis. This approach, in which situations corresponding to different values for the data are compared, has been called "comparative statics." We have seen, however, that there are not only immediate but also gradual processes of adaptation. In the latter, movements occur even though the data remain unchanged. It might be argued that such movements require at least a change in the data to be set into motion. But this is not necessarily the case. The process of change that consists in the accumulation of capital and that follows from the tendency to save and the tendency toward expansion of production need not be set into motion by any change in the data.

Movements that occur while the data remain constant are called "endogenous movements." As we shall discuss in more detail below, we consider cyclical movements as endogenous movements to a considerable extent. We mentioned, further, the process of accumulation. Movements that may be considered as the immediate, or the almost immediate, adaptation to changes in data are called "exogenous movements." An important part of the seasonal movements may be considered as such. The development of an economy in consequence of an increase in the population may also be considered as an exogenous movement. Here, the adaptation is not immediate in the limited sense of the word; it may take a year, for instance, before an increased supply of labor may lead to a corresponding reduction in the wage level. But compared to the periods over which relevant changes in population occur, a year is a relatively short span of time, and the adaptation may be considered as nearly immediate. It is assumed in this example that the movement of the wage rate is in fact an adaptation and not an undamped, or antidamped, process; there are good reasons for this assumption.

It will be clear from the preceding remarks that conventional economic statics cannot contribute to the explanation of endogenous processes. The theory which is necessary to explain these processes and which will follow step by step the process of adaptation and the succeeding movements will be called "economic dynamics." Economic dynamics has also been defined quite accurately as the economic theory of the relations between variables at different moments of time (Frisch). Yet dynamics is not so totally different from statics as is sometimes believed. It is based on much that has long been accepted by economic research workers but that, in statics, could be used only in part. An important difference between statics and dynamics is that the latter can never be indifferent to the question as to how much time a certain change takes. Economic dynamics must measure time also; it must incorporate time in its analysis as one of the variables.

As a consequence, economic dynamics is nearer to reality and, by being less abstract, is sometimes simpler. Economic statics may put forward the theorem that a certain commodity will not be produced in the long run if the production involves a loss. In the short run, however, production at a loss will occur. Economic dynamics will take this fact into consideration and will on that account be more realistic.

Let us analyze a slightly more complicated example to illustrate this point further. Economic statics shows us that a technical improvement which reduces the cost of production of a certain commodity will lead to a new equilibrium with a lower price and a larger quantity sold. Economic dynamics will describe the process in terms of the successive reactions of the economic subjects participating. Following a reduction in cost by, say, five cents, the suppliers may reduce the price by, e.g., three cents, with a view to selling so much more at this price as to maximize their profit. This implies a certain expectation concerning the quantity salable at the lower price, an expectation for which no empirical basis may be available. The price reduction will lead to a certain increase in the quantity sold. If, however, the increase in the quantity sold is greater than had been expected, it may be more profitable for the suppliers to raise the price again somewhat, depending on their cost curve. Let us assume that it is to their advantage to raise the price and that they raise it by one cent. This will again lead to a small reduction of the quantity sold. In this way the well-known process of trial and error will be executed. Static economic theory may make some reference to this process, but it makes no use of it; it does not study the process. Analysis by economic dynamics will lead to the conclusion that the process of trial and error will not necessarily lead to an equilibrium position. The well-known cobweb theorem—one of the theorems of dynamics—shows this in detail.[2] In this respect, economic dynamics is more realistic than economic statics. By its separation of the process of trial and error into a number of successive reactions, indicating at each stage clearly what is cause and what is effect, economic dynamics gives a picture which is much more readily understandable than that of economic statics.

SUPPLY AND DEMAND ANALYSIS

A very important instrument in both static and dynamic economics are the supply and demand schedules used to describe a market. We must devote some further attention to this subject. Various alternatives are possible; we shall deal here with the most usual one based on free competition. In a market, a sale of a certain commodity takes place. The sale reflects an

2. Cf. p. 235, *infra*.

agreement between sellers and buyers. The quantity sold is at the same time the quantity that the buyers are prepared to buy and the quantity that the sellers are prepared to sell. If we call the first quantity the quantity demanded and the second quantity the quantity supplied, then there must be equality between the quantity demanded and the quantity supplied. Both depend on a number of other variables. One of these is the price of the commodity in question. But the quantity demanded depends not only on the price but also on other variables which we may call "demand factors." For consumers' goods these demand factors may be, for instance, the income of the buyers and the prices of other commodities. In the case of producers' goods a number of other, technical factors may also be of importance. The quantity supplied depends not only on the price but also on a number of other variables which we shall call "supply factors." For most commodities the cost of production and the size of the productive capacity should be considered as supply factors.

Given the supply and demand factors, the quantity demanded and the quantity supplied will be determined by the price only. For every given price there will be a certain value of these two quantities. A relation of this nature may be expressed in a table, either a demand table or a supply table. The relations may be referred to as demand functions and supply functions; the quantity demanded and the quantity supplied are both "a function of the price." These functions or tables may be expressed in a diagram (see Fig. 40). In a rectangular system of co-ordinates XOY every point is characterized by two numbers, the X-co-ordinate and the Y-co-ordinate. According to the demand table, a certain value Y of the quantity demanded will correspond to a given value X of the price. These corresponding values can be represented by one point in the diagram. If the price is changed, another point is obtained. All these points together form a curve, the demand curve. A supply curve can be constructed in the same way. Both the demand curve and the supply curve correspond to given values for the demand factors and the supply factors.

In the market under consideration transactions will occur

only at that price at which the quantity supplied and the quantity demanded are equal. This price may readily be determined if the demand curve and the supply curve are known and are drawn in the same diagram. It is the price which corresponds to the point of intersection of the two curves (Y^S). At that price, the quantity supplied and the quantity demanded are equal, and X^S is the quantity sold and bought. The price and the quantity sold follow from the demand and supply functions, that is to say, from (*a*) the values of the demand and supply factors and (*b*) the coefficients reflected in the demand and supply functions. One might also say that they follow from the position and

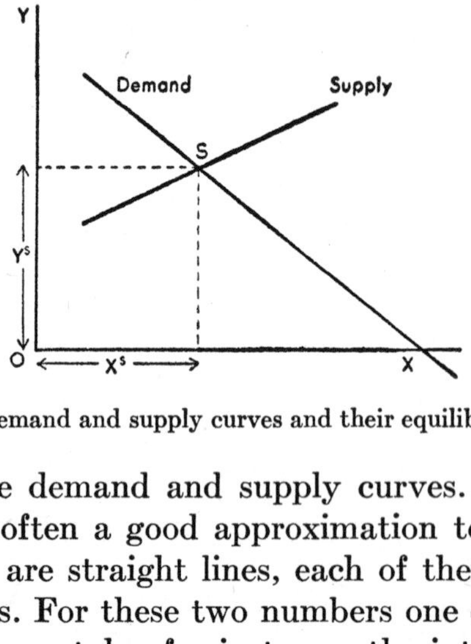

FIG. 40.—Demand and supply curves and their equilibrium point *S*

the slope of the demand and supply curves. In the simplest case—which is often a good approximation to reality—where the two curves are straight lines, each of them is determined by two numbers. For these two numbers one can select different pairs. One may take, for instance, the intercepts with the two axes. Or one may take the intercept with the *Y*-axis and the slope of the curve or the intercept with the *X*-axis and the slope of the curve. We select here the last-mentioned pair of numbers. The intercept with the *X*-axis represents the quantity demanded or supplied at a zero price. It may be rather difficult to see the economic sense of this particular number. One could take just as well the quantity demanded or supplied at any other fixed price. Graphically, however, the first concept is simpler because it does not require an additional vertical line in the diagram. It is also simpler algebraically; but, in line with the scope of this book, we shall not pursue this point. We shall call the intercept with the X-axis the "level" of the supply curve, or, respectively, of the demand curve. We state, therefore, that each of these two curves is determined by its level and its slope.

The level and the slope of the demand curve depend, among other things, on the values of the demand factors. They depend, further, on given data of a more fundamental character, such as the preference scales of the buyers. For other demand factors and other values of these data the level and slope of the demand curve will be diffierent. No general statement can be made as to which way the slope will be affected. On the other hand, it is

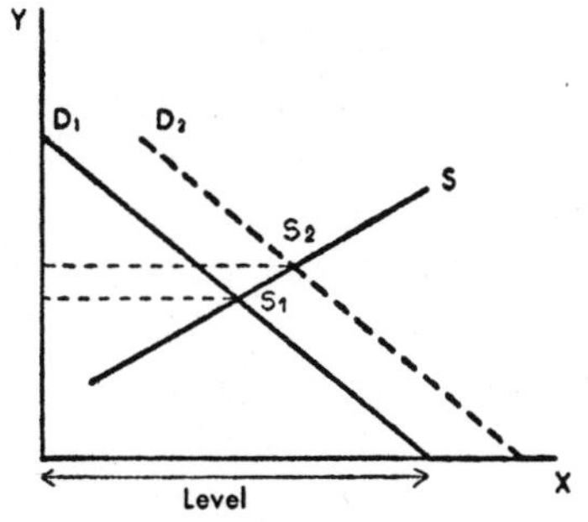

FIG. 41.—Change in level of the demand curve and its effect on the equilibrium point.

usually possible to state in which direction the level of the demand curve will move if income is increased or if the price of competing commodities is increased. In view of this, changes of the demand factors may as a first approximation be considered to affect only the level of the demand curve and not its slope. An increase in the income of the buyers will lead to a higher level of the demand curve and so will an increase in the price of a competing commodity; an increase in the price of a complementary commodity will lower the level of the demand curve. In all these cases we may assume a parallel shift of the demand curve. This shift, due to a change in demand factors, will lead to a shift in the point of intersection of the demand and the supply curves (see Fig. 41). Similar considerations apply to the supply factors. An increase in productive capacity will lead to a higher level of the supply curve and so will a decrease in costs.

As we have stated, the slopes of the demand and supply curves (which are closely related to the elasticities of demand and supply) may, as a first approximation, be considered as remaining unchanged when the demand and supply factors change. The slopes will change, however, when some of the more fundamental data change, such as the preference scales of the buyers or the production functions of the sellers.

Sometimes, when changes in some of the more fundamental economic data (not those of one market but of the entire economy) are the object of study, the analysis has to be focused also on changes in the slopes of the curves; this, however, raises much more difficult problems. A change in the slope by itself does not yet determine the new position of the curve; the slope may be changed by rotation around any one point of the curve, and it makes much difference which point is selected.

We have described in some detail the mechanism of demand and supply curves because this mechanism is used as an instrument of analysis in both static and dynamic economics. In the light of what was said earlier, this may also be understood in the sense that the demand and supply analysis can be used in the explanation both of exogenous and of endogenous movements. In the static type of analysis it is assumed, as we have said, that the values of the economic variables adapt themselves immediately to changes in the data—in this particular case the data of one market. Changes in prices and quantities are then explained by reference to changes in the level of the demand and supply curves.

In dynamic economics, on the other hand, other explanations of changes in prices and quantities are possible. One of the simplest cases of this is that in which there is a time lag between a change in the price and the consequent change in the quantity supplied. The instrument of the supply curve is then used in a different way: to indicate not in what way the quantity supplied will be determined by the price in the long run or after complete adaptation but how it depends on the price which prevailed at a certain specific earlier period. If one knows that the quantity is determined by the price with a certain lag, the supply curve indicating such a short-run reaction may be quite different from the supply curve indicating the ultimate adjustment.

It may very well be, for instance, that the seller will change the quantity supplied in response to a change in the market price in the direction of the ultimate change but not to the full extent. Different psychological and technical conditions will determine how large this initial and provisional adjustment will be. In a quantitative application of the supply curve to the short-run reaction, one will have to use figures different from those which apply to the reaction according to economic statics. Any knowledge concerning the quantities involved can be obtained only by statistical measurement of the curves. To the extent that we have any statistical knowledge of these curves, we know the provisional rather than the final reactions. In the explanation of reality the final reactions are of importance only to the extent that a sufficient time elapses before a new change in the relevant data occurs. In a qualitative sense it is possible in any case to operate with the same concepts of supply and demand curves in dynamics as in statics; it is possible that the quantitative differences are not too great either.

The same situation may also be described in other words. If we assume that the quantity supplied depends not on the price at the time of supply to the market but on an earlier price, one may say also that supply is completely inelastic but that there is an additional supply factor, namely, the price at an earlier period of time. Logically, this proposition is unexceptionable; in further analysis it is, however, often more convenient to extend the concept of the supply function in the way we did.

An important intermediate case is that in which the supply function depends both on the current price, as in economic statics, and on the price some time before, as in our dynamic case. In such a situation the preceding price must be counted as one of the supply factors.

The instrument of demand and supply curves may be generalized into a dynamic instrument in many other ways. One of these consists in assuming that the quantity demanded depends not only on the price, either current or past, but also on the change of the price compared to a preceding period. The change in price may often play a role, particularly in demand functions when speculative purchases are of importance.

In the preceding examples, dealing with situations in markets that represented only a very small part of the total economy, it was assumed that the demand and supply factors were independent of the result of the exchange, that is to say, independent of the price and the quantity in the market under consideration. In other words, the demand and supply factors were considered fully exogenous in the particular market. Strictly speaking, this can never be exactly true, since incomes must always be dependent on the price and the quantity sold in every market. When the market is small compared to the total economy, this point may be disregarded. This approximation, however, is not permissible in connection with a market that represents a large part of the economy, for instance, the labor market or the market for consumers' goods in general. In the analysis of such a market more complicated systems are required, particularly in economic statics. In economic dynamics, on the other hand, we have the advantage (indicating once more how economic dynamics is in some respects simpler than economic statics) that a more complicated system is often not required; this may in particular be the case if certain lags may be assumed between the formation of income and the exercise of demand in the market under consideration. The quantity sold in a market will determine current income but not income at a slightly preceding period; in that case, the preceding income may still be considered as exogenous with respect to the market under consideration.

In both statics and dynamics it will be necessary to deal with a large number of economic variables in order to explain developments in the economy as a whole. If we are to handle a large number of markets and all the relations applicable to them, the number of variables involved will usually be very large. Since our minds are not able to operate at one time with a system of so many relations between a great number of variables, the general scheme will often have to be simplified in many respects. A number of examples of this will be given below.

In addition to demand and supply relations, a number of other relations, equally well known from conventional theory, will have to be used. We may mention, for instance, technical relations, such as those which indicate the relation between the quantities produced of a certain commodity and the quantities of the factors of production employed in the production of that commodity. Further, we may mention certain definitional equations, such as the one stating that saving equals income minus consumption expenditure. We do not need to discuss these various types of relations at this stage since they present no particular problems.

The demand and supply functions as discussed in the preceding paragraphs indicate only one type of reaction, namely, the reaction of the quantity supplied or demanded to the price, the latter being considered as given. This is the normal reaction in certain markets, such as the security markets and the markets of the world's main staples. But this description of markets, in accordance with the classical theory of free competition, is not so suitable with respect to other markets. It is often more realistic to assume that the seller sets the price in response to the quantity sold, whereas the buyer determines the quantity he wants to buy in response to the given price. The buyer reacts in accordance with the classical scheme, but the seller does not. Both have specific reactions to either preceding or current economic variables, and these reactions can be described in a way similar to our description of supply and demand functions, even if they refer to variables other than quantities and prices. Much of what we discussed before, therefore, has very general validity and may also be used in the treatment of other problems of economic fluctuations.

CHAPTER TEN

THE PROCESS OF LONG-RUN DEVELOPMENT

THE CONDITIONS OF FULL UTILIZATION OF RESOURCES

ACCORDING to economic statics, a given status of population, technical knowledge, and stock of capital goods, combined with given values for a multitude of technical, psychological, and other coefficients, will, under certain conditions that we will have to analyze further, determine the levels of production, employment, relative prices, incomes, etc. As we said earlier, the instrument of economic statics is, therefore, not a fully adequate, although an important, instrument to explain the trend of economic development. Economic development occurs to a considerable extent as a result of changes in population, changes in technique, and changes in the stock of capital goods. These changes lead to certain problems that fall outside the scope of economic statics and also outside the scope of comparative statics. What will be the curves that production, employment, incomes, etc., describe over time? What is the influence on them of the rate of increase in population, in capital formation, and in technical development? What effect do interruptions such as wars have on this development? Will the income distribution tend to change in such a way that it will lead to socially intolerable situations? We shall have to expand economic statics into a theory which encompasses the process of long-run development and to try to apply this theory to the solution of the problems indicated. Before we make any use of the theorems of economic statics, it may be useful to make clear certain of their assumptions which have not always been realized clearly.

Economic statics in its more usual versions is characterized by a certain optimism concerning the question whether all productive factors will be used in the process of production. Often the equilibrium level of production is portrayed as the result of the happy co-operation of all labor, all natural resources, and all capital goods. Very generally speaking, this proposition is made plausible in the following way. If any workers or capitalists are involuntarily excluded from participation in the process of production, they will offer their services at a lower wage or a lower rate of interest and will in this way insure their acceptance in the process of production. In other words, full employment of all productive factors is believed to be guaranteed by considering only the supply of the factors of production. However, it would appear from experience that the importance of the changes mentioned, that is to say, the inducement exercised on entrepreneurs by price-cutting of the factors of production, is overestimated. This is indicated by the periods of long-drawn-out depressions that have occurred particularly since 1920 but also in earlier periods. It would seem clear from experience that a certain "suction" on the entire economy is necessary to have it run at full capacity.

More concretely and more exactly: the symmetry which is assumed in most conventional versions of economic statics between the demand and supply sides of the market would not appear to be in correspondence with reality. In particular, the volume of production of goods and services is determined mainly by the demand for them. In most markets the initiative concerning the quantities is with the buyers, that concerning the prices with the sellers.

We may go somewhat more deeply into this question and analyze at whose initiative important changes in the volume of total production are brought about. Total production may for this purpose be considered to consist of the production of consumption goods and the production of investment goods. For convenience we count services among goods. The demand for consumption goods is exercised to a very large extent by persons receiving moderate incomes and whose demand is determined by their income. They cannot spend much more, and they do not want to spend much less, than their income. The magnitude of their income is almost exclusively determined by the volume of total production and does not, therefore, add a new element to the determining factors. The consumption expenditure of persons receiving higher incomes has a greater degree of freedom; but it, too, is affected by the size of these incomes. Most independent, therefore, are the expenditures for investment. Except for the investment expenditures of small entrepreneurs who have no access to the capital market, investment expenditures are not limited by the size of incomes but can exceed them by recourse to credit.

The existence of strong motives to make investment expenditure is, therefore, of great importance in the determination of the total volume of production. If we look at the nature of large segments of investment expenditure, we are led to believe that a considerable influence is exercised by new technical possibilities, for instance, in railroad investment, electric-power stations, and the combustion engine, and by the discovery of natural resources in new countries. The nineteenth century has been rich in such new possibilities, which may have been responsible for keeping total demand for commodities at a relatively high level, thus providing the necessary "suction" to which we referred and the constant tendency to the use of all, or at least a very great part, of the productive resources of the economy. It may also be, as some have maintained, that the general mentality of entrepreneurs is subject to changes and that periods of greater optimism and audacity alternate with periods of caution and timidity. These differences have been associated with differences between succeeding generations and with the alternating domination of the male and female elements. Such suggestions, though interesting, do not appear to be very strongly founded scientifically; in any case, it is not the task of economics to analyze them further. These are data for economic science, and we cannot probe more deeply into them.

In any case, it will be necessary in our analysis to make a sharp distinction between two cases, that in which the total demand for commodities is intensive and that in which it is weak. In a period of intensive demand one may say approximately that the volume of production is determined by productive capacity; in periods of weak demand the influence of productive capacity is minor.

Both situations may be considered as special cases of one and the same demand and supply diagram in which the level of the demand curve changes (Fig. 42). According to usual practice, the quantities of production are indicated along the horizontal axis, prices along the vertical axis. The solid line S indicates the supply curve; the distance c indicates productive capacity. As the price increases from a very low level, only a very few enterprises will initially be able to produce; supply will approximate

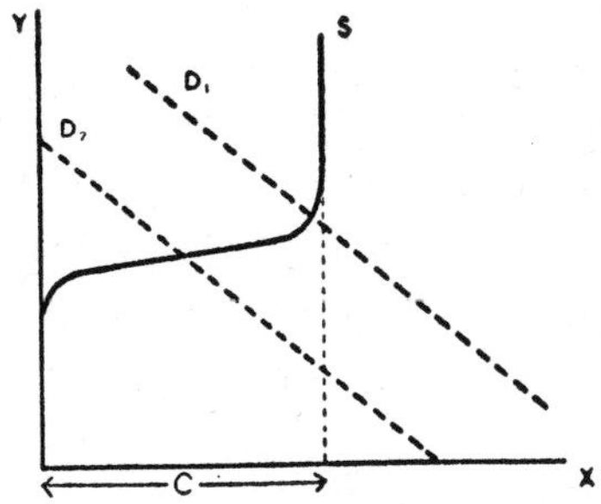

FIG. 42.—Influence of the intensity of demand on the quantity demanded and the price. In the case of strong demand (D_1), the quantity sold equals c (capacity); in the case of weak demand (D_2), c has no effect.

capacity only when the price has risen above the cost of production of the majority of producers. Obviously, supply cannot exceed capacity. The dotted lines, D_1 and D_2, indicate two positions of the demand curve. In case 1 there is a strong, in case 2 a weak, demand. In case 1 the quantity produced and sold is practically equal to c, whereas in case 2 this is not so; in case 2 the size of c is of minor consequence; but the level of the cost of production of the majority of enterprises is of importance in the determination of the quantity produced and sold.

SIMPLIFYING ASSUMPTIONS

We shall now analyze in more detail the contents of economic statics on the assumption of a strong demand. To repeat, our purpose in this analysis of statics is to gain an insight into the process of development and into the problems connected with it. In this context we shall apply simplification to all aspects that are not relevant to our purpose; if we did not, the system would become unmanageable. For instance, we shall not treat the markets for individual commodities separately but deal with only one product, which is assumed to be suitable for both consumption and investment purposes. We shall also distinguish only one type of labor and one type of capital goods. Often, we shall include the productive factor, nature, among the capital goods; in practice the distinction between nature and capital goods is in any case not an easy one. We shall at most consider only one type of land. We shall disregard the distinctions between the successive stages in the process of production, as well as the lack of mobility of labor and capital. We shall also leave out of consideration the difference in profitability of different enterprises. Some of the distinctions which fall victim to our simplifications are of importance primarily for the explanation of short-term movements; these movements are not the object of our present analysis. In the same train of thought, we shall leave out of consideration all phenomena of a speculative nature, such as the response of entrepreneurs or consumers to the rate of change in prices, as distinguished from the level of prices.

These simplifications raise a question of methodology on which we can touch only lightly. Is it permissible to disregard the phenomena mentioned? Is not the long-run development to some extent determined by them? A closely related question is whether any meaning can be attributed to the concept of a static equilibrium in a society that is subject to cyclical fluctuations. The following would appear to be a rough, provisional answer to these two questions. If the short-run fluctuations, in particular cyclical fluctuations, are damped or undamped but not antidamped, the long-run development is not affected by them, and in our study of the static equilibrium we may in this case legitimately disregard phenomena that are of importance only for the short-run fluctuations.

To offset these simplifications, we may enrich our analysis in directions that are of particular importance for our present purpose. Thus, for instance, we will not now consider the stock of capital goods as given but as a result of a process of accumulation: it is the sum of net investment over the entire period of the preceding years. We shall also admit changes in the data over time, according to certain laws. This will apply in particular to changes in population and in technical knowledge.

With respect to a number of other points, we shall work according to the well-known method of decreasing abstraction. This will apply in particular to the functions of money in the economy. We shall start out by considering an economy without money. We shall then introduce money first as a unit of account and then as a means of payment. Finally, we shall introduce money as an instrument of saving. There is much to be said for an analysis that starts out from an economy without money. Many disturbances of economic equilibrium that result from the existence of money, such as the "money illusion," are of short-run importance only; after a certain period the economic subjects will adapt themselves to changes in the value of money. If one considers only long-run developments, no great mistake is made by assuming that the adaptation to the changes in the value of money is immediate.

Within our analysis of an economy without money, we shall start again with the simplest case, following Cassel, in which we consider only increases in population and "horizontal" increases in the stock of capital goods; we shall subsequently take up the increase in capital intensity and only finally changes in technical knowledge.

THE BASIC RELATIONS OF THE SIMPLIFIED MODEL

In the economy simplified in the way indicated, two markets must be distinguished, namely, the labor market and the capital market. In the labor market there is an exchange of labor against commodities. In the capital market there is an exchange of claims to capital goods against commodities. Both markets are therefore also markets of commodities. The economic variables which relate to these markets and the development of which should be explained by economic theory are (*a*) the prices, namely, the real wage rate and the real rate of interest, and (*b*) the quantities traded, that is to say, the quantity of labor used, the quantity of capital used, and the volume of production. The quantity of labor used may also be regarded as the level of employment. The real rate of interest should be considered as the income of the owner of a unit of capital goods, expressed in terms of consumption goods. For simplicity, we shall drop the adjective "real" when we speak of prices. The level of prices and the magnitude of employment and of the use of capital are determined by the demand and supply functions in the two markets. The volume of production depends, further, by a technical relation, on the quantities of labor and capital used. This latter relation we will call the "production function."

a) The supply of labor

The supply function of labor indicates the number of workers who will offer their services at various wage rates. The most important supply factors affecting this function are the size of the population and the level of real wages considered normal or necessary. The larger the population, the larger will be the supply of labor, all other things being equal. The higher the conventional standard of living in a certain country, the lower will be the appreciation of a certain given real wage and the volume of labor supplied at that wage. The length of the working day may be considered as a third supply factor. One may want to go into further detail and consider, for instance, in addition to the size of the population, its composition, such as the distribution over productive and nonproductive age classes. These further details, however, need not be incorporated in our analysis.

A crucial question with respect to the supply function of labor is its slope. It is theoretically conceivable both that a higher real wage rate will increase the supply of labor and that it will decrease it. A higher wage will make employment more attractive and might therefore lead to a higher supply of labor; for the same reason, a lower wage might lead to a lower supply. This relation will be quite pronounced, for instance, if labor is unionized and would strike in case of a reduction of wages. It is also possible, however, that a higher wage will induce fewer members of a family to seek work because a certain minimum income, considered necessary, can be obtained with a smaller amount of work. For some members of the family the value of leisure may be greater at a higher wage than the wage which could be earned. This phenomenon is observed particularly in the case of colonial workers; in times of prosperity, however, it also applies to large families in Western economies.

Since both possibilities can exist theoretically, only observation can decide which of the two applies in a particular case. Very little empirical work has been done in this field, and the results do not always point in the same directions. In a number of cases Professor Douglas has found that an increase in wages was accompanied by a reduction in the supply of labor; this applies in particular to women and younger persons. Other studies, however, have shown opposite results. In theoretical studies of a more general character, concerning the long-run process of development, it has often been assumed that the influence of the wage rate on the supply of labor may be disregarded; it is assumed, then, that the entire population that is fit to work will desire to work.

b) The supply of capital

The supply function for capital indicates what amount of claims to capital goods will be supplied at any given rate of interest. This supply function has a higher degree of abstraction than that of the labor market. Suppliers in this market do not own the capital goods themselves but only claims to them. In reality, a considerable part of the supply of claims to capital goods is not under the control of the owners of these claims; the disposition over these claims is often made by entrepreneurs rather than by the owners. Only when enterprises attract new capital do the owners of claims decide whether they want to make the additional capital available to production. In line with our simplification we assume that the owners of capital goods receive a remuneration of interest in terms of commodities.

The supply will depend, in the first place, on the total stock of capital goods available. Here, as in the case of labor, it is uncertain in which way an increase of the remuneration, that is to say, of the rate of interest, will affect supply. Empirical studies are necessary in this case, too, to determine concretely in which direction the effect is. Little positive information is available at present; as in the case of labor, it is not unusual to assume that changes in the rate of interest will have only a small effect on the supply of capital. We shall make that assumption, and we shall consequently assume that, in times of intensive demand for commodities, the entire available stock of capital goods will be offered. Only very recently have tendencies toward monopoly on the part of savers made themselves felt; their influence has on the whole been so small that we may disregard it.

c) The production function

The demand for labor and for capital is exercised by the entrepreneurs. We may assume that the entrepreneurs are motivated by a desire to maximize their profits by the organization of production. They combine certain quantities of labor and of capital, in order to produce certain quantities of products. The yield of production, in real terms, will have to be used to pay wages and interest, both also in real terms; the remainder is the profit of the entrepreneurs. In order to determine the demand function of the entrepreneur, we have to ask this question: Up to which point will the entrepreneur continue to demand labor and capital, given a certain wage per unit of labor and a certain rate of interest for each unit of capital? He will clearly continue to purchase labor until the yield, in terms of product of additional labor, is no longer in excess of the wage, in other words, until the last worker no longer makes an addition to profits. The yield of the last worker is identical with the marginal productivity of the total quantity of labor employed. The marginal productivity will thus be equal to the wage rate. Similar considerations will lead to the conclusion that the quantity of capital employed will be such that the marginal productivity of capital is equal to the rate of interest.

The marginal productivities of labor and capital introduced in the preceding paragraph follow from the production function. This function indicates the quantity of product obtained by the application of given quantities of labor and capital.[1]

1. Followers of Boehm-Bawerk may prefer to state that the quantity of product depends on the quantity of labor and the degree of "roundaboutness" of production. The latter, however, may be derived from the quantity of capital; hence, there is no contradiction between the two ways of exposition.

Let us analyze the production function in somewhat greater detail. The definition just given has to be qualified in the sense that the application of labor and capital should be optimal. This implies that production takes place in enterprises of optimal size. We assume that the economy we consider is so large that the optimal enterprise is small in comparison to the total economy. If this condition is satisfied, it will be possible to make a small addition to total production by the addition of one new enterprise. In this situation we have to be concerned only with production functions in which the factors of production are combined in the optimal way; the extent of production that is taking place below the optimum may be disregarded because the total quantity of product which is produced in these circumstances—as the last enterprise does not work at full capacity—can only be small in comparison to total production. If these conditions are satisfied, a proportional increase of the quantities of labor, capital, and land employed (for instance, all increased by 10 per cent) will lead to an equiproportional increase in the quantity of product.

The production function will be quite different for different industries, and it may also be different for different enterprises within the same industry. It is also reasonable to assume that it changes over time. For our purposes, however, we need a production function of a rather general character, that is to say, one which would be applicable to the total production in an economy. Such a production function is of little interest to individual enterprises, and it is perhaps for this reason that relatively little research has been done with respect to it. Only a few research workers, in particular Professor Douglas,[2] have tried to establish production functions of this character on the basis of statistical data.

The simplest formula one might imagine is one in which the elasticities are constant. This is the formula which Professor Douglas has assumed for industry as a whole. The elasticity of production with respect to a certain factor of production, labor or capital, is defined similarly to the definition of elasticity of a demand or supply function, viz., as the ratio between a relative

2. Paul H. Douglas, *The Theory of Wages* (New York: Macmillan Co., 1934).

increase of the volume of output to a small relative increase of the factor of production which causes it. If an increase of 1 per cent in the quantity of labor were to produce an increase of 0.7 per cent in the quantity of product, the elasticity of production with respect to labor would be indicated as 0.7. Even if a constant elasticity function were not strictly applicable, it could still be used as an approximation for relatively small changes in the quantities. The changes that have taken place during the past century have, however, by no means been small. But the studies by Douglas do not give any indication to the effect that the elasticity would have changed considerably. If all enterprises are of optimal size, the sum of the elasticities of production with respect to the different factors of production should be equal to unity. If the three factors of production all increase by 1 per cent, the total volume of product will, as we have seen, increase also by 1 per cent, under the assumption made. The increase in the quantity of product is equal to the sum of the elasticities; thus, these elasticities together should be equal to unity. The following estimates for these elasticities have been found: for labor approximately 0.7, for capital approximately 0.2, and for land ("nature") approximately 0.1. This would imply that an increase in the application of the quantity of labor by 1 per cent, keeping the quantities of capital and land unchanged, would lead to an increase in the volume of output of 0.7 per cent, etc.

It would follow from this proposition that the percentage increase in the volume of production is equal to the weighted average of the percentage increases in the factors of production, with the elasticity coefficients as the weights.

The assumption of a constant elasticity, independent of the quantity of labor applied, would imply, strictly speaking, that there is complete substitutability among the factors of production, so that it would be possible to reduce the quantity used of any factor to as small a positive value as one likes. But it will never be necessary to carry this assumption to such an extreme point in the explanation of actual events.

At the other extreme, one might assume that the factors of production were strictly complementary. This would imply that for any given quantity of product the quantities of the factors of production required are entirely fixed and that it is not possible to change them, for instance in response to changes in the relative prices of the factors of production. Even with full complementarism, changes would, of course, be possible as technical knowledge changed. In the short run, a situation of strict complementarism may be approximated; the longer the period available for adaptation, the greater will be the substitutability.

From the assumption of constant elasticities of the volume of production with respect to the different factors of production, it would follow that the total national product will always be distributed in the same proportions over the various factors of production. An increase in the number of workers would, under that assumption, not lead to a greater share of workers in the national product; their larger number would be compensated by a lower wage rate, and in the case of a constant elasticity the two changes would exactly offset each other. The fact that the distribution of national income over wages, interest, and rent varies relatively little among countries and among periods would seem to indicate that the assumption of a production function with constant elasticities constitutes a reasonable approximation to reality. The actual figures of relative shares depend on the definitions selected, in particular on whether one includes in "labor" only manual or also intellectual and organizing labor. If labor is defined in the widest possible sense of the word, it is usually found that approximately 70 per cent of the national income is labor income, approximately 20–25 per cent capital income, and 5–10 per cent rent income.[3]

The demand and supply schedules for labor and capital sketched in the preceding paragraphs determine the prices and quantities used of these factors of production, provided that all the data in these schedules are given. The production function will then determine the quantity of commodities produced, which in our simplified economy would be equal to the real national income. The data of the economy would include the population, that wage rate which is considered normal, the length of the working day, the stock of capital goods available, the differ-

3. Cf. Table 8, p. 37, *supra*.

ent elasticity coefficients, etc. In the special case in which the elasticities of supply of labor and capital are equal to zero, the volume of employment would be equal to the size of the working population, and the quantity of capital used equal to the total stock of capital; these, with the production function, would determine the volume of production. The wage rate and the rate of interest would be equal to the marginal productivity for the given quantities of capital and labor. This would determine all economic variables in our model.

d) The formation of capital

We have stated already, however, that we will not consider the stock of capital goods as given but rather, in contrast to economic statics, will consider its explanation as one of our objectives. The total stock of capital goods may be considered as the sum of the net additions to the stock of capital goods in successive years, that is to say, as the cumulation of net real investment. We must, therefore, find out what determines the latter. It results mainly from savings and is therefore dependent on the use made of income. Savings will, first of all, depend on the magnitude of national income; the higher the income, the larger will be the amount saved and the greater the addition of capital goods to the existing stock. The fraction of income saved has remained relatively stable over time; as a first approximation it may therefore be stated that investment is proportional to income. On closer analysis, however, the propensity to save is found not to be a constant. It results, for the economy as a whole, from the propensities to save of individual persons, and these propensities depend to a large extent on the levels of individual incomes. As the average of individual incomes rises, the propensity to save will also rise. It may also depend on the rate of interest but, as we noticed, this influence is not great. There may be a number of other factors, all of which, however, are of secondary importance.

Investments may also be financed initially by the creation of credit; in real terms applicable to our model this implies that in addition to voluntary saving there is also a certain involuntary saving. Forced savings occur particularly in periods when there is a strong tendency to invest. In times of a weak tendency to invest, not all savings are absorbed; but we are not dealing here with these latter periods. In periods of a strong tendency to invest there will be a greater increment of the stock of capital than is compatible with the normal rate of saving. But there is no indication that there have been any great fluctuations in the tendency to invest during the course of the nineteenth century and the first decades of the twentieth century, excepting perhaps a certain relaxation in the period from 1919 to 1939.

Savings are made primarily from incomes received from capital since in the main these are the largest incomes. If we may assume that the production function has constant elasticities, income from capital will be a constant proportion of total income.

As a first approximation, it is therefore reasonable to assume that capital formation is proportional to income, that is, to production. As a closer approximation, it may be stated that the increase in the stock of capital will be slightly more than proportional to the increase in the volume of production.

ANALYSIS OF ECONOMIC DEVELOPMENT

a) *Horizontal growth*

Using the instruments developed in the preceding section, we now endeavor to explain the process of economic development. We may start with a simple case, already treated by Cassel.[4] We shall call this case "horizontal growth." This term refers to a case in which there is no change in the ratios between the quantities of labor, capital, and land used; the formation of capital and the exploitation of new natural resources are used only to provide for an increase in population at a constant level of consumption. Horizontal growth will occur if, at a certain period and perhaps by accident, the rate of saving is such that the relative increase in the stock of capital is equal to the relative increase in the population. If the population increases by a constant percentage per year, the population curve will be an exponential curve. If the population follows a growth curve, that

4. Gustav Cassel, *The Theory of Social Economy* (New York: Harcourt Brace, 1932), Book I, chap. vi, "The Uniformly Progressing State."

is to say, a curve with a declining rate of increase, and capital formation runs parallel, total production will also show a declining rate of increase.

With horizontal growth, prices will remain unchanged. At any one time, the economy will be an exact replica of the economy at an earlier time, with all quantities multiplied by a certain factor.

b) Capital formation

As our next slightly less simple case we consider an economy in which the rate of capital accumulation is more rapid than that of the increase in population. For convenience we assume that the quantity of land increases in proportion with the population; we assume, further, that there is no change in technical knowledge. In particular, the production function remains unchanged. However, there will now be a change in the relative quantities of labor and capital used; production will become more capital-intensive. Mechanization, the replacement of labor by capital, will occur. Since the increase in the volume of output will be equal to a weighted average of the rates of increase of the factors of production with the elasticities as weights, total production will now also increase more rapidly than the population. Per capita income will increase. As we have seen, capital formation may be considered as approximately proportional to the volume of production. It will increase, therefore, at the same rate as production, in other words, at a slower rate than the stock of capital goods. The latter, therefore, will increase by decreasing percentage amounts. Production will no longer follow an exponential curve. The exact nature of the curve which it will follow cannot be discussed without introducing certain mathematical complications.

At the next stage we assume that the state of technical knowledge increases. A technical improvement may be defined as a change in the function of production in such a way that the same quantities of labor, capital, and land will produce a greater volume of output. This may also be expressed in this way: the same quantity of product can be obtained with a smaller quantity of the factors of production. The former expression, however, is the simpler, particularly for the case to which we want to apply it. Technical improvement may occur both if substitution between the factors—labor, capital, and land—is possible and if the factors are fully complementary. In the former case the second description has to be used. A smaller quantity of the factors of production has to be interpreted, then, as quantities which together cost less than the quantities used previously. It may well be that larger quantities of one or two of the factors are used, provided that the higher costs are more than compensated by lower costs for the other factor or factors.

We shall concentrate, for the moment, on the case in which the factors of production are always fully employed and in which, moreover, some substitution is possible among them. In that case, technical improvement will always lead to a larger volume of output. The volume of production will increase more rapidly if we assume a continuous improvement in technical knowledge than without such improvement. Assuming, again, a capital formation proportional to the volume of output, the former will also increase at a more rapid rate. It is now again possible that the percentage increase of income and of capital formation is the same as that of the stock of capital goods, so that the volume of output may again follow an exponential curve. In that case, output will increase more rapidly than the population, if the latter follows a growth curve. It would seem that this case provides a good approximation to reality.

It is clear from these simple examples that production may follow different curves, among them exponential curves but also very many other curves. It is also clear that the rate of increase of population, the rate of capital formation, and the rate of the development of technical knowledge influence the shape of this curve. These influences may be calculated numerically in certain simple cases, but in more complicated cases, particularly if account has to be taken also of changes in wage demands and of an elasticity of the supply of labor different from zero, the problem can be solved only by mathematical treatment.

In the last case it will follow from the production function that the percentage rate of increase of production per annum would be equal to the sum of (*a*) 0.7 times the percentage increase of the population, (*b*) 0.2–0.25 times the percentage increase of the stock of capital goods, and (*c*) 1 times the percentage increase of production as a result of technical improvement, that is to say, the increase of production which occurs if the quantities of capital and labor remain unchanged.

The percentage increase under (*b*) may be related further to the propensity to save, which is a more basic datum than the percentage increase in the stock of capital goods. If the ratio of the value of the stock of capital goods to the annual national income is assumed to be 5—a rather realistic figure—then we may substitute for (*b*) 0.04–0.05 times the propensity to save (expressed as the percentage of national income saved). In order to obtain an impression of the relative importance of the three components, one should know the percentage increase in the population, the propensity to save, and the increase in production as a consequence of technical improvements. Certain provisional measurements (of which the latter magnitude is the most provisional) would lead to the following numerical values. In the period of four decades preceding the first World War the rate of increase in the population in the four largest industrial countries was on the average about 1 per cent. The propensity to save may be put at 10–15 per cent of income; the increase of production as a consequence of technical improvement amounted to about 1 per cent per year. On the basis of these figures the three components indicated would be as follows: (*a*) 0.7 per cent to be attributed to the increase in the population, (*b*) 0.4–0.8 per cent to be attributed to capital accumulation, and (*c*) 1 per cent to be attributed to technical improvement.

It is clear from the preceding reflections that the relative significance of these components may be changed very considerably, for instance, if the rate of increase of the population slows down; the coefficient would also be affected if the elasticity of supply of labor were different from zero.

If the elasticity of supply of labor were equal to -1, the propensity to save would have no influence whatsoever, whereas the influence of the population increase would be greater; if, on the other hand, the elasticity were equal to 0.5, the influence of the propensity to save and of technical improvement would be twice as large and that of the rate of increase in the population would be less than the one given above.[5]

DISTRIBUTION OF INCOME

After dealing with the development of production, we may now turn to the wage rate and the rate of interest. As we have seen, they will be equal to the marginal productivity of labor and capital, respectively. In the case of horizontal growth, neither of these will change, and the wage rate and the rate of interest in real terms will remain constant. If the capital intensity increases without technical improvement, the marginal productivity of labor will increase and that of capital will fall. Technical improvement, however, will add an increasing component to these two movements. Technical improvement would also make possible an increase in the rate of interest. In actual fact, the wage rate has shown a sharply increasing tendency, whereas the rate of interest seems to be falling in the long run.

We may now come to the question of the changes in the distribution of income. We have seen that under free competition, with constant elasticities of the production function, the distribution of income over the different factors of production would be in a constant proportion. This proposition does not depend on the existence of free competition in the labor and the capital markets, since it follows directly from the proposition that entrepreneurs will employ labor only when and up to the point where the increase in output is in excess of the wage. Income per head of the labor population, in comparison to income per head of other groups of the population, will depend on the number of persons in each group. If the number of persons in the working class increased more rapidly than that of the owners of capital and land, then the wage rate per head would develop relatively unfavorably. In practice, this question is complicated by the fact that one person may receive both labor and capital income. Our proposition, however, does indicate in any case that income per head is determined not only by economic factors but also

5. For a systematic treatment on a mathematical basis, reference is made to J. Tinbergen, "Zur Theorie der langfristigen Entwicklung," *Weltwirtschaftliches Archiv*, LV (1942), 511.

by population factors. The tendency shown by the labor population in the last decades toward a smaller rate of increase would tend to be beneficial to their per capita income, assuming no unemployment.

If it is correct to assume that the elasticities of the production function are approximately constant, it will follow that attempts to raise the wage rate by association on the part of the workers could not increase the total labor income. Such attempts would, on the other hand, increase total labor income if labor and capital were complementary factors of production. In that case the demand for labor would be determined by the total volume of capital and would, within certain limits, be independent of the wage rate. This applies to some extent to changes in the short run. In these circumstances an increase of labor income would be possible at the expense of the incomes of capital and land. In the longer run, however, account would then have to be taken of the following facts: the lower incomes of capitalists would lead to a lower rate of capital formation, resulting in a less favorable development of the demand for labor at a later time. It might be that, in the longer run, total labor income would be lower than it would have been without the increase in the wage rate.

If the production function had rigidly constant elasticities, an increase in the share of labor in national income could be achieved only by taxation policy and by various social policies.

It is to be noted that all this refers to the distribution of incomes and not to the absolute level of incomes. The latter might be considered the more important; the distribution of income does, however, also have a considerable importance, in particular because it is mainly responsible for tensions between different classes of the population. An increased total income, accompanied by an increase in the inequality of distribution, may have dangerous consequences for the stability of society.

It has to be borne in mind that our knowledge of the production function is limited and that there are no clear facts to prove that the elasticities of this function are in fact constant. If they are not, any conclusions based on their constancy will, of course, have to be revised.

CONSEQUENCES OF WARS

Following approximately the chronological order in which some of the basic problems have presented themselves to our Western society, we will now, after our treatment of the social problem, devote a few paragraphs to the influence of a large war on the long-run process of development. We do not deal here with the problems of the war economy as such (they are treated in chap. xi) but rather with the consequences of wars on the long-run process of development.

Seen from that point of view, wars have the following characteristics. Human lives and capital goods are destroyed; as a consequence, smaller quantities of the production factors, labor and capital, are available. In addition, the regular accumulation of capital goods is interrupted for a certin period of time. In two respects, therefore, the stock of capital falls behind what it would have been without a war. The remaining population is thus likely to have a smaller stock of capital goods per head. The money side of the process of accumulation has continued, however; the population has continued to make savings, in terms of money, which have been invested in government obligations for the financing of the war. At the end of the war these savings are not matched by capital goods; there is, nevertheless, the obligation on the part of the community to make available to the holders of these government obligations a portion of the national product. We may say that there is a fictitious capital which participates in the distribution of national income but not in its production.

If the supply of labor and capital were entirely inelastic (our simplest hypothesis), all labor and all real capital would participate in production and would yield a volume of output per head lower than before the war. Of this output, part has to be ceded to the owners of fictitious capital, leaving even less for the productive factors.

If the supply functions are not entirely inelastic, the situation will be more complicated. If the elasticity of supply of labor is negative, more work will be done because the heavy burden on account of the service of fictitious capital will reduce the worker's wage. If the elasticity is positive, there will be the opposite result: since less is paid for work, it will be less attractive. The same may apply to entrepreneurs who, in view of their reduced income, especially marginal income due to high and progressive taxation, may relax their efforts.

Much concrete research will be necessary before all the consequences of the accumulation of fictitious capital have been established; it would appear clear, however, that the existence of large amounts of fictitious capital created by the succession of two large wars may entail great dangers with respect to the volume of output.

STAGNATION

So far we have analyzed the process of development on the assumption of a continuous intensive demand, particularly for investment goods. On this assumption the volume of output was primarily determined by the capacity of production.

An entirely different picture is obtained when the autonomous demand factors are not strong. In that case, the capacity of production will be no longer the determinant of the volume of production; part of the capacity may remain unused. This situation may be described in the following simplified way: the total volume of production is determined by demand, and the total use of the factors of production is determined by the attempt on the part of the entrepreneurs to meet this demand in the cheapest possible way. Given the volume of production, the choice of the quantity of one or the two factors of production is free; the quantity of the other factor of production is then determined by the production function, in accordance with the principle of the lowest total cost. It is then possible that neither the total quantity of labor nor the total quantity of capital will be fully absorbed. Under this assumption the rate of development is relatively independent of the level of investment. The rate of increase in the population has also only an indirect and not very important influence on the development of production. The volume of production will now develop primarily as a result of changes in the autonomous demand factors. In the years since 1918 autonomous factors in a number of countries have tended to produce a low level of general demand. It appeared as if the opening-up of new territories were either impossible or politically too risky, as if all new inventions were in the direction of economizing capital, and as if a general tendency toward economy tended to stifle all public expenditure.

These factors must be considered as responsible for the high average level of unemployment in some of the Western countries in the interwar period. They were, however, not the only causes. Shifts from these countries to the younger industrial countries on the periphery of the world economy were also in part responsible. We do not want to discuss the actual details of this development within the limits of this book.

Let us see in somewhat closer detail in which ways unemployment can occur, in situations both of intensive and of weak demand. We shall make a distinction between voluntary and involuntary unemployment. Voluntary unemployment occurs if part of the working population does not offer its services for production. This will occur when the supply of labor has a certain elasticity. In the case of a negative elasticity, voluntary unemployment will occur when the wage rate is relatively high; leisure, in particular that of women and children, is preferred to additional income. In the case of a positive elasticity, voluntary unemployment will occur when the wage rate is relatively low; the wage offered is not considered sufficiently attractive to compensate for the additional disutility of labor. This latter situation may occur in particular when the population has other sources of income at its disposal, e.g., unemployment assistance. It may also occur when there is a high standard of living. In the absence of other sources of income, reduction of the wage rate must in the somewhat longer run lead to a position of negative elasticity of the supply of labor.

Voluntary unemployment might also be considered to exist as a special case of the situation of positive elasticity when unions declare a strike to achieve a higher wage rate.

Involuntary unemployment, on the other hand, will occur when workers are prepared to work but cannot find work because the demand for labor is insufficient. If the labor market has the form which has been assumed by Walras and his followers as typical of all markets, this type of unemployment can occur in the equilibrium position in one case only. According to

Walras, the market operates in such a way that each supplier and each demander assumes the price as given. In the equilibrium position the price is such that the quantity demanded equals the quantity supplied. There would then be work for everybody who offers his services for work. There would be only one exception to this reasoning, namely, if the supply curve were horizontal at the equilibrium point. This would mean that a large number of workers would be prepared to work just at the current wage rate but not at a somewhat lower rate (see Fig. 43). It would then be possible that, at the current wage rate, demand would be smaller than the total number of workers who offer their services, whereas at the lower wage rate supply would be smaller than demand.

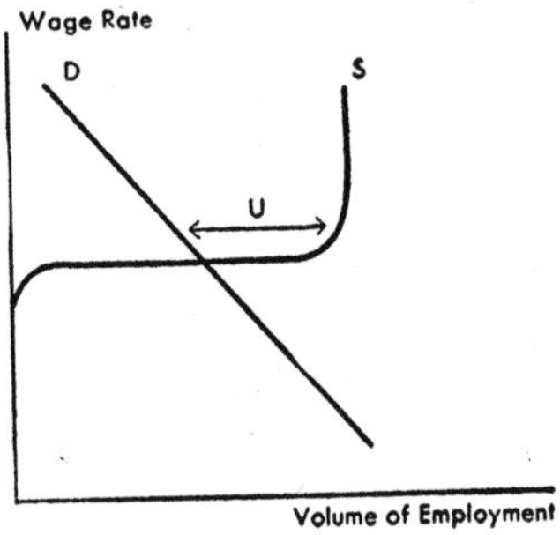

FIG. 43.—Equilibrium in the labor market if the supply curve has a horizontal part (u = unemployment).

This situation may also be described in another way. One may say that the type of market is not the one generally assumed by Walras but rather the following. In the labor market, as in many other markets, the suppliers determine the price at which they are prepared to supply; the buyers determine the quantity they are prepared to take at that price. On this assumption it is quite possible that the total supply, in this particular case the total supply of labor, will actually not be absorbed.

Within the framework of the Walrasian assumptions concerning the organization of the market, it would still theoretically be possible that there was no point of equilibrium, because the demand curve would have no point of intersection with the supply curve. In practice, however, this will probably amount to the same as the preceding case, because in reality there will always be a price, if only a price determined by the preceding period.

Involuntary unemployment is therefore possible at a relatively low level of demand. As we have mentioned, such a situation can occur, and in all probability did occur after 1918 in a number of countries, as a result of a low level of the autonomous demand factors.

MONEY

So far we have abstracted from the "veil of money." In order to approximate reality further, we must take money into account. Now, therefore, we picture all transactions as paid in money: the worker receives his wage, the capitalist his interest, in money; both use this money for the purchase of commodities. The factors of production and the product itself now have a price in terms of money, and the real wage rate to which we have referred so far is represented by the ratio between the money wage rate and the money price of the product. If, in fact, everybody were guided by real prices, nothing would be changed in the physical sphere. All relations and tendencies would remain unchanged. It would be necessary only to add a monetary sphere to our picture. This monetary sphere would be simplest in character if the economic subjects considered money only as a means of exchange and a unit of account and not as an instrument of saving, that is, a means for the accumulation of wealth. They would then hold money only for what Keynes has called the "transactions motive," that is, to meet payments they have to make before new money income becomes available. For any given level of money prices a fixed amount of cash will be needed; if prices are twice as high, double the quantity of money will be required. Conversely, if the quantity of money is given, the level of money prices will adjust itself to this quantity. Assuming no changes in the physical sphere, prices will change in proportion to changes in the quantity of money. If, further, owing to peculiarities of banking legislation (itself based on the beliefs of the economic subjects concerning the requirements of a sound monetary system), the quantity of money is proportional to the gold stock, the price level will be proportional to the latter at constant levels of production. If there are changes in the volume of output, the level of money prices will be proportional to the ratio of the gold stock over the volume of turnover. Studies by Cassel have shown that, in particular, the long waves in the price level satisfy approximately this relationship.

The picture becomes somewhat more complicated if money is used not only as a means of payment but also as a form of accumulation of wealth. There will then be a tendency to keep part of one's capital in the form of cash because cash has the advantage of liquidity. The greater the importance attached to liquidity, the larger the amount of cash held for the liquidity motive and hence not used for purchases of commodities. If the liquidity preference increases, the money price level will tend to fall. An increase in the liquidity preference will occur, for instance, in times of great uncertainty. The best-known example of such a tendency to increase liquidity occurred during the great depression of 1932.

The amount of money held will depend also on the rate of interest. By keeping money in the form of cash, one foregoes the possibility of investing it at interest; a possible interest return is sacrificed. The higher the rate of interest, the less will be the preparedness to accept this sacrifice. The level of money prices will depend, accordingly, also on the rate of interest.

Additional complications will occur if the economic subjects are guided in their decisions concerning the real sphere not only by real prices but also by money prices. In that case the "money illusion" makes itself felt. This will occur, for instance, if the satisfaction of the worker depends to some extent on the level of his nominal wage. It would lead us too far to follow the consequences of the money illusion. With respect to long-run movements, it has to be borne in mind that this illusion is usually only a temporary phenomenon, based on the fact that the subjective valuation of money is based on a previous level of prices. Essentially, the money illusion is an error which has only a second-order effect on the longer-run developments. For short-run movements its consequences may be much more important, but these are not the subject of this chapter. We must break off here our discussions of the long-run development, particularly because statistical observation has not proceeded far enough to permit more than establishing the very general tendencies which we have discussed so far.

CHAPTER ELEVEN

PERIODS OF WAR AND INFLATION

IN THIS chapter we shall endeavor to give an explanation of some of the most characteristic aspects of economic movements in periods of inflation. The two phenomena mentioned in the chapter title, war and inflation, are intimately bound up with each other in history. It is true that some wars, particularly minor wars, may have been fought without significant inflationary effects; and inflation, particularly moderate inflation, may occur in a normal business boom in peacetime, as a result, for instance, of high government spending or of unusually favorable export conditions. But all the most pronounced instances of inflation in history have occurred in or shortly after great wars.

A war period or an immediate postwar period will usually be characterized by specific commodity shortages. All three factors of production—labor, capital, and land—will tend to be supplied in lesser quantities than before. The supply of labor will be reduced by the absorption of a large number of men into the armed forces. The interruption of free ocean shipping will reduce the supply of overseas materials. After a certain time, these scarcities may lead to others: land and labor may become less productive, and the stock of capital will deteriorate. The reduced productivity of land is usually the effect of a reduced application of fertilizer and reduced care in tilling, owing to lack of labor. Labor productivity per head is likely to be reduced further by inadequate nutrition, psychic tensions, and the undermaintenance or actual destruction of capital goods.

If, however, unused resources are available, the increased demand that is characteristic of inflation may lead to an increase in output as resources previously unemployed are drawn into employment. The extent to which this will be possible will depend on the conditions in each country. Often the absence of an adequate supply of imported raw materials may present a bottleneck that will make it impossible to increase total output. However, even if a considerable increase in total output is possible, the physical volume of production will in any case be determined by certain technical limits. After an initial increase, therefore, total output will to a large extent be insensitive to further incentives, such as might be provided by increased prices. Developments in the sphere of prices will, however, affect the distribution of total output over the different groups of the population, both during the war period itself and even for long periods thereafter. The distribution rather than the production of goods and services has therefore received the greatest attention, in particular as regards the past, of economists studying the phenomenon of inflation.

INFLATION IN A CLOSED ECONOMY

In studying inflation we shall deal with it first in its simplest case, that is, in a "closed economy" in which no foreign trade occurs. In a closed economy the most important phenomenon that may be considered as an indicator of the rate of inflation is the general level of prices. At a later stage, we shall expand our analysis to include inflation in open economies; at that time the second important variable to be explained will be the rate of exchange of the currency of the country concerned. When we deal with an open economy, we shall first consider the case of inflation with a stable rate of exchange; subsequently, we shall consider also the rate of exchange as a free variable, the movement of which results from the process of inflation.

In explaining first the price level and then the rate of exchange, we shall have to reduce the movements of these variables to the movements of data or exogenous factors that lie behind them and to establish the mechanism of causation. In doing so we may find that this mechanism leads toward endogenous movements. In explaining the movement in the general price level, it seems reasonable to use the general scheme of demand and supply. It will be our task, therefore, to find the general supply and demand factors that are operative particularly in a situation of inflation and that determine the general price level.

We have mentioned that on the supply side there will be a number of tendencies operating in the direction of increased scarcity. The level of production will, in any case, be limited by certain technical conditions that may be considered as a datum. The productive capacity will change at a much slower rate than prices and the quantity of money.

More important, therefore, than the factors on the supply side is the increase in total demand. We have mentioned before, and we will return to this point later, that total demand may be considered to consist of demand for consumption and demand for investment. In that simple distinction no allowance is made for demand exercised by the government, which may be considered to be subsumed, as a relatively minor factor, under demand for consumption purposes and demand for investment purposes. This treatment is satisfactory when the objects of study are trend movements, or business-cycle movements in general, in conditions where the government plays a relatively passive role. But it is clearly not appropriate is discussing a war economy, one of the main characteristics of which is the unusually large demand exercised by the government. In wartime the government requires, and acquires by its purchases, a large proportion of the nation's real annual output. To a considerable extent the government will simultaneously take measures to offset its increased demands for the output of resources of the country by measures which will lead to a reduction of demand for resources on the part of the population. Taxes are increased, thus reducing purchasing power and hence demand on the part of the population at constant incomes. By savings propaganda an attempt is made to increase the amount of income saved and hence to reduce the proportion of income spent on consumption goods. Restrictions on investment may force business enterprises to invest less than they would have done otherwise and, possibly, actually to run down their capital. Generally speaking, these government measures toward offsetting the increased government demand were more successful in World War II than they were in World War I. Nevertheless, they result only in a mitigation of the excess demand of the government; they are never adequate fully to offset that excess demand. In wartime there will always remain a very considerable net additional demand exercised by the government. Although this is not quite accurate, one might, for purposes of convenience, associate this net additional demand by the government with the amount of the budget deficit.

If, at the outbreak of war, considerable unused resources are available, they may be drawn into use first to meet the additional demand. But the increase in supply will at the same time be accompanied by an increase in national income of the same amount. As workers previously unemployed are finding jobs, they will also receive incomes. A considerable portion of the additional income, created by the employment of resources previously unemployed, is likely to be spent on consumption goods. Thus only a small proportion and not the total of the resources previously unused can act to offset the net additional demand on the part of the government. Hence, whenever the additional government demand is large, as in any major war, only a relatively small part of it can be met by drawing into use previously unused resources. This partial offset is not likely to reduce by much the net additional demand on the part of the government.

Whence, then, come the resources that are to meet this demand on the part of the government? We may recall that we have assumed a closed economy. The additional resources, therefore, cannot come from abroad. To some minor extent, they can be obtained by using up commodity stocks. But the results obtainable in this way will be limited both in amount and in time. Hence, the resources the government requires will have to be found mainly by reduction in private consumption. This reduction in consumption is brought about by the movements of the price level. Total demand increased because of the addition of government demand, facing a supply which is reduced or, at best, constant, will tend to push up the prices of all commodities. Let us assume that prices were initially at a level of 100. Now the government requires for war purposes a net additional amount of resources to the equivalent of, say, 10 per cent of the gross national product. As a result of this increased demand, prices will go up from 100 to, say, 125.

Why does this rise in prices free resources for government use? The rise in prices reduces the real purchasing power of two important groups of the population: (*a*) those with fixed incomes, such as pensioners, persons living on annuities or on income from bonds, etc., and (*b*) those with wage and salary incomes which, though not fixed, are not automatically and immediately increased when prices go up. While the real income of these two groups of the population is reduced, the real income of the remainder of the population, mainly the entrepreneurial group, is at the same time increased by the same amount, assuming unchanged total production. There is thus not a reduction in real income but primarily a shift in real income. This shift, however, will reduce consumption demand. It will do so for two reasons. The important factor in this connection is that, broadly speaking, those whose real income has been lowered are the low-income groups, whereas those whose real income has gone up are the high-income groups. The high-income groups are likely to be subject to a higher rate of taxation; hence inflation will tend to reduce the government deficit; and high-income groups will also tend to save a larger proportion of their income. Hence, a good deal of real income shifted by inflation will lead to a reduction of consumption on the part of those who lose income but not to an increase in consumption of those who gain the additional income. If the net amount of reduction in consumption thus produced by a 25 per cent rise in prices equals 10 per cent of the gross national product, no further pressure on prices will remain. An equilibrium position will have been reached in which a reduced consumption matches the increased demand on the part of the government.

The equilibrium will, however, be temporary. Wage-earners will not be prepared to accept for any great length of time a 25 per cent reduction in real wages. Some time after prices have gone up, most wages will tend to be increased, perhaps not fully in proportion to the increase in prices but nevertheless considerably. As a result of this increase in wages, a certain amount of real income will be shifted back from the entrepreneurs to the wage-earners. By this fact, part of the stabilizing effect of the original increase in prices will have been nullified. There will again be excess purchasing power; prices will rise further until a new temporary equilibrium is reached. But then wages will be adjusted anew, and the spiral of increasing wages and increasing prices will have started.

In actual fact, this process is not likely to proceed by successive steps but rather gradually in a smoothly curved line. As the mobilization of resources for war purposes progresses, the government will gradually require a greater share of national income. Prices of some commodities in ample supply will initially remain unchanged; others will start rising immediately. Gradually, also wage increases will occur, first in one industry, then in another. Thus the index numbers of prices and wages will both tend to go up in smooth curves.

It should be noted that inflation as described in the preceding paragraph is not a rise in prices to a higher level, at which level it would be compatible with the net additional demand of the government. This would be so only if wages were not adjusted at all and if one group of the population were to accept, for the duration of the war, the reduction in real income and consumption necessary to satisfy the requirements of the government. But as wages are adjusted from time to time, inflation will take the form of a constantly rising price level. Thus the equilibrium established is not, as in ordinary supply and demand analysis, one of an equilibrium price level but one of an equilibrium rate of increase of prices. This may be shown in a diagram similar to that used in ordinary demand and supply analysis. We shall presently refer to a diagram of this nature. In the simplest case the rate of price increase per unit of time will be a constant, and prices will accordingly describe a logarithmic curve over time. The rate of price increase will be determined by two sets of factors: (*a*) the extent of the net additional government demand which, as we saw before, consisted of (1) the increase in demand by the government for resources for war purposes, less (2) the reduction in demand of the population imposed by the government through such measures as increased taxation, propaganda for increased saving at constant incomes, and restrictions on investment and (*b*) the degree to which and the speed with which wage rates are adjusted to increases in prices, the progressiveness of the system of taxation, and the tendency to save in the higher-income groups.

The larger the factor under (*a*), the net additional government demand, the more rapid will be the rise in prices. Similarly, the fuller and the quicker the adjustment of wages, the more rapid will be the rise in prices. The two factors are shown in Figure 44.

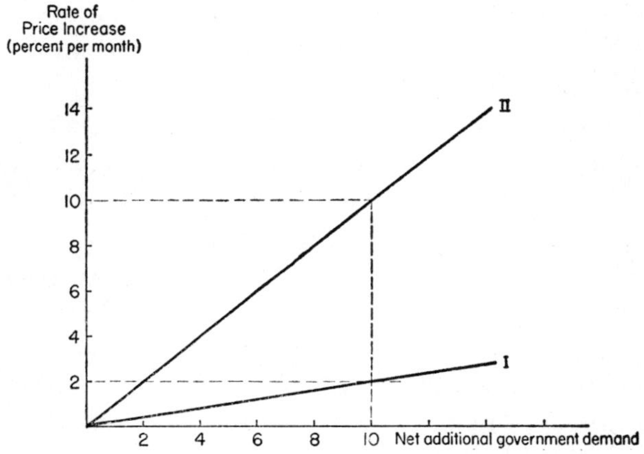

FIG. 44.—Rate of increase of prices as a function of net additional government demand.

Line *I* shows conditions favorable to a limited rate of inflation: slow wage adjustment, highly progressive taxation, a high marginal propensity to save on the part of entrepreneurs. Line *II* has been drawn to reflect conditions that would lead to rapid inflation. At the same level of inflationary pressure as expressed by the net additional government demand, the price rise resulting in case *I* will be much less than that in case *II;* e.g., if net additional demand is 5 per cent of gross national product, the equilibrium rate of price increase will be 2 per cent per month in case *I*, according to the diagram, but 10 per cent per month in case *II*. It is possible, however, that the greater slope of line *II* may be offset by a smaller amount of inflationary pressure as shown along the horizontal axis. Thus, if *I* and *II* refer to two countries, it may be possible that prices in both countries rise at the same speed. This will occur if in country *I* inflationary pressure is much greater. Country *I* might have the same rate of price increase at a net additional demand of 25 per cent of its gross national product as country *II* would at a net additional demand of only 5 per cent of its gross national product.

We have dealt so far with conditions that lead to a constant rate of inflation, that is to say, to a movement of prices along an exponential curve. As a matter of fact it is likely that inflation, when it has lasted for a certain period of time, will become more rapid. This will be so for two reasons: (1) Workers who have been caught time after time by rising prices after each adjustment of wages will insist on a more rapid adjustment of their money wages in the future. If in the beginning the lag may have been one-half year, it will tend gradually to be reduced to three months, one month, a week, and, ultimately, even as little as a day. As a result of this and other factors tending toward more rapid adjustment, the curve in Figure 44 will tend to become steeper. Gradually the curve, which initially may have been at the level of line *I*, will tend in the direction of line *II* and even beyond that. (2) To the net additional demand on the part of the government (which may remain constant), further factors will be added as inflation proceeds. Manufacturers and traders who have seen prices rising for a long period of time will tend to anticipate further price rises and buy for inventory. Consumers, rather than saving part of their income, will spend the part previously saved on additional consumption goods, either for immediate consumption (since "money loses its value anyway") or for accumulation of stocks of consumption goods. The result of these various actions on the part of the population will be the same as if the government had absorbed a larger proportion of the nation's annual output for war purposes. The point of intersection on the steeper curve caused by the factors under (1) will therefore be moved further to the right, owing to the factors mentioned in this paragraph. For both reasons the equilibrium rate of price increase will tend to be higher.

Figure 44 will readily make clear what the extreme position

will be. If, ultimately, prices and wages are adjusted immediately—if, in other words, the monetary mechanism permits the government no longer to reduce anybody's real income by any finite rate of increase in prices per unit of time—prices will tend to increase at practically an infinite rate. As curve *II* becomes steeper and steeper, it may finally coincide with the vertical axis of the diagram. At that point any positive net additional demand will lead to an infinitely high rate of price increase: any perpendicular line to the right of the origin will intersect the vertical axis in a point "infinitely far away." Strictly speaking, of course, prices cannot increase at an infinitely fast rate. Various cases in history, however, closely approximate this situation. In the conditions of hyperinflation in Germany after the first World War and in Greece, Hungary, and China after World War II, prices in the last stages did increase at rates which for all practical purposes may be described as infinite. In certain other countries, such as in Poland and Austria after World War I, inflation came very near to this point.

THE QUANTITY OF MONEY

The reader may have observed that no reference has been made so far to the quantity of money, whereas usually an explanation of inflation runs primarily in terms of that quantity. We have preferred to give our exposition initially in real terms because in that way a clearer insight is gained into the shift in real resources which is at the basis of any process of inflation. The quantity of money does, however, come in at two points. The government deficit is normally financed to a considerable extent by the creation of money either directly by the issue of government paper or indirectly by the sale of government debt to the central bank or commercial banks. Thus, if we said that the rate of increase of prices per month was a function of the amount of net additional government demand, we might also have said that the rate of increase of prices was a function of the increase in the quantity of money per month. By the same token we might say that the level of prices, which is the cumulation over time of the price increases, is a function of the quantity of money, which is the cumulation over time of the increases in the quantity of money. There is nothing in this argument, however, that would lead to the conclusion that the increase in prices and the increase in the quantity of money would be proportional, as most theories have held in the past and as has also been found to be approximately true statistically. No such proportional relation may be assumed since we have seen that the rate of price increase depends not only on the net additional demand on the part of the government but also on the responsiveness of the economy (the slope of the curve in Fig. 44). Thus it may be, particularly in modest inflations, that prices increase less than proportionally to the quantity of money and that, accordingly, the velocity of circulation is reduced (assuming a constant volume of output). In periods of rapid inflation, on the other hand, prices may often tend to increase faster than the quantity of money, thus leading to a decrease in the velocity of circulation. Here certain limits exist. The velocity of circulation cannot be reduced infinitely. If, therefore, the mechanism of inflation had in itself the tendency to make prices increase much faster than the quantity of money, a pressure on the banks would result to increase the quantity of money, not to finance the government deficit, but to accommodate the needs of the population at the increased level of prices. The quantity of money will then tend to follow the level of prices.

In attempts to explain the movements of the general price level, use is often made of the formula developed by Professor Irving Fisher. We may review this method in the light of the discussion in the preceding pages. A number of variants of the formula have been used. We select the simplest of these; with respect to the more complicated ones, considerations similar to those which we will develop apply. The simplest formula is as follows:

$$M \times V = P \times T,$$

in which M equals the quantity of money, V equals the velocity of circulation of money, P equals the general level of prices, and T equals an index of the physical volume of production. The formula expresses the fact that the amount of all payments made is equal to the value of all commodities and services sold.

It disregards changes in the quantity of turnover sold on credit; this simplification is of little consequence for our analysis.

It is well known by now that this formula should be considered as an identity if each of the four quantities mentioned is properly interpreted. Therefore, there can be no question whether the formula is right or wrong. It must always be right. What may be discussed, however, is the question whether the formula can be used for the explanation of the fluctuations of one of these four variables on the basis of the three others. An explanation in a static theory, as the one we are now discussing, should then be a reduction to autonomous factors. Since all four variables in this formula are economic variables, none of them can, strictly speaking, be considered as an autonomous variable. Some of them, however, may be autonomous by approximation. It all depends upon the question whether, in certain situations, three of these four variables may, with sufficient approximation, be considered as autonomous variables to provide an explanation of the developments of the fourth variable. Such situations are possible, and we may mention a few of them.

1. If M is determined by pressing causes, such as war conditions dictating the creation of additional money, while V is given by the relatively stable payment habits of the population and T by the technical limits of production, then one may indeed say that, approximately, the movement of P is determined by that of the three other variables. In that sense the formula has often been applied—and, with the qualifications stated, properly applied—to the situation during World War I.

2. If P, in an open economy, is determined primarily by the movement of the rate of exchange, V again by payment habits, and T by the productive capacity of the country, the formula may similarly be used to explain fluctuations in the quantity of money. The situation is then one in which "the banks follow the needs of the economy," the needs being determined in this case by the factors to which we have referred. In this way the formula has been applied to certain periods in the early twenties.[1]

3. In dealing with a more limited problem, in which not the economy as a whole but only part of it is subject to analysis, the

1. Cf. chap. iii.

concept of datum may be somewhat modified.[2] Thus, for instance, in dealing with a depression in a small country it may be that the course of prices and turnover is determined by conditions abroad and that the volume of money is primarily determined by development in the economy in the immediate past and by the policy of the central bank. In that case, the formula may be used to determine V. It may be used to show that in a period of depression the velocity of circulation will have a tendency to fall; usually the product PT will fall more rapidly than M. In a period of recovery and boom, on the other hand, the velocity of circulation will tend to increase: PT will increase more rapidly than M. This phenomenon will also occur in a closed or nearly closed economy; in this case, however, P and T cannot be considered as determined by foreign factors. Even then one might still say that, of the four variables, V is least of all determined by autonomous factors and may therefore be considered most as the "effect" of the other variables.

It will be clear from the preceding remarks that the Fisher formula cannot be used as the only theory to explain certain phenomena if less than three of the four magnitudes— P, T, M, and V—are wholly or nearly wholly determined by autonomous factors. If, for instance, two of these factors are determined, one would require one additional relation in addition to the Fisher formula, in order to specify the magnitude of the other two variables. In other words, additional theoretical considerations would be necessary; the theory implied in the Fisher formula should not be considered as incorrect but rather as incomplete in that case.

INFLATION IN AN OPEN ECONOMY

We have dealt, so far, with inflation in a closed economy. We must now generalize our treatment and incorporate in it the phenomena that occur in a country which has foreign trade. This introduces two new elements. First, the resources to meet inflationary pressure in a country are now no longer necessarily limited to the domestic supply of goods and services. Foreign resources may be available to the country either as a result of

2. Cf. chap. ix.

foreign loans or by the use of the country's gold and foreign-exchange holdings. Second, an open economy is characterized by an additional variable—the rate of exchange.

We shall deal first with the case in which the rate of exchange is constant as a result, for instance, of the central bank's supplying gold or foreign exchange at the gold-export point. In that case, part of the inflationary pressure will be met by the use of foreign resources. Imports will increase as a result of increased demand for commodities in general and possibly also as a result of a tendency of prices within the country to rise compared to prices abroad. Hence part of the inflationary pressure will be drained off; the pressure will be reduced by the amount of the import surplus. Furthermore, if there is a general feeling that prices will continue to rise and that the rate of exchange will continue to fall, a flight of capital is likely to occur; foreign exchange is bought from the central bank, in exchange for local currency, for speculative purposes. As long as the demand can be met, it will also exercise a deflationary pressure, inasmuch as demand which might otherwise have been exercised for domestic resources will now be satisfied by foreign resources.

The use of foreign resources permits a country to have a temporary deficit in its balance of payments. But when the exchange resources have been exhausted by inflation or, even earlier, when the government is no longer prepared to support the rate by losing reserves, an equilibrium in the balance of payments will have to be established. In periods of serious inflation in the past this equilibrium was established almost always by a free rate of exchange. When demand for foreign commodities became too strong, depreciation of the currency ensued automatically.

Depreciation, or an increase in the price of foreign exchange, means an increase in terms of the national currency of the prices of imported commodities and a decrease in terms of foreign currency of the prices of exported commodities. Hence depreciation will tend to increase the volume of exports and to decrease the volume of imports. In normal circumstances this will mean an increase of the supply of foreign exchange and a reduction in the demand for foreign exchange. The exchange market, therefore, shows characteristics similar to those of a normal market: a price is found by balancing supply and demand, with demand depending negatively and supply positively on price, the equilibrium price being found at the point of intersection of the demand and the supply curve. We treated the market for commodities by reference to autonomous supply and demand factors. We may apply the same terms to the exchange market. The most important autonomous demand factor, in a period of war or in the immediate postwar period, is the strong autonomous need for imports. In wartime the need may be for armaments, raw materials, and foodstuffs. After the war it may be for reconstruction goods, for foodstuffs, and for restocking. This demand often originates by the creation of credit in the country, the inflationary pressure thus created spilling over into the exchange market. It is a matter of choice whether to consider the creation of credit or the autonomous import needs as the factor determining demand. Much will depend on whether one considers the credit creation as necessary and inevitable or not. Similarly, in the case of reparations payments, one may consider either the imposition of these payments or the way in which they were met by inflationary domestic financing as the cause of the additional demand for foreign exchange.

In periods of advanced inflation such as the German and the French inflations after World War I, an additional factor tended to increase the autonomous demand, namely, the lack of confidence in the national currency. Thus an additional speculative element of demand was added to the existing demand for imports. As the rate of exchange increased steadily, there was a tendency to convert holdings of national currency into foreign exchange in order to make an exchange profit.

In a market for an individual commodity it is normally assumed that appropriate price adjustment will bring the market into equilibrium. With respect to the foreign-exchange market in a period of inflation, two very important qualifications of this statement should be mentioned, however.

1. Depreciation may not lead to an equilibrium position if the foreign demand for the export products of the depreciating country and that country's own demand for imports are insufficiently elastic. Depreciation will decrease the volume of im-

ports and hence, assuming constant prices in terms of foreign currencies, the foreign-currency value of imports. Depreciation will increase the volume of exports, but it will not necessarily increase the foreign-currency value of exports. It will do the latter only if the increase in the volume exported is proportionately greater than the decrease in price, expressed in foreign currency. It is conceivable, therefore, that the country would suffer a loss (in terms of foreign currency) in its export proceeds, and this loss might exceed the savings in foreign currency on imports. In that case, depreciation would worsen a country's balance of payments, and the rate of exchange, instead of bringing equilibrium by an initial fall, would tend to fall further and further. Although it is conceivable, it is not very probable that the balance of payments of a country would be unstable with respect to the rate of exchange in the way indicated. A constantly falling rate of exchange is, nevertheless, a real possibility which has occurred frequently in the last twenty years. The explanation of this phenomenon must be found along the following lines.

2. We have seen that in a closed economy the equilibrium established by an initial rise in prices may be only temporary. The same applies in an open economy with respect to changes in the rate of exchange. The equilibrium in the balance of payments established by an initial fall in the rate of exchange may also be only temporary in character. Domestic price adjustment which follows depreciation will tend to raise demand for resources in general, and hence for imports in particular, and will thus lead to a renewed pressure on the balance of payments. As long as inflationary conditions continue, the initial fall in the rate of exchange may lead to further and further declines. The price of foreign currency, like the domestic price index, will rise further and further; in the simplest case, both will move along an exponential curve. The rate of increase of domestic prices and of the price of foreign exchange will depend on the factors which we mention in our discussion of inflation in a closed economy. The fall of the exchange rate may be accelerated as capital flight adds additional demand for foreign exchange to the demand that results from the import need of commodities.

With respect to fluctuations in the rate of exchange during

periods of inflation, reference is often made to the "purchasing-power parity" theory. In a somewhat oversimplified form, this theory holds that the rate of exchange for the dollar in a foreign country should be equal to the ratio of the purchasing power of the dollar to the purchasing power of the currency of that country. If a certain basket of goods costs $100 in the United States and 30,000 francs in France, the rate of exchange of the dollar should be 300 francs.

This theory has this in common with the quantity theory, that it, too, appears to give a much simpler solution for the exchange-rate problems than the much more general theory of the formation of exchange rates we have just developed. It differs, however, from the quantity theory in that it cannot be considered as strictly accurate. It should be considered rather as an approximation. Strictly speaking, it will hold only for commodities that can be purchased in both countries and can be transported between them and other countries without cost, duties, etc. For the total of all goods in the economy this condition is clearly not fulfilled; the very existence of international trade presupposes that the two countries do not produce the same commodities. If, however, the two countries do not produce the same commodities, the theory should be given in a somewhat more refined form.

In that case, two periods, I and II, have to be compared, and the change in the rate of exchange from the first period to the second has to be taken as the object of explanation. A different package of commodities for each country is considered. This package has a price in the country in period I and in period II. For each country the price change in terms of its national currency for its package may be calculated, and these price changes are compared. If, for instance, the price increase in the one country is three times as large as the price increase in the other country, the rate of exchange between the two countries would have changed, at a ratio of one to three, according to the purchasing-power parity theory. The value of the currency of the country in which prices have risen most would have fallen to one-third its previous value in terms of the currency of the other country.

Various objections may be raised against this theory as an

explanation of rates of exchange. The prices of all commodities do not move together, and the ratio of price increases observed will depend therefore on the package of commodities taken. Perhaps this objection is not the most serious one since it may be assumed that, generally speaking, the movement of prices of the most important commodities in any one country will be at least approximately parallel. But two other sets of factors may make possible, or necessary, a rate of exchange which deviates from that calculated on the basis of the purchasing-power parity theory. Both these factors follow from a shift in the position of demand and supply curves of the countries under consideration.

a) If a country has a high level of investment (for instance, in order to reconstruct war damage), its demand curve will move to the right and, with a similar price ratio as in a prewar period, it will require more imports. If, at the same time, there is no similar high investment activity in the rest of the world, the country under consideration will have an import surplus even though its rate of exchange may be at its purchasing-power parity level.

b) Structural changes may affect both the demand and the supply curves for international trade of the country itself or of foreign countries. Exhaustion of the country's natural resources will move its supply curve to the left, and an increased preference for foreign commodities compared to domestic commodities will move its demand curve to the right; in both cases this will lead to a deterioration of the country's balance of payments at a constant price ratio. The same effect will result from movements of the supply or the demand curve in foreign countries in the opposite direction, such as the discovery of more productive natural resources abroad or the development abroad of a preference for national, as against imported, commodities. On this account, too, the balance of payments may be in disequilibrium, notwithstanding the fact that the exchange rate is at the purchasing-power parity point. In all such cases the equilibrium rate, i.e., the rate which would bring the balance of payments into equilibrium,[3] would be different from the purchasing power parity.

In view of these limitations, the purchasing-power parity

3. Assuming that there is an equilibrium rate. Cf. p. 151, *supra*.

theory can be considered only as an approximate theory of the rate of exchange, valid only in cases of large price discrepancies. Where the price discrepancies are relatively small, the disturbing factors mentioned above may far outweight any disequilibrating tendency resulting from price disparity.

We must make a further observation with respect to the purchasing-power parity theory, and one which is similar to an observation made earlier with respect to the quantity theory: the purchasing-power parity theory may be considered as a theory of the rate of exchange only if the causes to which this theory links the rate, that is, the price changes in the two countries, may be considered as autonomous. In the period immediately after World War I there were indeed good grounds to consider the process of causation in this way. Prices were to a considerable extent determined by monetary conditions resulting from war financing; they could be considered approximately as autonomous factors. Other situations are conceivable, however, where this is by no means the case. If, for instance, the rate of exchange of a smaller country is linked by law to the value of the currency of another, larger, country, then it may be quite possible that the price level in the smaller country is practically determined by prices in the leading country and the legally determined rate of exchange. In that case the rate of exchange cannot be explained on the basis of purchasing parity, but rather the level of prices in one country can be explained on the basis of prices in the other country and of the rate of exchange.

CHAPTER TWELVE

LONG WAVES

THE explanation of the phenomenon of the so-called "long" waves has not advanced very far. To some extent this is a consequence of the very length of these waves: few of them have occurred. It is, therefore, particularly difficulty to establish regularities in their movement. Statistical data are, moreover, extremely scarce for the first half of the nineteenth century and still quite inadequate for the second half of that century.

The question has often been raised whether there is actually any justification for speaking of long waves. Is there anything more than an accidental alternation between increasing and decreasing tendencies? Against this skepticism, certain authors have maintained that there are indeed long waves which should be considered as actual waves. The explanation of these waves has been sought in two different directions.

MONETARY THEORIES

One group of authors has looked for an explanation in the monetary sphere. None of these has tried strictly to prove that the phenomena explained had necessarily a periodic character. But it may be possible to link together into a picture of a certain wave movement some of the regularities to which they have referred. We think here in particular of the studies by Cassel and Warren and Pearson, on the one hand, and by various others, in particular Wagemann, on the other. Cassel has seen an explanation for the movement of prices in fluctuations of the monetary gold stocks of the world. According to his findings, the latter increased much more rapidly than the general rate of increase of production (which he assumes at about 3 per cent) during certain decades, e.g., between 1850 and 1873 and between 1895 and 1920; in other periods, however, such as between 1873 and 1895 and after 1920, the rate of increase in the gold stock was less than that of production. On the basis of the quantity theory we would, therefore, expect prices to rise in the former and to fall in the latter period, as in fact they did. Cassel does not, however, give any reasons why the increase of the gold stock should show alternatively periods of more rapid and less rapid growth. In part this is no doubt due to chance. The rate of increase of gold stocks has been greatly affected by the discoveries of new gold fields, such as those of Australia and California in the 1850's and those of South Africa around the beginning of the twentieth century. Cassel's arguments have been criticized by many, in particular on the ground that the influence of gold stocks on prices is quite limited, on the one hand, because silver played an important monetary role, especially in earlier days, and, on the other hand, because the money supply consists to a large and increasing extent of banknotes and deposits, the creation of which is only in part and indirectly determined by gold stocks. This has led Professors Warren and Pearson to make additional studies in this field which have led them to the conclusion that Cassel's proposition should on the whole be accepted.[1] They found that there was a satisfactory parallel movement between fluctuations in the gold stock, in the total money supply, and in the price level.

A further contribution to the explanation of fluctuations in gold stocks has been made by the authors who have pointed to the systematic factors affecting the production of gold that operate in addition to the accidental findings of new gold fields. Wagemann has provided impressive statistical data showing that gold production has a tendency to be high when the general level of prices is low and low when the general level of prices is high. This is due to the fact that the cost of gold production fluctuates with the general price level, whereas the yield of this production has a constant value, except for incidental changes in the gold par value of currencies. It might be possible to explain the long waves by a combination of these two theories. When prices are low, gold production would be high. This would

1. G. F. Warren and F. A. Pearson, *Gold and Prices* (New York: Wiley, 1935).

lead to a relatively rapid increase of the gold stock and hence to an increase of prices. As prices reach a higher level, gold production will tend to level off. This would lower the rate of increase of the gold stock, leading to a reduction in the rate of increase of prices which would finally turn into a decline. This in turn would, after a certain time, lead to a new starting point of low prices.

Mathematical analysis of these propositions would indicate that they are correct only if the intensity of the reactions and the lags involved satisfy certain numerical conditions. Research with respect to these points has not yet led to definitive results.

OTHER THEORIES

Another attempt to explain the long waves has been provided by the Dutch economist S. de Wolff.[2] He considers these waves as a particular case of the "echo principle" to which we shall refer in more detail below. In brief, the echo principle amounts to this. If at any time, by whatever cause, there has been a period of active production of a certain type of durable capital goods, this high production will repeat itself after a certain period equal to the lifetime of the particular category of capital goods. According to figures given by De Wolff, the average lifetime of certain categories of very durable capital goods would approximate forty years. On this basis he argues that the long waves reflect the echo principle for these categories of capital goods. He considers these waves, therefore, as reinvestment waves of capital goods with a long lifetime.

Professor Wagemann has made some suggestions for an explanation of the long waves on a sociological basis. He attributes great importance to the ideas, put forward by certain writers in the field of sociology, that each generation has a mentality which is different from that of the preceding one. Wagemann sees periods in which the expansive, bellicose, and wasteful mentality dominates and others in which the conservative and parsimonious mentality dominates. Since the generations succeed each other with intervals of approximately thirty years, one might expect waves with a period of some sixty years. A much

2. *Het economisch Getij* (Amsterdam: Emmering, 1929).

more detailed statistical and factual study would be necessary before any great weight could be attributed to this explanation.

As we have mentioned, many observers question the very fact that there are any long waves and would be satisfied with an explanation of the price fall between 1873 and 1895, the subsequent price rise until 1920, and the fall of prices between 1920 and 1933. They make use, on the one hand, of Cassel's explanation and, on the other hand, of the occurrences in the field of agriculture. Between 1873 and 1895 and also after 1920 agriculture was afflicted by a long-drawn-out expression. In the former period this depression was due in part to the opening-up of the overseas grain-producing areas made possible by the new developments in transportation, particularly in ocean transportation. With respect to the period after 1920, reference is made to the consequences of World War I which again stimulated agricultural production in the overseas territories and to the mechanization of agriculture. After the resumption of agricultural production in Europe, total productive capacity was too large for world demand. Since the demand for most agricultural products is very inelastic, in particular for bread grains and potatoes, which satisfy the most elementary needs, a relatively small excess capacity might be sufficient to create a very severe fall in prices.

The period between 1895 and 1920, on the other hand, is considered as the period during which the rapidly increasing world population and its increasing demand outran the productive capacity of the agricultural resources of that time and during which the law of decreasing returns made itself felt. The higher prices of that period were, according to this line of thought, a necessary condition for the required increase in agricultural production.

As far as we know, no satisfactory comparison or synthesis of these different points of views has been achieved. The question of the long waves remains, therefore, one of the fields in which scientific energy may obtain some rich fruit.

CHAPTER THIRTEEN

BUSINESS-CYCLE FLUCTUATIONS

INTRODUCTION

THIS chapter deals with the theory of the business cycle. In our explanation of the phenomenon of business cycles we shall have to bear in mind that this phenomenon occurs in quite divergent forms in different countries and in different periods. We shall discuss these differences in some detail.[1] In view of these differences any generalizations concerning the business cycle have to be made, and to be used, with considerable caution. For the moment, however, we shall concentrate on those characteristics that are common to the great majority of business cycles, without implying that they occur necessarily in every cycle.

As we have mentioned, the separation between a trend movement and a cyclical movement, although to some extent artificial, offers considerable advantages in the analysis. In this chapter we are dealing, therefore, with the explanation of the cyclical component by itself.

Before entering into the discussion of actual business-cycle theories, we must mention three fundamental questions, even though full answers to these questions can be given only at a later stage.

1. Should the succession of prosperity and depression be considered as a real cyclical movement in which one phase necessarily follows the other as part of an integral process? Or should this succession be considered as the result of a random series of disturbances which lead sometimes to upward, sometimes to downward, movements, without any necessary link between

1. Pp. 227 ff., *infra*.

them? We shall see that recent investigations lead to a satisfactory theoretical synthesis of these two viewpoints.

2. Granted that there is a tendency for the economy to develop in cycles, should each cycle be considered as a separate identity, or does one cycle necessarily lead to the succeeding cycle? With respect to this question, too, it will be shown that neither viewpoint is exclusively acceptable.

3. Should an explanation of the cyclical movement consist of a separate analysis of the four phases of the cycle: the upward movement, the upper turning point, the downward movement, the lower turning point? Or should all four phases be explained simultaneously on the basis of one and the same set of economic relationships? Here again it will be shown that the explanations should be partly of the former, partly of the latter, type.

The general observation should be made at this stage that business cycles are so complicated in nature that they cannot satisfactorily be described in all their aspects by reference to one single principle or to one single feature of the economy. This same reason makes it particularly difficult to give an integrated picture of business cycles. It is difficult to decide with what aspect of the phenomenon or with what part of the economy to start. No single approach is the best one, and many different approaches lead to the same goal.

THE TWO MONEY STREAMS

As a starting point of our discussions we select a description of the economy which, by its general nature, is particularly suitable to facilitate a general understanding of the phenomenon on which we shall concentrate. We describe the economy as a circular flow of money streams consisting of two parts: (*a*) the formation of income and (*b*) the use of this income. This circular flow repeats itself without end, since the use of income creates at the same time new income which can be used in turn. The circular flow may be described by reference to two amounts per unit of time (year, quarter, or month): the total income of the population and the total expenditure representing the use of this income. These two amounts, it will be noted, do not include all payments. They exclude, in particular, payments that cannot be considered as the use of income, such as entrepreneurs' outlay for raw materials, wages, etc. These latter payments are not given a separate place in our outline of the circular flow; the entrepreneur is rather considered as representing the ultimate consumer who buys his product. Through the intermediary of the entrepreneur, the consumer pays an income to the workers who produce this product. At a later stage of our discussion, however, we shall treat such successive payments separately.

For our purposes, national income may be described as the sum of the net incomes of individuals and institutions, including among the latter business enterprises, the government and its various agencies, nonprofit institutions, etc. Net income will be defined as the amount that can be consumed without impairing the capital of the individual or institution concerned. For practical purposes, net income may be considered to be equal to the remuneration of all types of labor, interest, rent, dividends, profits of unincorporated business, and undistributed profits of corporations. This summary description does not attempt to resolve all points of doubt concerning the definition of national income. Any remaining problems, however, are not of particular consequence in connection with our study; the reader is referred to the existing literature on the subject.

In modern business-cycle theory it is usually found convenient to start from the concept of the two money streams. The problem of business cycles can then, in its simplest form, be formulated in this way: How can one explain the fluctuations which, according to our observation, occur in the magnitude of these two streams? A description of the entire economic process by reference to two global money amounts, which comprise many different elements, may appear objectionable in its simplicity. Yet, since the various elements usually show predominantly parallel movements, it would generally appear permissible to group them together in this way, at least as a first approximation. In one respect, however, a differentiation in total expenditure should be made from the start, namely, between expenditure for consumption and expenditure for investment, including in both types of expenditure both commodities and services. This distinction appears indicated since fluctuations in these two flows of expenditure are determined by different causes.

Since every expenditure may be considered as a payment of income to the economic subject whose products one acquires, we may write this first equation for income formation:

$$\text{Consumption expenditure} + \text{Investment expenditure} = \text{Income}\,. \quad (1)$$

Since income has been defined "net," investment is also net in this equation, i.e., gross investment *minus* depreciation allowances.

All income is either spent on consumption or saved. Hence:

$$\text{Income} = \text{Consumption expenditure} + \text{Saving}\,. \quad (2)$$

It follows from equations (1) and (2) that

$$\text{Investment} = \text{Saving}\,. \quad (3)$$

This result appears paradoxical, if one thinks of saving and investment as two different variables, both dependent on the rate of interest which is assumed to equate these two variables by assuming the proper level. The equations given would, however, show that the two variables were identical.

This apparent paradox need not detain us. The concepts of saving and investment which enter into these two equations are such that they may both contain "unintended" components. Thus, if consumption depends not on current income but on income some time earlier,[2] current saving will be the somewhat arbitrary difference between current income and consumption expenditure corresponding to past income. Similarly, investment includes unintentional accumulations or decumulations of inventories. The statistical identity of total saving and total investment is therefore logically compatible with an equalization of intentional saving and intentional investment by means of the rate of interest. However, according to the views of the Keynes school (which would appear reasonable to us), the rate of interest would in practice have only a minor effect in equating these two variables, the primary, if not the only, adjusting factor being the level of total national income.

Our objective is the explanation of fluctuations in the total amount spent. This stream of money may be considered as the

2. Cf. p. 188, *infra*.

product of the total stock of money and the income velocity of money. Inasmuch as the velocity of money can, in normal periods, increase to a limited extent only, one may mention the fact that the possibility of an increase in the quantity of money during the boom is a condition for an expansion of the flow of money payments. A certain elasticity of the monetary system is necessary to permit cyclical fluctuations. This elasticity does not have to be very large, however, because, as has been shown clearly by Carl Snyder's investigations, the velocity of circulation increases also in periods of boom.

FLUCTUATIONS IN INVESTMENT

We shall start our attempt to give an explanation of fluctuations in total expenditure with a closer analysis of the causes of fluctuations in investment. The total amount spent on investment may be considered as the product of the volume of investment and the price of investment goods. We shall concern ourselves first with fluctuations in the volume of investment. In order to do this, we must immediately make a subdivision of investment. The accompanying division accords with the nature of investment and provides at the same time an opportunity to appraise the various investment theories.

- Investment
  - Fixed Capital
    - New Investment
    - Reinvestment
  - Inventories (Raw Materials and Semimanufactured Products)

New investment is considered investment leading to an increase in the stock of capital; reinvestment is all other investment. The latter may either replace specific capital goods, which have been used up or become obsolete, or compensate, by means of different capital goods, for the reduction of capital in other places in the productive apparatus of the economy.

A) New investment in fixed capital

First we shall treat new investment in fixed capital. The most interesting theories in this field consider the demand for new investment in fixed capital goods as a derived demand. The primary demand, they state, is for consumption goods or services, to be produced with these capital goods. The demand for these final commodities determines the demand for capital of the different sorts necessary for their production. Given the quantity of fixed capital available, the amount of necessary new investment follows.

This line of reasoning has been worked out further in the theory of the "acceleration principle," which has gained considerable currency in recent years. In accordance with this principle the demand for investment goods will be proportional to the increase in the demand for consumption goods over a certain period. This may most conveniently be shown by a simple example. Suppose that the production of shoes in a certain year is five million pairs, which require a thousand machines of a certain type. If in the two succeeding years six and six and a half million pairs are required, respectively, then twelve hundred machines will be needed in the first of these years and thirteen hundred in the next. New investment of two hundred machines will then be required in the first and of one hundred machines in the second year, that is, in proportion to the increases of one million and a half million, respectively, in the number of pairs of shoes produced.

This theory makes certain tacit assumptions which it is well to state explicitly:

1. There are no severe declines in the production of consumption goods, for such declines would require a proportional reduction in the quantities of fixed capital which is not possible. Negative new investment is possible but cannot exceed the quantity of machines that is eliminated each year on account of obsolescence or usage. If we put this percentage as 10 per cent of the total, then a decrease in the production of shoes by 20 per cent could not lead to a proportional reduction in new investment.

2. There should be no abrupt changes in the methods of production.

3. The means of production are used either always at full capacity or always at a constant percentage of full capacity. In other words, it is assumed that entrepreneurs are able to esti-

mate future production with such accuracy that they will always have either the capacity which corresponds to this production or a certain fixed percentage excess capacity. The principle implies perfect technical adjustment of new investment, according to very simple principles, to changes in the level of production, disregarding in particular the time period required for the production of means of production.

The acceleration principle has been expanded into a much more general principle by the interesting studies of Dr. Chait.[3] He considers not only durable goods but also goods of a shorter lifetime, such as raw materials, and not only processes in which one capital good is used for the production of one final product but also processes consisting of many more chains and ramifications. He, further, takes explicit account of the formation of inventories, which he assumes to change proportionate to turnover. He follows the acceleration principle in its assumption that there is immediate adjustment of the stocks of capital goods and raw materials to the requirements of demand; he also disregards the time involved in the production of capital goods, an omission to which we must make some objections. The results of the much more general problems with which he deals cannot be expressed without the use of mathematical formulas. We may, therefore, return to the simpler statement of the acceleration principle.

It would appear to us that in particular the third assumption of this principle is not in accordance with reality. On account of the relatively long period involved in the production of investment goods, it is impossible for entrepreneurs in advance to estimate accurately the level of production at the moment the goods will become available; as a result, productive capacity is not always adapted to the demand for production, nor is there a constant excess percentage. Statistical data, concerning the percentage of capacity used, indicate clearly that excess capacity fluctuates very greatly. Apparently, entrepreneurs do not succeed in anticipating exactly the future level of demand, as might indeed have been expected. New investments on the part of en-

3. B. A. Chait, *Les Fluctuations économiques et l'interdépendance des marchés* (Brussels, 1938).

trepreneurs should be considered rather as attempts to adapt capacity to demand than as measures of actual and precise adaptation.

Moreover, the question for most enterprises is not purely a technical one, one in which quantities only play a role. Prices and particularly profit expectations are of great importance. Most new investments are made for the purpose of making greater profits. Profit expectations will, therefore, be among the most important determinants of new investment. It should be noted that these are "expectations" containing a considerable amount of uncertainty. Modern Anglo-Saxon and Swedish economists have paid particular attention to this aspect of profits.

The adherents of the acceleration principle will not deny, of course, that profits are the purpose of investment, but they may point to the fact that one of the conditions for making profits is the sale of products. This, however, is not the only element in profits. The price of the products and the cost of production are also of importance. All these elements enter here in precisely the same way in which they enter into the calculation of profits. It is, therefore, much simpler to say that profits are the determinant of investment.

But how are profit expectations determined? They may be affected by extra-economic exogenous factors, such as new technical possibilities or measures of economic policy. For these reasons, some economists consider profit expectations as an entirely exogenous factor which determines investment and thereby indirectly the entire business-cycle position. But this separation of profit expectations from the entrepreneurs' experience appears to us to be exaggerated. To a very large extent, profit expectations will be based on current facts, in particular on the actual magnitude of profits. This may be observed in many sectors of the economy. In determining the acreage to be planted with a certain crop, farmers are guided usually by the last known prices, sometimes to some extent also by the prices of earlier years. Share prices are determined to a large extent by the latest dividend. There is always a strong and well-understandable tendency to extrapolate the recent past and current events into the future.

There is, therefore, very much to be said for the proposition that the volume of investment depends to a considerable extent on the level of profits at the time when investment plans are made.

There is a second reason why investment depends on profits. The larger the profits, the larger the possibility toward self-financing. Since each entrepreneur prefers to invest in his own enterprise and many enterprises do not have easy access to the capital market or even to bank credit, the level of profits is an important limitation of investment. Large profits may even be the cause of investments that in themselves would be hardly justified, or not at all. The inflation period in Germany in 1923 gave clear examples of this.

Certain industries, however, will be in a position to make new investment by use of bank credit or capital derived from the capital market. The investment decisions of these industries will be determined in part by the rate of interest at which these resources can be procured. For bank credit, this will be the rate of interest for short-term credit, particularly the rate for advances to customers. This rate fluctuates, usually in accordance with the discount rate of the central bank. Since these credits will, however, require to be consolidated at some time in the future, the rate of interest in the capital market should also be of importance. Most enterprises will try to attract capital by the issue of shares; the corresponding rate of interest is the yield on shares. This yield is equal to the ratio between the dividend and the market price of the share. An annual dividend of $3.75 on a share quoted at 50 would represent a yield of 7½ per cent. It will be found in practice that the share yield neither is equal to the yield of first-class bonds (which is usually considered as the typical representative rate of interest in the capital market) nor does it show parallel movements. Since dividends are largely determined by profits, and share prices in turn by dividends, the yield of shares will also depend to a considerable extent on the level of profits. Part of the influence of the rate of interest on investment would, therefore, again be the influence of profits on investments.

Share prices, however, depend also to some extent on the bond yield; in this way, there is an indirect influence of the latter.

To the extent, further, that investment is financed by the issue of bonds in the capital market—a form of financing of particular importance for railroads and public utilities—the rate of interest in the conventional sense of the word would also influence the volume of investment. Generally speaking, even in the other cases quoted, a proper calculation of the use of capital will have to be performed on the basis of this rate of interest instead of on the basis of the other rates. It may be questioned, however, how many enterprises are in fact guided by such a proper method of calculation.

The consideration that the gross rate of profit should be reduced by the interest to be paid on credit or capital obtained has induced economists of the Swedish school in particular to argue that the volume of investment would be determined by the difference between what they call the "natural rate of interest" and the market rate of interest. Sometimes the natural rate of interest has been identified with the rate of profit. In that case, the line of argument would seem to be realistic from a practical point of view and quite in accordance with the theory given here.

Usually, however, the concept of a natural rate of interest has been defined in a much more abstract way. It has been defined, for instance, as the rate of interest that would prevail if the supply in the capital market consisted exclusively of savings and did not include credit creation by the banking system. The word "natural" is then used to indicate that the creation of credit by the banks would be an "unnatural" disturbance of that economic equilibrium which would have been established in an economy without money. The creation of credit in the market depresses the rate of interest below its natural level, and in this way a larger amount of investment is induced that would have taken place in the equilibrium situation.

We have given some reasons for believing that not each decision to invest is reached by a comparison of the rate of profit as a positive item and the market rate of interest (either the discount rate or the bond yield) as a negative element. We would expect, therefore, that the positive coefficient of the rate of profit would be larger than the negative coefficient of the market rate of interest. In other words, an increase of profits by 1 per cent will increase the volume of investment more than a decrease by 1 per cent of the market rate of interest. And even if we were to accept the theory of the Swedish school that the volume of investment is determined by the difference between the natural rate of interest (to be defined, for simplicity, in the realistic sense, that is to say, as the rate of profit) and the market rate of interest, even then the influence of the fluctuations in the latter would be of secondary significance in the explanation of fluctuations in investment, because the rate of profit fluctuates much more strongly than the market rate of interest. It is doubtful whether the older Swedish writers had realized this point.

It will be clear from the preceding paragraphs that we do not consider the influence of the rate of interest on investment to be very great. There has been a considerable divergency of views on this subject; particular attention to the influence of the rate of interest may be noted among British economists. Some hold that investment in long-lived capital goods is particularly susceptible to fluctuations in the rate of interest; others, on the contrary, that this influence is felt particularly in investments in raw materials and semimanufactured products and first of all in inventories held by merchants. Sensitivity of investment in long-lived capital goods would be attributable to the large amounts of capital which are required. On the other hand, the fluctuations in profits connected with these investments are still greater. The sensitivity of investment by merchants is motivated by the argument that the amounts paid for interest may be of considerable importance compared to the small margins on which merchants operate. But here, too, fluctuations in profits are much greater. This will be readily plausible if one realizes that profits may become negative whereas the rate of interest will never fall below zero.

Recently, attempts have been made in two ways to determine empirically the actual influence of the rate of interest on investment. A group of economists at Oxford University has made an investigation with a large number of business leaders, requesting information on the basis of an extensive questionnaire, about the motives which guided them in their investment decisions. It appeared from this study that the influence of the rate of interest in the decisions was quite minor.[4]

Another attempt has been made in connection with the statistical testing of business-cycle theories, undertaken by the League of Nations Secretariat shortly before the war,[5] to find an answer to these questions by mathematical-statistical methods. The details of these studies cannot be explained here. Mention is made, however, of an attempt to approximate the fluctuations in investment in a number of countries, for the period 1870–1914 and 1919–32, by a formula including profits and various rates of interest, as well as a number of other variables which could be considered to be important. The results of these calculations showed in almost all cases that the fluctuations in the rate of interest had a very secondary significance in the explanation of fluctuations in investment. The influence appeared to be larger in the case of railroads, whose capital goods have a very long lifetime and whose financing of investment is often done by bond issues, than of investment in general. In the nineteenth century, railroad investments constituted an important part of total investment; after 1920 this is no longer the case. This indicates a structural change that is of importance in this connection.

It appeared also that the rate of interest was of some significance for investment in residential construction. This conclusion, however, was subject to some reservation, owing to the relatively inadequate statistical material available for this part of the investigation. Some students of this problem point to the

4. J. E. Meade and P. W. S. Andrews, "Summary of Replies to Questions on Effects of Interest Rates," *Oxford Economic Papers*, Vol. I (1938).

5. J. Tinbergen, *Statistical Testing of Business Cycle Theories*, Vol. I, *A Method and Its Application to Investment Activity*, and Vol. II, *Business Cycles in the United States, 1919–1932* (Geneva: League of Nations, 1938–39).

fact that in residential construction it is the preparedness to grant credit rather than the actual rate of interest which is of importance. We shall return later to this question in connection with the special waves in residential construction in the United States.[6] In the same studies a statistical verification was also attempted of the significance of the acceleration principle. It appeared that this principle is clearly applicable only to investment in railroads, with respect to which it had been formulated first by its discoverer, Professor J. M. Clark. It is not impossible that the predominance of this technical principle in the case of the railroads should be seen in connection with the conditions of exploitation of railroads. In most countries railroads have an obligation to provide transportation and can therefore sometimes be guided less completely by considerations of profitability.

Our main theme in the preceding paragraphs has been that the volume of investment is determined by profit expectations and that profit expectations are determined mainly by the level of profits at the time the investment plans are made. We have further mentioned the influence of the rate of interest. The latter, however, may also be seen as a correction on the profit figures. Usually, although this is not the most correct way of calculation, profits are computed on the basis of interest actually paid. Actual interest payments, at least for the economy as a whole, are based on credits taken in a large number of years in the past. The average rate of interest over a long series of years shows practically no fluctuations. To the extent that credit has to be attracted, new investment will be financed, however, at the current rate of interest. This rate may differ from the average rate. The difference may sometimes be large, sometimes small, sometimes positive, sometimes negative. There is some reason, therefore, to refrain from identifying profit expectations with the current rate of profit and to adjust the calculation of profit with respect to the rate of interest used.

The effect of prices of capital goods that are to be purchased may be interpreted in a similar fashion. In computing current profits, use is made of depreciation allowances based on the

6. P. 241, *infra*.

prices of capital goods of many years in the past. The average of these prices, again, will fluctuate very little from year to year. The profit expectations of new investments, however, will have to be based on prices of new capital goods. These prices fluctuate very strongly from year to year. It might therefore be expected that investment activity would show certain fluctuations from year to year which do not reflect fluctuations in profits as computed in the usual way but which are connected with fluctuations in the prices of capital goods.

The effect of the price of capital goods may also be interpreted in a different way, namely, as a normal price-demand relationship. The opinion has sometimes been held that this relationship is even very pronounced, that is to say, that the demand for capital goods would be very elastic with respect to price. The studies made by the League of Nations Secretariat have led, however, to the conclusion that these demand functions are not elastic.

Since fluctuations in national income run approximately parallel with fluctuations in profits (the latter forming the most fluctuating part of income), it may also be stated as a reasonable approximation that fluctuations in investment are largely determined by fluctuations in income.

The preceding paragraphs have referred in general to the volume of investment demanded. The expenditure on investment is obviously equal to the product of this volume and the price. The amount spent on investment will therefore depend on the same factors as those determining the volume, plus the price, which, however, is itself among these factors.

Profit expectations reflect, in an indirect way, the scarcity of productive capacity. It is conceivable that, apart from this indirect influence, there is a direct influence of this scarcity of capacity on the volume of net investment. Other things being equal, the larger the existing productive capacity, the smaller the demand for new investment; the smaller the existing productive capacity, the larger the demand for new investment. Thus, there may be grounds to consider available capacity as an additional factor determining investment. Since the fluctuations in total capacity are, as a rule, rather weak, we shall disregard this factor in our simpler models.

The effect of the rate of interest, to which we referred in more detail before, may be considered as a brake restraining investment on the part of the credit system. It tends to prevent the expansion of the productive apparatus from becoming excessive, excessive as measured by standards of the capacity of the credit system. A more direct force operating in this direction is sometimes exercised by a certain rationing of credits applied in periods of credit tension. In economic terms this means that the law of demand and supply is temporarily put out of action: given all factors, that is to say, profits, prices, and the rate of interest, prospective borrowers would like to obtain a larger volume of credit than is actually supplied. There is not much information available whether the extent of credit-rationing has ever been considerable. There would seem to be some indication that its influence was rather modest in the boom year 1929; it is not impossible, however, that in some of the boom years before 1914 its influence was more considerable.

We have dealt so far with fluctuations in profits, in the rate of interest, and in prices of capital goods as determinants of investment. It would seem probable that other factors in addition had some influence. Among such, mention may be made of new inventions, which may lead to the creation of new enterprises or to the expansion of existing ones; it is probable that new inventions are of considerable importance, particularly for developing industries. The significance of these industries in the total volume of production should not be overestimated, however. The very industries that are in the experimental stage are normally of relatively small size. It may perhaps be assumed, further, that the occurrence of new inventions is distributed over time in a way that is not systematically connected with the business cycle. There may be some tendency toward a certain relation between the two, as the pressure toward research may be greater in a depression than in a boom; for this reason there may be a tendency to find more important results shortly after a depression than in any other phase of the business cycle. But chance will always play a large role in these matters. For these reasons, new technical possibilities may thus be considered as random disturbances of the systematic pattern of business cycles, disturbances which may give impulses toward a more rapid recovery.

A point of very great importance for a full understanding of the mechanism of the business cycle is the question of the lag between the factors mentioned and investment expenditure. For a number of reasons, a certain time must elapse between a given increase in profits and the corresponding increase in the amount spent on new investment.

a) First, it takes a certain time before profit figures, even those of one's own enterprise, are actually known. It would seem that this period was greater before 1914 than thereafter and greater in England than in the United States.

b) A certain period must elapse before an increase in profit leads to the stimulation of investment plans—a psychological reaction period. Since fluctuations of profits have many irregular characteristics, it is not always possible to decide on the basis of an increase for one month whether the change should be expected to be lasting. This may require waiting a second and a third month.

c) A certain amount of time is involved in the elaboration of investment plans or the adaptation of existing plans to a new situation.

d) Finally, the actual production of the investment goods, or their installation, will require a certain amount of time.

For these various reasons there will be a time lag of at least some months before increased profits will be reflected in increased investment expenditures.

This lag will be very different for different industries and for different types of investment. The installation of machines that are on hand can happen in a very short time; the building of a factory will take half a year or a year; the building of new railroads—a very important component of total investment in the nineteenth century—may take a number of years. For purposes of the cyclical mechanism it is necessary to take some sort of weighted average of these lags. It would seem plausible that this average lag would be between one-half year and one year.

In the League of Nations study referred to, a lag of one-half year was found for the United States for the period from 1919 to 1933 and a lag of one year for the United Kingdom for the period from 1870 to 1914. It will be seen from Figure 45 that it is possible to explain a very large part of the fluctuations in the volume of investments in the United States for the period from 1919 to 1933 on the basis of fluctuations in profits, the price of capital goods, the rate of interest of short-term credits, and the

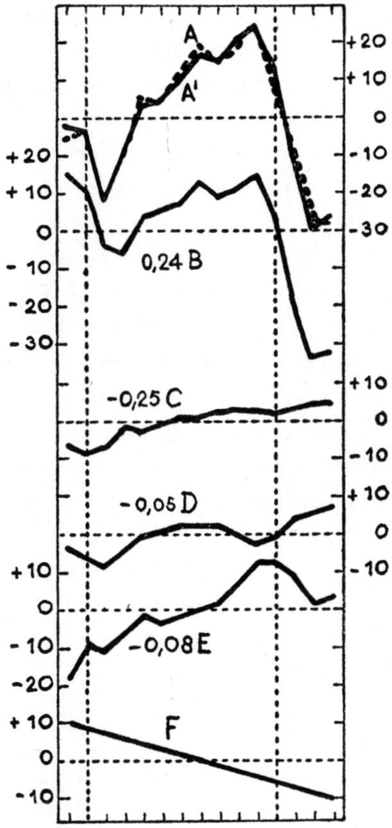

FIG. 45.—Explanation of fluctuations in *A:* investment in the United States, on the basis of *B:* profits of corporations, *C:* iron prices, *D:* the rate of interest for short-term credits, *E:* the yield of shares, and *F:* a trend component. The line $A' = 0.24\ B - 0.25\ C - 0.05\ D - 0.08\ E + F$ has been selected to approximate line *A* as well as possible. The variables *B*, *C*, *D*, and *E* all refer to a time one-half year earlier than series *A*.

share yield, all the latter series taken one-half year earlier. The sum of these series and the trend series, each of them multiplied with the appropriate coefficient indicating its influence, yields a total series which shows almost exactly the same fluctuations as the investment series itself. It is necessary, however, to add a smoothly declining series of figures (a negative trend) which represents the influence of the slowly changing factors (e.g., technical changes).

The significance of each of the factors mentioned in the explanation of fluctuations in investment is further illustrated in Figure 46. Along the horizontal axis of section I are plotted profits (series B) one-half year earlier and along the vertical axis the volume of investment after correction for the influence of the other explanatory variables (the price of capital goods, the rate of interest, share yield, and the trend component), in order to give the investment figures as *ceteris paribus*. This section of the diagram indicates the relationship between profits and the volume of investment. Similarly, section II reflects the influence of the price of capital goods on investment, section III the influence of the short-term rate of interest, and section IV the influence of the share yield. The significance of the influences shown by these various sections is qualified, of course, by the condition that by the statistical method employed the intensity of the influence of each of the variables on the total volume of investment is in fact accurately determined. One can rarely be absolutely certain about this, but there is a reasonable probability in the cases such as the present one, in which it is possible to explain the fluctuations in the determined variable with a very high degree of approximation.

B) *Reinvestment in fixed capital*

We shall now give some consideration to the factors that determine reinvestment in capital goods. These factors are to a large extent similar to those determining the volume of new investment. In a sense, the distinction between the two is artificial. If an old factory is replaced by a new one with a greater capacity and involving more capital, there is at the same time, and inseparably, new investment and reinvestment.

It is, however, also possible to mention certain factors which

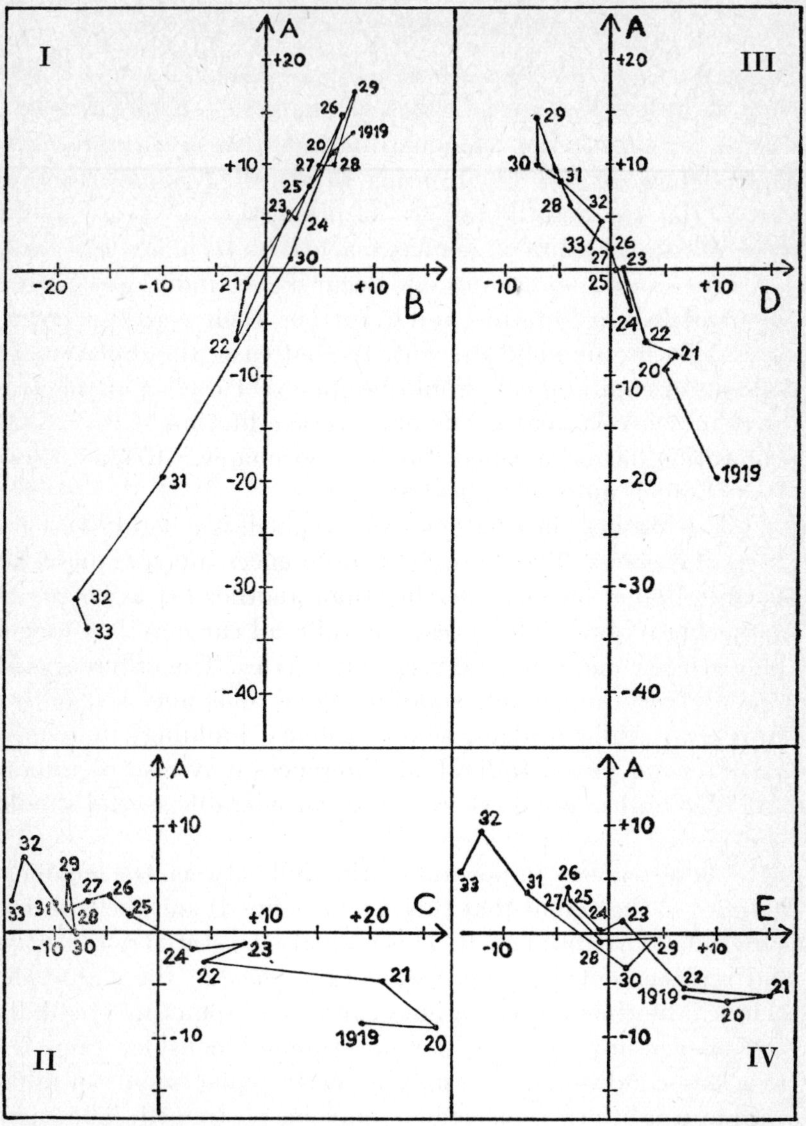

FIG. 46.—The influence on investment (A) of variables B, C, D, and E given in Figure 45. The four sections show the following:

Section	Along Horizontal Axis	Along Vertical Axis
I..........	B	A corrected for the influences of C, D, E, and F, i.e., $A+0.25\,C+0.05\,D+0.08\,E-F$
II..........	C	A corrected for the influences of B, D, E, and F, i.e., $A-0.24\,B+0.05\,D+0.08\,E-F$
III........	D	A corrected for the influences of B, C, E, and F, i.e., $A-0.24\,B+0.25\,C+0.08\,E-F$
IV........	E	A corrected for the influences of B, C, D, and F, i.e., $A-0.24\,B+0.25\,C+0.05\,D-F$

are of particular importance for reinvestment. These are especially of a technical nature. There is, namely, a compelling reason to reinvest if the technical lifetime of a given individual capital good has run out. In other words, the tendency to reinvest is the greater, the larger the proportion of the available stock of capital goods which has reached its technical age limit.

A very simple situation would occur if each individual capital good had an equal lifetime and if, further, each were replaced as soon as its lifetime had run out. In that case, the replacement demand of capital goods would be the exact replica of the production of investment goods one average lifetime earlier. This proposition has been called the "echo principle." Reality, however, is much more complicated.

a) The lifetime, in whatever way defined, is not the same for all capital goods. There are, first, differences in type: one type of capital good has a longer life than another type. There are further individual differences: one railroad car may last longer than another one from the very same series. The differences in type are very important: small machine tools may last only a few years, while bridges, sewer systems, buildings, may last many tens of years. Individual differences may also be important. For both reasons, therefore, a considerable spread should be expected.

b) There is a very important distinction between the technical lifetime (to the extent that this can be defined) and the economic lifetime of a capital good. This may also be stated in this way, that replacement does not always take place at the end of the technical lifetime but sometimes earlier and sometimes actually later, depending in particular on economic considerations. In favorable conditions there may be early replacement; in unfavorable conditions replacement may be postponed. The same thing may be expressed in another way (although the two expressions are not exactly the same): in a year of favorable economic circumstances, replacement will be larger than the number of capital goods whose technical lifetime has run out, and it will be the larger, the more favorable are economic conditions.

c) We have hinted already at the fact that the technical lifetime may not always be definable. Take, for example, a complicated machine different parts of which may be replaced successively. In the end, the whole machine may have been renewed. But it is not easy to indicate any particular time at which replacement has taken place.

The simple echo principle just formulated would require to be replaced by a much more complicated system of reinvestment fluctuations, on account of the complications mentioned under (*a*). A number of different echoes are, as it were, superimposed, the result of which is a damped wave movement. This may readily be understood on the basis of a few numerical examples. Assume that there has been a pronounced peak in the production of capital goods in year 3, as indicated by the following figures:

Year	1	2	3	4	5
Production	0	0	100	0	0

Assume, now, that the frequency distribution of the lifetime of capital goods is as follows:

Lifetime in Years	Percentage of Capital Goods
3	20
4	50
5	20
6	10

It is easy to calculate the number of investment goods that will be replaced each year. The one hundred produced in year 3 will be replaced as follows:

Year	6	7	8	9
Replacement	20	50	20	10

Of the twenty that have been produced in year 6, replacement will be as follows:

Year	9	10	11	12
Replacement	4	10	4	2

Of the fifty produced in year 7, the replacement program will be as follows:

Year	10	11	12	13
Replacement	10	25	10	5

Proceeding in this way, the total replacement demand is found as follows:

Year	6	7	8	9	10	11	12
Replacement	20	50	20	14	20	33	22

It will be noted that the peak of one hundred is not reached again; successive peaks and troughs become flatter and flatter. The movement is damped as compared to the undamped movement assumed in the simple echo principle.

The complication mentioned in (*b*) has an opposite influence to the extent that the general economic position would determine to some extent the volume of reinvestment. The general economic condition has a tendency again to concentrate reinvestment in years of prosperity; replacement in depression years preceding that peak is postponed until the prosperity years, and replacement in depression years following that peak has to some extent already taken place in the prosperity years, in any case more than would have taken place if the boom had not occurred. It might occur, therefore, that in the example given the relatively low peak of fifty in year 7 might again be increased, even to one hundred.

If reinvestment amounts show a wavelike movement, then the amounts set aside for depreciation each year, which are much more regular, will not be equal to the expenditure on reinvestment. In depression years, depreciation allowances will to some extent be hoarded, and these reserves will be used in boom years when replacement exceeds depreciation.

C) *Investment in inventories*

We may now deal with the last category of investment, namely, the investment in inventories. These are also quite important in the cyclical mechanism; fluctuations in stocks of raw materials and semimanufactured products (working capital as distinguished from fixed capital) are quite considerable. The size of minimum inventories is determined by technical factors. But extra stocks in excess of these minimum inventories are often kept. On the part of the producers of agricultural commodities, these extra stocks may be considered as the result of unusually large crops; on the part of the processing industry, they should more properly be considered as speculative stocks. To the extent that there are excess stocks for products other than those of agriculture, e.g., mineral raw materials, the considerations on the part of the producers should normally also be considered as speculative; in other words, the stocks have been produced in anticipation of increased demand or increased prices.

We shall deal later with the particular factors operating in the case of agricultural products.[7] They are not systematically connected with cyclical fluctuations. There remains, then, the technical factor as the most important systematic factor determining investment in stocks. In the simplest cases this may be considered as a special case of the acceleration principle. There is a pronounced tendency to keep stocks, not only stocks of raw materials and semimanufactured products but also of finished products, in proportion to the volume of sales. This tendency would produce a reaction quite similar to that described by the

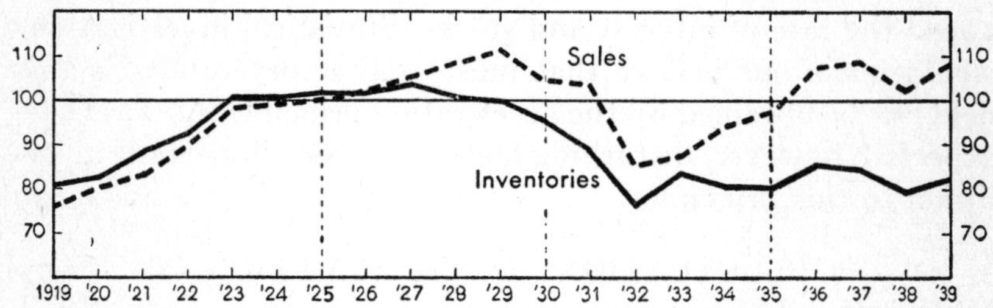

FIG. 47.—Fluctuations in stocks at the end of the year and sales during the year for department stores in the United States (index numbers, 1923–25 = 100).

acceleration principle. In some cases where there is no proportionality, there is nevertheless correlation in the sense that increases of stocks per unit of time (positive or negative) fluctuate proportionate to changes in the volume of production (see Fig. 47). The increase in stocks per unit of time accounts itself for part of the production, since part of production has to be used to increase stocks. This leads to the interesting mathematical construction that production depends in part on its own rate of increase a short time before. From this we shall derive certain important conclusions with respect to the movement of production.[8]

In more complicated cases the formulas developed by Chait provide a solution; but, since these formulas involve higher

7. Chap. xv, *infra*.

8. P. 199, *infra*.

mathematics, we must leave them out of consideration in this connection.

Various authors, in particular Hawtrey, have argued that changes in the rate of interest for short-term credits would have an important influence on investment in stocks. However, they have not made quite clear whether they intended that a high rate of interest would correspond to a low level of new investment in stocks or to a low level of stocks *in toto*. This case is typical of the precision of thought which is imposed by a mathematically exact way of expression and the danger of vagueness whenever less accurate modes of expression are used. But, as a matter of fact, it has never been possible to obtain any statistical verification of either of these two possible relationships between the rate of interest and stocks. Statistical investigations would make one believe that most satisfactory results in this field can be obtained by the acceleration principle. As was to be expected, however, disturbing factors are very important in addition to this principle.

FLUCTUATIONS IN CONSUMPTION

Next to investment expenditure, expenditure for consumption is the most important component in total national income. Expressed as a percentage of the average value of the series over a whole cycle, fluctuations in consumption are not so large as fluctuations in investment. But the average value of consumption is so much higher than that of investment that the amplitude of consumption expenditure in absolute terms is greater than that of investment expenditure. This fact, which has often been neglected, makes it very important to go into the factors determining fluctuations in consumption as a preliminary to a good understanding of the cyclical mechanism. It is Keynes's great merit to have drawn attention to this point.

The considerations that determine the part of income spent on consumption will determine at the same time the part of income saved.

We may concentrate first on the demand of an individual family for an individual consumption good. Here, the determining factors will be income, size of the family, and prices. This applies not only to the quantity demanded but also to the amount spent, since the latter represents the product of the quantity demanded and the appropriate price. It would also apply to the total amount spent by the family under consideration for all consumption goods, because this amount may be obtained by the addition of the amounts spent on individual commodities. When we consider finally the total amount spent on consumption by all families together, we would expect to find first of all the influence of the incomes of all families, of the size of these families, and of the level of prices. The latter are in principle the same for all families, so that there are in this category no more determining factors than for one individual family. But in the categories of incomes and of the size of families there is a great increase in the number of determining factors.

Let us first consider the effect of total income on total consumption expenditure. Strictly speaking, it would appear as if, to know this effect, the size of each income would have to be known or, in other words, as if both national income and its distribution would have to be known. This, however, is not necessary in all circumstances, and the situation can be represented with a very good degree of approximation in a much simpler way. If families are grouped according to the size of their income, it appears from budget studies that a certain increase of income, for instance, by $100, will lead to approximately an equally large increase in consumption expenditure for groups with very differing incomes, namely, of approximately $80. It would follow that it does not matter much in which class a certain increase in income takes place and that changes in total income are the determining factor much more than the distribution of income or the distribution of changes in income. It is, therefore, legitimate to use the approximation that an increase in income of consumers affects consumption expenditure in a fixed relationship. In other words, the relation between total income and total consumption expenditure may be represented by a straight line, the slope of which is the reverse of the relationship just mentioned. This slope is therefore an important factor; following Keynes, it is usually indicated by the term "marginal propensity to consume."

From the theoretical point of view, there is also no objection to the assumption of a constant proportion between changes in income and changes in consumption; as shown by Allen and Bowley, this assumption is justified if one assumes that the utility surfaces are functions of the second degree, the simplest acceptable hypothesis for these functions. It is important, further, not to confuse the marginal propensity to consume with the average propensity to consume, the latter representing the ratio between total consumption expenditure and total income. For the country as a whole the average propensity to consume surpasses 0.8 because there is normally an excess of consumption over income (negative saving) at very low levels of income.

If the relationship between income and consumption expenditure for the individual family could not be represented by a straight line, information on total national income would not be sufficient to determine total consumption expenditure of all families; in that case, additional information on the distribution of income would be required. The distribution of incomes is a complicated concept. It is completely known only if we have the full frequency distribution. Less complete information may, however, sometimes be used as a substitute as is often done in statistics; e.g., the standard deviation or quartiles may be used. In the case of the income distribution, it is usual to employ other indices, in particular the number α of the law of distribution of Pareto. It may be assumed that Pareto's law describes accurately the distribution of incomes and that α acts as a measure for the inequality of incomes. The smaller α, the greater is the inequality.

As a first approximation, in cases where the individual consumption function is not linear, we try to explain total consumption of the population by total income and the index α. It appears, however, that in many cases the fluctuations in total income are almost parallel with those of α; therefore, it would appear, provisionally and on empirical grounds only, that fluctuations in income may be considered as representative of fluctuations in α and hence that fluctuations in consumption may again be explained by reference to fluctuations in income only.

Considerations similar to those applied to the influence of

changes of income apply to the effect of changes in the size of families. For large groups of the population, arranged according to the size of the family, it may be assumed approximately that consumption expenditure is a straight-line function of the size of the family, that is to say, that changes in expenditure reflecting changes in the size of families are proportional to the latter. If this is so, then only the average size of families is of importance for the total consumption expenditure, while the distribution of the population over the different size classes is irrelevant. Since, moreover, the average size of families changes only very slowly, its influence can be disregarded in the study of cyclical problems.

Both considerations—that of the influence of income and that of the influence of changes in the size of the family—apply to a population with a constant number of families. In addition, there are increases and decreases in the number of families, owing to marriages and divorces. The change in the structure of the population for these reasons has a separate influence on consumption expenditure. For a study of the cyclical problem, however, the significance of changes in the size of families as well as changes in the numbers of families is of very secondary importance, since both types of changes occur very regularly in the course of time and can be expected, therefore, to affect trend movements but not cyclical movements. Therefore, we shall not deal with them any further.

We shall now analyze the effect of changes in prices on consumption expenditure. Strictly speaking, a change in prices is known fully only if we know the price of every individual commodity. In order to obtain a general picture of the frequency distribution of prices, one will again often be satisfied by the indication of certain characteristic magnitudes of this distribution. First, one will have recourse to some sort of average and use an index number of prices to reflect the movement of prices. The calculation of such an index number may be adapted to the special purpose for which it is intended to be used by the choice of appropriate weights. In order to measure the effect of the movement of prices on the volume of consumption, one could use an index number that would be weighted somewhat differently from the conventional index number. It is probable that the effect of a change of prices of commodities with a very elastic demand will be greater, all other things being equal, than the effect of changes of prices of commodities with an inelastic demand. Strictly speaking, therefore, the index number that would be ideal to measure the effect of changes in prices on the expenditure on consumption would be a different one from that which would be ideal to measure the changes in the volume of consumption. In an actual study of fluctuations of consumption expenditure in total, these differences usually have to be disregarded, however, and the conventional index number of the cost of living will have to be considered as representative for the price level of consumption goods; it will be necessary to assume that fluctuations in this index number will determine changes in consumption expenditure which have been induced by changes in prices. This assumption is the more legitimate, the more parallel the changes in the prices of the various commodities are. Over the course of a business cycle there is usually a high degree of parallelism since the systematic causes of price changes are the same: changes in costs, on the one hand, and changes in demand, on the other hand.

With respect to the magnitude of the influence of changes in prices on changes in the quantity consumed, it may be stated that the elasticity of this total demand for consumption goods must be smaller than unity; persons with a very small income which is used entirely for consumption will have the same amount to spend as prices go up, which would indicate that for them the elasticity would be equal to unity. Those with a more comfortable income would tend to keep the quantity of consumption constant; this would correspond to zero elasticity. The average value will therefore be between zero and unity.

In summary, we may state that fluctuations in consumption expenditure depend, first of all, on changes in total income of consumers and changes in the index number of the cost of living. At a constant level of prices the ratio between the change in consumption and the change in income will be equal to the marginal propensity to consume. Fluctuations in prices are usually in the same direction as fluctuations in income. Their effect on consumption will therefore on the whole be parallel to the effect of changes in income. Whenever the price level fluctuates approximately simultaneously with changes in income, the ratio between changes in consumption and changes in income will be larger than the marginal propensity to consume. We make, therefore, a distinction between the net marginal propensity to consume (assuming prices constant) and the gross marginal propensity to consume (incorporating changes in consumption due to changes in prices).

So far we have sought a relationship between the total value of consumption and the total income of consumers. For purposes of cyclical analysis it is advantageous, however, to consider total national income as the starting point. This figure includes, in addition to income of consumers, another component with strong fluctuations, namely, undistributed profits. On the whole, these will show fluctuations parallel to those of income of consumers, so that it would be legitimate to seek a relationship between consumption expenditure and total national income. If this is done, however, the figure found for the marginal propensity to consume will be smaller and that for the marginal propensity to save larger, since undistributed profits are saved *in toto*.

On the basis of Keynes's identity of saving and investment, then, the ratio of the amplitude of consumption expenditure and investment expenditure would be determined by the ratio between the gross marginal propensity to consume and the gross marginal propensity to save, both measured with respect to total national income. On the basis of statistical investigations by Mr. and Mrs. Stone, these two coefficients are to be put at 0.7 and 0.3, respectively, for most countries.[9]

Whether one considers consumption expenditure as determined either by income of consumers or (theoretically less accurate) by total national income, there is always another aspect in this relationship which deserves attention, that is, the time lag between a change in income and the corresponding change in consumption. As in the case of investment, this lag is of great

9. R. and W. M. Stone, "The Marginal Propensity To Consume and the Multiplier," *Review of Economic Studies*, VI (October, 1938), 1 24.

importance for the understanding of the cyclical mechanism. There are a number of causes explaining the existence of this lag:

a) First, there is for certain categories of income a certain lapse of time before income becomes available. Dividends and interest payments are the clearest example, in particular in Europe, where dividends earned during a certain year are paid out four to six months after the end of the year. In the United States, with quarterly dividend payments, this lag is obviously smaller.

b) A second cause of lag is the seasonal character of certain important expenditure items, especially of the higher income groups. Travel expenditure is concentrated in summer, expenditure for presents in December. An increase in income in the spring will therefore affect expenditure partly in the summer, partly only in the fall.

c) A third cause is the length of certain contracts which fix expenditure. A rent contract or an instalment-credit contract cannot be adjusted immediately to a lowered income. There will therefore be a tendency to adjust these types of expenditure to changing circumstances after a considerable period only.

d) A fourth cause for a lag may be found in the psychological inertia of most people. Only slowly do they fully realize their higher or, especially, lower income and adapt their expenditure to it.

Since the lag may be different for different expenditure items, different persons, and different groups of persons, it is essentially a distributed lag. It may also be different for upward and downward changes in income. As a first approximation, however, a good picture of reality can be obtained by assuming that there is one single lag between fluctuations in income and fluctuations in total consumption expenditure. Statistical investigation would make it plausible that for nonlabor income in England in the last decades of the nineteenth and the first decade of the twentieth centuries, the lag was approximately one year. For the United States in the period 1919–32 practically no lag is found. For the Netherlands in the same period a lag of about one-half year is found.

Since both investment expenditure and consumption expenditure show a certain lag with respect to income, it might be expected that fluctuations in investment and in consumption are practically simultaneous. This is confirmed by a direct comparison of the respective time series (compare Fig. 48). There are certain periods in which investment fluctuates slightly earlier. It has sometimes been held that this was generally the case; but there are also cycles in which consumption leads slightly; there are many cycles in which no lag in either direction can be distinguished. It would seem doubtful, therefore, whether toward the end of the boom

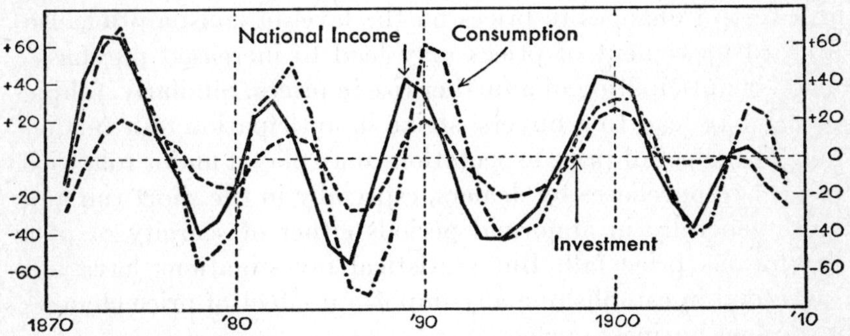

Fig. 48.—Fluctuations in investment, consumption, and national income in the United Kingdom. (Deviations from nine-year moving averages, millions of pounds of 1907 purchasing power.) Note that the fluctuations in the three series are practically simultaneous.

there is an expansion of the production of consumption goods at the expense of the production of investment goods, as held by certain cycle theories. Normally it would seem that both categories of production expand simultaneously.

A clear example of what the theories referred to consider as normal occurred in the period of extreme inflation in Germany in 1923. There was full employment of all factors of production, owing to hyperinflation, and investment goods industries and consumption goods industries actually competed for labor; it was impossible for both to expand at the same time. Such a complete employment of all labor occurred also occasionally in boom years before 1914, especially in Germany; in other major countries it rarely occurred after 1920. The German inflation period of 1923 can therefore hardly be considered as an example of normal cyclical relationships. It indicates rather the pathological excesses of hyperinflation.

A few, normally secondary, factors affecting consumption expenditure may be mentioned. Most important among them are changes in prices, as distinguished from the level of prices. It is necessary to make a sharp distinction between these two concepts. In the preceding paragraphs we have dealt with the influence of the level of prices on the level of consumption or, what comes to the same, with the influence of changes in prices on changes in consumption. However, there is in addition to this an effect of changes in prices on the level of consumption. An upward movement of prices may lead to increased purchases made in anticipation of a further rise in prices. Similarly, falling prices may lead to a buyers' strike in anticipation of a further fall. The effect of price expectations may play a major role with respect to purchases by dealers, especially in the short run and more generally in abnormal periods either of scarcity or of a precipitous price fall. But statistical investigations have not succeeded in establishing any important effect of price changes in normal business cycles.

A second factor, the rate of interest, is sometimes mentioned, in particular because it would affect savings and thereby indirectly consumption. Economic theory is uncertain, however, as to the direction of the effect of the rate of interest. On the one hand, it is argued that a lower rate of interest will reduce the attractiveness of saving since the price paid for saving is reduced. On the other hand, it is pointed out that the purpose of saving is often to obtain a given income in the future and that in order to achieve this income a larger capital will have to be saved at a lower rate of interest.

Statistical evidence would lead to the conclusion that changes in the rate of interest exercise little effect on the volume of consumption and of saving. It may be shown that the rate of interest granted by individual institutions may affect the amount of savings made in those institutions; but this reflects primarily shifts between different forms of saving which, as one might expect, react more to interest differentials than the total amount of saving can react to the average rate of interest.

Finally, the availability of new products will have some influence on the demand for commodities in general and on the demand for commodities immediately competing in particular. In general, the possibility of satisfying a specific demand which could not be satisfied before will lead to an increase in demand. Initially, only a few people will be prepared to spend on the new experiment. As experience spreads, more layers of the population will gradually become interested. A large stream of buyers follows suit, while a few conservatives require a still longer period to make up their minds. In the case of articles which are not durable and which, when once consumed, must be purchased at regular intervals, the sale of the new product will show a growth curve. This has interesting consequences for the adaptation of production to demand. Initially, the rate of increase will be more and more rapid, which may produce a tendency to expand productive capacity more and more. Hence it will be easy to overshoot the mark, since it is extremely difficult to estimate the pattern of the growth curve and in particular its maximum height on the basis of its initial phase only. There is then a great possibility of overproduction of new products. The business-cycle theories of "generalized partial overproduction" pay particular attention to this problem and then indicate, further, how such a partial overproduction will propagate through the entire economy. We do not want to enter upon a discussion of these theories at this stage, since, as we have mentioned, new commodities have only a relatively minor significance in the total demand for all commodities.

FLUCTUATIONS IN INCOME

We have considered above[10] the circulation process in its two component parts, the use of income and the formation of income. In the two preceding sections we analyzed the factors which determine fluctuations in expenditure. We will take up now the formation of income, that is, the factors which determine the fluctuations in the magnitude of the national income.

10. P. 160, *supra*.

As a starting point in the definition of national income we take the total value of the sale of finished goods and services for consumption and investment (including those sold abroad as exports). Looked at from the other side, the same magnitude represents the total expenditure on investment and consumption goods and services. Both concepts, however, are gross rather than net, and for that reason they are in some aspects in excess of total national income.

Part of the receipts from sales, though not representing income of the firm which receives them, is passed on by it as income to others. This applies to wages passed on to the employees, dividends passed on to the shareholders, interest passed on to the bondholders, etc. Similarly, payments made by the firm to other firms for raw materials and semimanufactured products within the country under consideration represent income passed on. Payments to foreigners, however, for imported materials, are not part of the national income of the country and must therefore be deducted from the value of total sales if we are to arrive at the net figure of national income.

The amounts received from sales which correspond to depreciation allowances do not represent income at any stage of the process of production and should therefore not be included in a figure for net national income. For purposes of cyclical analysis, depreciation is of secondary importance, since the amounts involved fluctuate only very little from year to year. The amount of depreciation is normally based on the value of the total stock of capital goods installed. On account of the long lifetime of capital goods, the physical stock shows very gradual changes. Since the price of capital goods used for purposes of depreciation is usually the original purchase price, the fluctuations in the value of the stock of capital reflect the prices of a great many years in the past and, therefore, will also be quite small. Only depreciation on account of special losses may occasionally, for particular industries, give a sharp dent to the depreciation curve; but for business as a whole writeoffs of this nature are usually of minor importance, except in years of very sharp and severe depression.

If we follow the conventional way in which income is computed, another income element still has to be taken into account. To assume equality between gross income and the total value of gross expenditure on final consumption and investment goods implies the assumption that the final producers charge the same amounts for the raw materials and semimanufactured products contained in these goods that they are currently paying for them. Only on this assumption would the costs paid by final producers equal the receipts of the producer of the raw materials and would these two amounts cancel out for all enterprises taken together. This assumption is fully justified only if all raw materials either are used immediately or, if used later, are charged as cost at the price ruling at the time when they are used. Normally, however, the existence of inventories of raw materials makes for a considerable lag between purchase and use; and also, normally, costs are charged on the basis of purchase price rather than of replacement price. Thus, the prices calculated reflect actual purchase prices at an earlier time, say, three months earlier. If, during this period, prices have risen, the amount calculated as costs is smaller than the receipts for the sale of raw materials by the enterprises producing them during the same period. An amount of extra profit is contained in the total value of consumption and investment goods to final users. The amount of this income equals the average volume of all stocks in the hands of producers during the period under consideration times the increase in price. Thus, if income is calculated for a calendar year and stocks represent one quarter's consumption of raw materials, these extra profits are equal to the average stock during the year times the price increase between the last quarter of the previous year and the last quarter of the current year. Similarly, losses of the same character occur in times of falling prices. Such profits and losses are in nature, even if not in intention, speculative. Their pattern over time is determined by changes in the price level. They show therefore a lead[11] with respect to prices themselves and usually also with respect to such other cyclical developments as the volume of production.

11. Cf. p. 19, *supra*.

In very much the same way, income is created by the increase in prices of shares, since stock-exchange profits and losses are often treated as if they were fluctuations in income both by many business firms holding shares and by speculators. Other investors, however, whose primary interest is the regular income from investment, may not consider changes in the value of their holdings as income. In disregarding paper profits and losses, these latter investors act in accordance with modern theoretical conceptions as to what constitutes income. But for the purpose of explaining business-cycle fluctuations we are not primarily interested in what income "is" or "should be." We have to concentrate on the concept of income as seen by those who receive the income. It is income according to this concept which determines their decisions with respect to consumption, and these decisions are one of the important chains in the cyclical mechanism.

As a final adjustment in passing from gross sales to national income, we still have to take account of the lag between gross receipts at the final stage of production and the income earned at earlier stages of the same production.

It will be shown later that the movement in prices of commodities and shares can be explained to a large extent by reference to fluctuations in income. In the case of commodity prices this is due mainly to the fact that changes in demand factors are the most important systematic causes of price movements, and income is the most important demand factor. Share prices are determined primarily by dividends and expected dividends, the movement of which is very nearly parallel to that of national income, because profits, from which dividends are derived, constitute the most fluctuating element in national income.

The movement of the price level is thus approximately parallel to that of national income, though with a short lag. The rise of the price level from one quarter to the next is therefore also parallel with the increase in national income, but again with a short lag. If we take this lag as three months, then the increase of the price level from the third to the fourth quarter would be determined by the increase of national income from the second quarter to the third quarter. Changes in share prices are determined similarly by changes in national income, again sometimes with a certain lag which need not be constant.

On the basis of the two relations developed, we come to the important conclusion that that part of income (as seen by consumers) which represents speculative income is determined by the rate of increase in national income some short time earlier.

THE MAIN ELEMENTS OF THE CYCLICAL PROCESS

We have made clear in the preceding pages (1) that fluctuations in investment and in consumption expenditure may be attributed largely to fluctuations in national income a short time previously and (2) that fluctuations in national income can be explained largely by (*a*) fluctuations in total expenditure for consumption and investment and (*b*) the increase of income itself taken over a slightly earlier period. In our example at the end of the preceding paragraph we assumed that the level of income due to factor (*b*) in the fourth quarter of a year was determined by the rate of increase of income between the second and the third quarters of the same year. We shall further assume that the lag between changes in income and the corresponding changes in expenditure on consumption and investment is also one quarter. The essence of the argument which is to follow is independent of the magnitude of these lags; but it is convenient at this stage to make specific assumptions concerning their magnitude.

We assume further that the relations to which we have made reference hold exactly and not only as approximations. We may then state that we have a system of relations, or a "mechanism," the properties of which we want to study.

It might appear that the two statements—that investment expenditure and consumption expenditure depend on income and that income depends on total expenditure—constitute circular reasoning. However, this is not the case. Circular reasoning occurs only when one and the same relation is first used to explain A on the basis of B and then to explain B on the basis of A. To give an example, we take the relationship that the price is equal to cost plus profit. If, now, in order to determine profit one uses once more the same relation, viz., that profits are equal to the difference between the price and costs, then there is circular reasoning and price and profit are not determined. Our mechanism, however, is different in two respects. In the first place, the two relations used are not the same. For this reason alone there is no circular reasoning. If, to go back to our example, we would state that profit were 10 per cent of costs, this relation, together with the first one, would indicate that the price was 110 per cent of costs; both variables would then be determined. The second reason why our mechanism does not constitute circular reasoning is that the magnitudes occurring in them do not refer to the same time period. Expenditure in period 2 depends on income in period 1, while income in period 1 depends on expenditure in period 1.

If we indicate income by Y and expenditure by E and the period to which they refer by a subscript, then we may say that E_2 enters in the first relation and E_1 in the second relation. The first relation indicates how E_2 is determined by Y_1, while the second indicates how Y_1 is determined by E_1. Therefore the two relations together specify how E_2 is determined by E_1. The quantities E_1 and E_2 need not have the same value. The relations do not determine one constant value for the variable E but a series of successive different values. The mechanism in our previous example does not permit of more than one solution. It refers to a stationary position. But the mechanism connecting Y and E can refer to variable positions. It relates magnitudes of different time units and is therefore dynamic in the sense in which we have defined dynamic relations.

Since these relations are valid not only for periods 1 and 2 but also for all successive periods, they may also be used to determine E_3 on the basis of E_2, E_4 on the basis of E_3, etc. In other words, the fluctuations of E over time can be determined by it provided that we know one initial value, E_1.

The same applies to the values of Y, since the second relation determines, on the basis of any value of E, the simultaneous value of Y. Therefore, if one knows the sequence of figures representing E, one can determine the sequence of figures representing Y. But it is also possible to determine the sequence of Y

values directly. The second relation determines Y_1 on the basis of E_1. The first relation, if applied to periods 0 and 1, determines the value of E_1 on the basis of Y_0. Together, therefore, they determine the relationship between Y_0 and Y_1. If we repeat this process, we can find Y_2 on the basis of Y_1, subsequently Y_3 on the basis of Y_2, etc. Here too, therefore, a sequence of figures can be obtained provided that we have one initial value, Y_0.

It is important to illustrate these processes by some numerical examples. We shall treat a number of them in succession and shall try to draw some lessons from the differences which occur between these various examples.

EXAMPLE I

In this example we assume that expenditure and income have an equilibrium value of 100. If, by some random cause which interrupts the relationship between the two variables in one time period, income is higher or lower than this equilibrium value, expenditure in the succeeding quarter will also be higher or lower and, we assume, 1.1 times as much as the deviation shown by income. Thus if income will be at 120, expenditure in the succeeding quarter will be at 122. One may assume that this relationship indicates a case of excessive optimism on the part of consumers. Assume, now, that, in fact, income in a certain quarter has been brought to the level of 120 by some external cause, for instance, an excessively large crop, and that according to our assumption expenditure will be 122 in the next quarter. We further assume that income is equal to expenditure in the same quarter. Income in the second quarter will then amount to 122. It follows, then, that expenditure in the third quarter will be 124.2. Thus, computing from one quarter to the next one, we find:

Quarter	1	2	3	4	5
Expenditure		122	124.2	126.6	129.2
Income	120	122	124.2	126.6	129.2

The deviations which income and expenditure form from the equilibrium value of 100 form together the terms of a geometric series: each successive deviation is 1.1 times as large as the preceding one. The increase will go further and further, in an upward cumulative process.

If, on the other hand, we had taken as our starting point a value below the equilibrium value, for instance, 80, a downward cumulative process would have developed in an analogous way.

EXAMPLE II

We change Example I in one respect only, namely, by substituting 0.9 for the factor 1.1. In other words, "excessive" income will lead again to "excessive" expenditure, but the level of expenditure will be only 0.9 times in excess of the deviation of income from normal. Along the same lines we then compute the following sequence of figures:

Quarter	1	2	3	4	5
Expenditure		118	116.2	114.6	113.2
Income	120	118	116.2	114.6	113.2

There is now again a geometric series, but the ratio between two successive deviations from the equilibrium position is now 0.9, so that the equilibrium position is again gradually approached. There is now a process of adaptation to the initial equilibrium position. If we had started from a downward deviation, for instance, an income of 80, the process of adaptation would have been upward.

For convenience we shall in subsequent examples indicate only the deviations from the equilibrium position; in these terms the last example will appear as follows:

Quarter	1	2	3	4	5
Expenditure (deviations)		18	16.2	14.6	13.2
Income (deviations)	20	18	16.2	14.6	13.2

EXAMPLE III

We shall now reintroduce a complication which we had left out of account temporarily, namely, the assumption that income is not equal to expenditure in the same quarter but contains, as a further item, speculative income equal to the increase in income of the preceding quarter over the quarter before the preceding one. We start again from an equilibrium income in quarter 0 of 100 (deviation = 0), which by a random cause is brought to 120 in quarter 1 (deviation = 20). Hence, expenditure in the second quarter measured as a deviation from normal will equal 0.9 × 20 = 18. Income in the second quarter is now not equal to 18 but to 18 + 20, the latter figure representing the increase of income in the first quarter over income in quarter 0. Hence income is 38 above normal. This will lead in the third quarter to expenditure at 34 above normal (rounded to integral numbers). Hence, income in the third quarter will be equal to 34 plus the increase between the first and the second quarters, namely, 18. The further process of computation will become clear from the following figures:

Quarter	0	1	2	3	4	5	6	7	8	9	10
Expenditure (deviation)		0	18	34	47	55	58	55	47	34	18
Income (deviation)	0	20	38	52	61	64	61	52	38	20	0
Increase in income		20	18	14	9	3	−3	−9	−14	−18	−20

Quarter	11	12	13	14	15	16	17	18	19	20	21
Expenditure (deviation)	0	−18	−34	−47	−55	−58	−55	−47	−34	−18	0
Income (deviation)	−20	−38	−52	−61	−64	−61	−52	−38	−20	0	20
Increase in income	−20	−18	−14	−9	−3	3	9	14	18	20	20

We had to continue this computation somewhat further because the further course of events is not so easily seen in this example as in the preceding ones, where the sequence of figures turned out to have simple properties. The development of the figures in the later part of the period shown is of particular interest. Initially, that is, up to the fifth quarter inclusive, there is an upward cumulative process: incomes increase more and more. However, the rate of increase slows down. By the sixth quarter income has decrease compared to the fifth quarter.[12] Although total expenditure is still higher than in the preceding quarter (58 as against 55), speculative incomes are so small that the total computed income is lower now than in the preceding quarter. This is the sign of the reversal. Up to the fifteenth quarter there is now a downward cumulative process which initially proceeds at increasing speed, then at a decreasing speed. After the fifteenth quarter there is again a cumulative increase which initially is also at increasing speed. In the twenty-first quarter the position is exactly the same as in quarter 1. From here on out the movement will repeat itself; it is purely periodic.

The most interesting aspect of this example is that it proves that constant relationships can produce a fluctuating process. Apart from the initial disturbance of the equilibrium, expenditure depends continuously in the same way on income and income depends continuously in the same way on expenditure and the rate of increase in income. After a disruption of equilibrium by one single exogenous event these relationships produce a fluctuating movement. It will be noted that the movement here, as in the preceding example, is an endogenous movement: it occurs without any further change in the data. This, then, is an example of an endogenous fluctuation. The assumptions underlying our calculations, in other words the economic theory which has been used, explain both the development of a cumulative process and its turning points. It is difficult to put this explanation into words. It is particularly difficult to indicate "the cause of the turning point." In fact, the belief that there must be a cause for each turning point is erroneous. It is not so

12. If another choice had been made of the initial values, this turning point could have come at another point of time.

that each turning point has a cause of its own. This may be so when the turning point has been brought about by a new change in the data. Many theories introduce such a change in data, often as a *deus ex machina,* at the appropriate moment; it is then, however, difficult to prove that the turning point is a necessary one.

In our last example it would have been impossible, moreover, to explain the turning point on qualitative grounds. The fact that a turning point occurs depends on the numerical values which enter into the relationships. If the ratio 0.9 between the excess of expenditure and the excess of income were changed into 1.1, no cyclical movement would occur. The occurrence of fluctuations, therefore, depends on the numerical values of the coefficients used. These values also determine the period of the waves and their degree of damping or antidamping. The various problems which arise in this connection can be solved satisfactorily only by means of mathematical methods.

It may have become clear from our examples that the movements of an economic system are determined by two sets of data: (*a*) the initial position, in particular the disturbance of equilibrium which occurs at the beginning, and (*b*) the nature of the relations among the various economic variables. What exactly has to be known concerning the initial position depends on the particular structure of these relations. If they should contain values for the variables for more quarters than occur in our examples, then a larger number of initial values would have to be known to determine the movement. In our third example, two values of income were necessary; whereas, in Examples I and II, one value was sufficient. These initial disturbances of the equilibrium should be considered as the operation of temporary factors, such as, for instance, large or small crops. The properties of the relations, however, are not of a temporary but of a more permanent character. They may in fact be considered as reflecting the economic structure of the economy or the market concerned.

These examples should not be considered as anything more than, indeed, examples; at best they indicate a few of the most important characteristics of actual cyclical movements. To prevent misunderstanding, we want to mention at this stage a number of other characteristics which need to be added to obtain a reasonably realistic picture. In the following paragraphs we shall expand these additional characteristics gradually, in order to come gradually closer to reality.

In the first place, one should realize that the disturbances are not limited to one: after the cyclical movement has run its course for a certain time, another disturbance is likely to occur; there may be many disturbances in one cycle; hence a cycle will not in reality show the smooth, regular pattern of our example.

The relations between the various economic variables will, moreover, be of a more complicated nature. More variables than the two we mentioned will occur in them. We have referred to some of them already in preceding paragraphs. Thus, we assumed in our examples that expenditure was determined by the level of income only. But we have seen, above,[13] that, in addition to income, the level of prices, too, has a certain influence on expenditure. It is true that with a reasonable degree of approximation one may assume that the fluctuations in prices are parallel to those in incomes, so that prices as a separate variable may be eliminated; but this remains always an approximation. There are many examples of other similar approximations which would disappear in a more exact and complete theory.

Furthermore, a larger number of time units will occur in our relations. In Example III the level of income in the third quarter depended in part on the levels in the second and the first quarters. In reality, however, influences of quarters further back will make themselves felt. Part of expenditure, for instance, that for investment in commodities which have a very long construction period, will depend on the level of income many more quarters earlier. Since income is determined by expenditure in the same quarter, it, too, will in part depend on incomes a number of years ago.

Much longer lags may play a role as a consequence of the echo principle;[14] according to that principle, reinvestments are in part determined by investments which occurred one lifetime ago.

13. Pp. 185 ff.

14. Cf. p. 179, *supra.*

Then again, there may be relations of a more complicated structure. We have given some indications of these in chapter i. If they are taken into account, a more complicated and less regular pattern of waves may emerge, even without the occurrence of new disturbances.

EXAMPLE IV

A relatively simple example of a more complicated relation (which incidentally does not lead to waves of a less regular pattern) may be derived from the theories of Kalecki.[15] The purpose of this example is also to show that it is not particularly necessary to introduce the phenomenon of speculative income to obtain a cyclical movement.

Kalecki's theory may be interpreted in this way, that, in contrast to our Example III, he assumes that expenditure does not depend on the level of income but on the ratio of income to capital. He bases this assumption on the following considerations:

a) Expenditures for investment will determine all other expenditure, since they determine the level of income of consumers.[16]

b) Investments are determined by the rate of profit, that is, the ratio of profit to capital, rather than by the absolute level of profits.

c) Since fluctuations in profits are parallel with those in national income (profits forming the most fluctuating part of national income), it may also be concluded as an approximation that investments are determined by the ratio between total national income and capital.

We have now introduced a new variable, capital. In order to establish a system of computation, we have to determine how capital depends on the other variables. Capital is formed by the accumulation of successive investments. Assuming a certain initial capital, we find the capital at the end of a quarter by adding the amount of investment during that quarter; capital at the

15. M. Kalecki, *Essays in the Theory of Economic Fluctuations* (London: Allen & Unwin, 1938).

16. Cf. p. 113, *supra*.

end of the second quarter, by adding again investment during the second quarter, etc. Investment itself is part of total expenditure and indeed a systematically determined part.

For illustrative purposes we will put these relationships in the following specific forms which form the basis of Example IV. The amount of investment, I, shown on line 1, is 225 times the profit rate z of the preceding quarter, if both are measured in deviations from their normal value. Total national income Y (line 2) is twice the amount of investment (again both measured as deviations from normal). The normal value of national income is taken as 100, so that the absolute value of national income ($\bar{\bar{Y}}$) is equal to $100 + Y$ (line 3). The normal value of investment is 10, so that the absolute value $\bar{\bar{I}}$ equals $10 + I$. Hence the value of capital, $\bar{\bar{K}}_t$, at the beginning of quarter t is equal to the value at the beginning of the preceding quarter ($\bar{\bar{K}}_{t-1}$) plus $10 + I_{t-1}$, the latter symbol indicating the amount of investment in the quarter $t - 1$ (line 4). The profit percentage $\bar{\bar{z}}$ (in absolute value) is equal to the ratio of $\bar{\bar{Y}}$ to $\bar{\bar{K}}$ (line 5). The deviation from normal can be obtained by deducting 20 per cent so that $z = \bar{\bar{z}} - 0.2$ (line 6).

The choice of these numerical values, although somewhat arbitrary, is realistic. For a value of national income of 100 the value of new investment will indeed be approximately 10. The normal relation between national income and national capital is about 1 to 5; hence the normal value of $\bar{\bar{z}}$ would be 0.2. Of the total income, roughly one-fourth may be income of entrepreneurs, and the corresponding relationship to capital is therefore 0.05. The fluctuations in z will be mainly attributable to variations in this 0.05. The choice of 225 in the first line indicates that an increase of this ratio of 5 per cent of capital by 1 per cent would lead to an additional investment of 2.25 at a normal level of 10; this is also a realistic assumption.

In order to determine the movement of the variables, it is necessary to assume certain initial values. For this purpose we select a value of 450 of capital at the beginning of the period under consideration and a value of 2 for investment in excess of normal. The computation for Example IV then proceeds in a way similar to that in the preceding example:

EXAMPLE IV

Line	Quarter	1	2	3	4	5	6	7	8	9	10	11	12	13
1........	$I = 225\,z$	2	7.0	10.6	11.9	10.8	7.7	2.7	− 2.9	− 8.1	− 12.4	− 16.0	− 18.7	− 20.3
2........	$Y = 2\,I$	4	14.0	21.2	23.8	21.6	15.4	5.4	− 5.8	− 16.2	− 24.8	− 32.0	− 37.4	− 40.6
3........	$\overline{\overline{Y}} = 100 + Y$	104	114	121	124	122	115	105	94	84	75	68	63	59
4........	$\overline{\overline{K}}_t = K_{t-1} + I_{t-1} + 10$	450	462	479	500	522	543	561	574	581	583	581	575	566
5........	$\overline{\overline{z}} = \overline{\overline{Y}}/\overline{\overline{K}}$	0.231	0.247	0.253	0.248	0.234	0.212	0.187	0.164	0.145	0.129	0.117	0.110	0.104
6........	$z = \overline{\overline{z}} - 0.2$	0.031	0.047	0.053	0.048	0.034	0.012	− 0.013	− 0.036	− 0.055	− 0.071	− 0.083	− 0.090	− 0.096

Line	14	15	16	17	18	19	20	21	22	23	24	25	26	27
1........	− 21.6	− 21.8	− 21.8	− 21.4	− 20.3	− 18.9	− 17.1	− 14.6	− 11.9	− 9.2	− 6.3	− 4.1	− 2.0	− 0.7
2........	− 43.2	− 43.6	− 43.6	− 42.8	− 40.6	− 37.8	− 34.2	− 29.2	− 23.8	− 18.4	− 12.6	− 8.2	− 4.0	− 1.4
3........	57	56	56	57	59	62	66	71	76	82	87	92	96	99
4........	556	544	532	520	509	499	490	483	478	476	477	481	487	495
5........	0.103	0.103	0.105	0.110	0.116	0.124	0.135	0.147	0.159	0.172	0.182	0.191	0.197	0.200
6........	− 0.097	− 0.097	− 0.095	− 0.090	− 0.084	− 0.076	− 0.065	− 0.053	− 0.041	− 0.028	− 0.018	− 0.009	− 0.003	0.000

Since the relationship between the variables is more complicated, the resulting movement is also more complicated than that in the preceding examples. The primary movement is again a wave movement. In addition, a trend occurs, the character of which does not interest us in this connection. We suggest to the reader a very close study of this example. It has a number of interesting characteristics, many more than can be discussed in this text. It will be noted in particular, as we have mentioned already, that a wave movement is obtained without the introduction of speculative income, as a result of the assumption that not profits but the rate of profit determines investment. The example indicates the proposition which can be proved easily that fluctuating endogenous movements can occur in many different ways. For purposes of business-cycle theory it is important to determine which of these ways is actually operating in reality.

EXPANSION OF CYCLICAL MODELS

In the preceding example we have introduced a number of simplifying assumptions in order to explain the broad outlines of the cyclical process. In particular, we have assumed that total expenditure (apart from incidental disturbances) depended only on the size of national income.

a) Prices

This assumption implies that no separate influence is attributed to price. The assumption is justified if either of the following conditions is satisfied: (1) the elasticity of demand for all commodities combined, as a function of the general price level is equal to 1; (2) prices themselves depend on income only. As a first rough approximation we may say that both conditions are approximately satisfied so that our method is in two ways justified as a first step. A more precise analysis, however, will have to take account of deviations of these assumptions from reality. This will require the conventional demand and supply analysis. The quantities demanded and prices, and hence also the values, depend on the joint operation of demand and supply factors. We will therefore have to proceed to an enumeration and treatment of these factors, bearing in mind that the size of their effects depends on the magnitude of the elasticities of demand and of supply. The latter will normally be taken as data. In this connection we do not have to pay attention to all demand and supply factors but only to those that are of importance in the cyclical process. The demand factors have already been discussed in this respect when we analyzed fluctuations in investment and consumption; a brief recapitulation will suffice.

The most important demand factor remains income; in addition, the rate of interest, the lifetime of the stock of capital goods, the rate of increase in prices and of share prices, and possibly the income distribution are of importance as demand factors.

We may now turn to the supply factors. Goods and services are supplied from production or, as far as goods are concerned, from stock. Supply from production is by far the most important. Factors that determine production are (*a*) those which determine the cost curve—we may mention, as the most important, the prices of factors of production (the wage rate, the rate of interest, and the rate of rent) and (*b*) the quantities of the factors of productions which are required per unit of product. For practical purposes, the latter are given by the size of the capital, the productivity of labor, and, in the case of agriculture, the yield per acre. Some further, more incidental, factors may for the moment be left out of consideration.

How can we depict the changes in the mechanism which follow from the introduction of these variables? For this purpose we shall have to expand the calculations given in our examples by as many new lines as there are new variables. Thus, if some of the magnitudes concerned, such as expenditure, depended also on prices, this factor could be taken into account. A new relation would then have to be added to compute the level of prices for each period and, similarly, for the computation of each new variable. No new relation is necessary when new data are introduced; their course over time is known in advance and is therefore independent of the figures computed on the basis of the other relations.

Two steps are therefore necessary: the new relations have to be determined, and with their help the course of the variables in the more complicated model has to be computed. In general, it is by no means simple to anticipate the results of this computation simply on the basis of the knowledge of an individual new relation. The required mathematical method of handling can be replaced by reasoning only in exceptional cases, when one deals with exceedingly simple economic structures.

The relation which we need in each case is to inform us about the direct causes of changes in the variable under consideration; the indirect causes have to be left out of this relation. Indirect causes of changes in a given variable are always at the same time direct causes of changes in another variable. If we attribute changes in expenditure partly to changes in the level of prices and the latter again partly to changes in yields, then the latter are an indirect cause of changes in expenditure but at the same time a direct cause of changes in the price level. When we know the direct causes of all variables, we know all the elements in the general structure of relations. By concentrating our attention on direct causes, we can be sure that each link occurs only once. These questions are demonstrated clearly by the systems of arrows shown in Examples I, II, and III. Each of these systems consists of an endless repetition in time of a certain basic pattern which reflects the structure of the relations in the model. Each arrow indicates a direct cause of change of the variable to which the arrow points. The basic model is completely described by the enumeration of all direct causes. This may imply that more than one arrow points to one variable. We have already seen in chapter i that the total change in one variable may be composed of changes due to more than one cause.

We will now first consider the direct causes of changes in the price level. It is a reasonable approximation to reality to postulate that prices are determined by suppliers on the basis of the quantities demanded and of the supply factors. It is true that this is not the usual description of a market in economic theory. It is more normal to postulate that the suppliers determine the quantity they are prepared to supply on the basis of prices and supply factors.[17] In a sense, we turn the supply relation around and interchange quantity and price. As long as we assume im-

17. Cf. p. 113, *supra*.

mediate adaptation of these two variables, this interchange does not make any difference. But if it is assumed that a certain time elapses before the quantity supplied responds to a change in the market price, it does make a difference. In this case, we deliberately choose the relation in the sense in which we have formulated it because we believe that it better reflects actual changes in the short run. In economic theory, however, the supply relation is customarily not used to indicate changes in the short run but rather to describe the adaptation in the long run.

We assume further—a good approximation in most cases—that total costs for each enterprise consist of fixed and proportional costs, that is to say, that the cost curve is a straight line until very near total capacity. The slope of this line, however, may be different for different enterprises.

We specify now as a supply relation that the price will be equal to the marginal cost of the best firm plus profits such that the marginal firm will just cover its marginal costs. We mean by the best firm the one with the lowest variable cost per unit of time. Of course, it would be shorter to state that the price is equal to the marginal cost of the marginal firm, but in this connection it should be borne in mind that the marginal firm is not a given firm: it changes with the volume of production. For this reason the former formulation is preferable. The best firm may not be the same for eternity, but changes in this respect are in any case much slower. The concept of the representative firm may also be used, provided that one does not consider this as the firm which is midway between the best one and the marginal firm, since a firm so defined would also change too much over the course of a cycle.

The marginal costs of the best firm will be primarily wage costs and raw-material costs. If we consider a vertical integration of the economy, as we shall do to prevent too many complications, all raw-material costs vanish and instead of them we have wage costs of the firms producing raw materials. The wage costs are the product of the wage rate and the quantity of labor per unit of product. The latter variable is the inverse of labor productivity.

The profit margin which we mentioned is, as it were, the margin that the market permits. It will be the larger, the greater the distance between the best firm and the marginal firm. This distance may be measured by the volume of production. The size of the profit margin per unit of product depends on the spread of costs among the various enterprises. If this spread is small, the margin will also be small and will change little when the volume of production changes. In that case we would say that the supply price would have little flexibility, or that supply is very elastic. This will usually be the case for industrial products as long as there is unused productive capacity. If the volume of production reaches the limit of capacity, a further increase of production can take place only when the price promises profitability of the necessary new investment. At that stage, price suddenly becomes much more flexible; the further increase of the quantity supplied is accompanied by a relatively much stronger increase in prices. In the graphic representation between quantity and price the slope of the supply curve would show a definite change at this point.

In these various relations there may be a certain lag between cause and effect, that is to say, between a change in wage, labor productivity, or volume of production and a change in price. In particular, the tendency to compute costs on the basis of actual past expenditure will lead in this direction. If this method of calculation is used, a lag will occur equal to the period for which raw materials or semifinished products are kept in stock.

b) Wages

The wage rate, itself a price, may in its turn be considered as determined by the quantity turned over in the labor market, that is to say, the volume of employment, and by a number of supply factors. The most important supply factor with respect to changes in the wage rate in the short run is the cost of living. An increase in the cost of living will on the part of workers lead to requests and active measures for an increase in wages, whereas a decrease in the cost of living will lead to attempts on the part of entrepreneurs to lower wages. There are, of course, a number of other factors which determine supply, such as increases in the population, changes in social views, changes in educational facilities, etc. But these factors are as a rule the cause only of very gradual changes in the wage rate and are therefore not of importance in this connection.[18] We are, therefore, not far from reality when we consider that changes in the wage rate are determined by changes in the volume of employment and in the cost of living; the latter may be considered as the general level of prices of consumption goods. Changes in productivity of labor occur on the whole very regularly also; they are primarily trend changes and may therefore remain undiscussed in an explanation of cyclical movements. On closer analysis and particularly in individual industries, certain changes connected with the cycle may also be discerned. We may make a distinction here between changes that are more or less automatic and changes of a more spontaneous character. Automatic changes are the direct and automatic consequences of changes in the degree of capacity used. At a high level of utilization of capacity the efficiency of the total system of production is usually greatest, but, on the other hand, it is often necessary in these conditions to use workers who are less capable. The opposite occurs at a low degree of utilization of capacity.

As to spontaneous changes in labor productivity, these would be due to changes in the method of production, introduced by management as a result of its continuous attempt to improve the organization, to employ new methods, etc. These changes are likely to be pursued with the more intensity, the lower the activity of the firm. Sometimes these attempts will have more success than at other times. Abstracting from these differences in success which are of a more incidental character and assuming that the actual changes are also greatest in the periods of greatest adversity, it still does not follow that labor productivity itself would also be highest in depression periods. The increase in labor productivity is greatest in such times; hence labor productivity itself would be highest (as a deviation from its trend) approximately one-quarter of a cycle later. Since the process of spontaneous changes takes a certain time, the relative maximum of labor productivity is, according to statistical investigations, reached still later (approximately half a year),

18. Cf. p. 118, *supra*.

hence in total some two and a half years after the minimum of employment or of production has been passed. As we have mentioned, however, the influence of the cyclical movement on labor productivity is not very large for production as a whole, and we will pay no further attention to it in this connection. We may postulate, therefore, that the cyclical movements in employment and production are practically parallel; this is confirmed by statistical investigations.

If we try to summarize the preceding reflections, we arrive at the following conclusions, first of all for periods in which the full productive capacity is not used. The quantity of commodities demanded depends also on price, in addition to income. Price is determined by the wage rate and the volume of production; the wage rate itself by the price level and the volume of production. If all these relations for the variables mentioned referred to the same unit of time, one would have three variables with three unknowns, namely, the quantity demanded, the price, and the wage rate. By mathematical operation it would then be possible to express all in terms of income. In other words, the fluctuations in income would pull along the other variables; again, in other words, the three variables, quantity, price, and wage, would adapt themselves immediately to changes in income. In that case our original model would remain valid. The meaning of some of the numerical coefficients which we used, such as the marginal propensity to consume, would have become somewhat more complicated. These coefficients would then represent some sort of net result of the joint operation of a number of relations.

If, however, the various relations operate with a certain lag, the entire model becomes much more complicated. But if the lags are not great, the differences from an unlagged system would not be very great either, so that we might expect that the quantities produced, the level of prices, and the wage rates would follow approximately the fluctuations in income.

But this would hold only as long as production does not reach capacity. When it does and when we reach the region of bottlenecks, the general picture changes. At that stage, production can increase only slowly. There will now be a discrepancy between the movement of incomes and the movements of the other variables. The quantity produced and the quantity traded will show a tendency to increase only slightly, while prices start to rise more rapidly. It is now not certain how their product—total expenditure—will move; this depends on the elasticity coefficients entering into the various relations. Speculative income will now show more rapid increases than before. Hence the general development may become different. As a rule, however, there will still be a turning point. The curve of the volume of production will now reach its maximum first, but this does not mean that it will also show a decline first; a practically horizontal part may be expected, and this in itself will not always be a reason for a turning point. Whether a turning point does or does not occur can be determined only on the basis of a precise calculation and not by reasoning alone.

c) *Fluctuations in crops*

Another deviation in the pattern of the examples that can be attributed to factors in the commodity sphere is provided by changes in crops, changes to which we have referred a number of times before. In a year of excessively large crops, prices will be lower and the quantities consumed higher than they would have been in a normal year, given the same income of the preceding quarter. Here again one cannot say a priori whether total expenditure and hence income in a subsequent period will be larger or smaller, and a special pattern of developments may well occur. In this case there is not a systematic deviation from the cyclical pattern, since fluctuations in crops may be considered largely as random movements. As we mentioned in our examples, they may, therefore, rather be considered as disturbances of equilibrium which from time to time impart an impulse to the cyclical mechanism.

In this connection, it may be useful for a moment to assume that all lags are reduced to zero, that is to say, that the adaptations which are involved in this mechanism occur so rapidly that there is always an immediate adaptation of all economic variables to changes in the data. Thus, expenditure will correspond to a change in incomes not after a certain lag but immediately; prices will be adjusted immediately to increases in costs, wages to changes in the cost of living, etc.; and there will be no speculative incomes. All economic variables would then follow the pattern of fluctuations in the data, in this particular case the fluctuations in crops. What would then be their pattern? Since the natural time unit of these fluctuations is one year,[19] and random fluctuations have a quasi-period of three time units, there would then be quasi-periodic movements with a period of three years. One might in this way derive a cycle which shows a high degree of approximation to the short American cycle (the Kitchin), although not to that of the European cycle. It is worth noting in this connection that the reaction periods in the United States are relatively short. Hence the particular assumptions made in this paragraph may approximate reality in the United States much better than in Europe. This example, however, should be considered as an extreme approximation in which the disturbances would dominate completely the endogenous reactions of the system, which again might be more acceptable for the United States than for Europe. We may add to this the remark that, as we trust the reader will have realized from what has been said, it is inaccurate to consider the "agricultural" theories of the business cycle as an alternative to other theories. Rather, they complete these other theories by giving a further specification of the disturbances whereas most other theories concentrate on the reactions of the economy to these disturbances.

Apart from the question whether the adaptation of the economic variables to changes in crops occurs rapidly or slowly, another question of importance remains, namely, in which direction total expenditure will move in the case, for instance, of a positive deviation of yields, i.e., relatively large crops. In this respect, the agricultural theories of business cycles contradict each other. There need be no argument that in such a situation the degree of activity in agriculture and in the processing and transportation industries depending on it will be increased or that prices will be below normal. These facts, however, do not indicate anything about the direction into which money incomes and money expenditure will move, unless one has a cer-

19. Cf. p. 77, *supra*.

tain amount of information concerning the elasticities of demand for the different agricultural products. A solution of this problem on the basis of a statistical determination of these elasticities would be possible but has not yet been achieved. A further complication should still be mentioned. Since in reality the various reactions indicated take a certain amount of time and since, further, speculative influences based on the movement of prices from one year to the next play a role, not all reactions caused by one change in crops coincide, and the later reactions of one crop year become mixed with the early reactions of the next crop year.

d) Short-term rate of interest

Adjustments similar to those which should be made in our simple models given in Examples I–IV, in order to take account of the influence of the price level on the demand for goods and services, should be made to take account of the influence of the rate of interest on demand and hence on expenditure. This will mean that certain influences originating in what we may call "the financial sphere" will make themselves felt. We consider this sphere as consisting of the variables—prices and quantities—relating to the more liquid assets, in particular to money, claims, and evidences of ownership. In the last two categories we would include short-term claims such as drafts, current account advances, etc., and claims with a longer period to maturity, such as bonds and shares. Each of these relatively liquid assets yields a certain income to its owner, and hence a certain rate of interest corresponds to each of them. The various short-term rates of interest correspond to the short claims, the rate of interest in the capital market to bonds, and the yield on shares to stock certificates. Of total expenditure, especially that for investment will depend on one or more of these rates of interest.

By the same token, these rates of interest will have a certain effect on business-cycle fluctuations. Here again, however, we may observe that the effect of these factors is quite moderate, because the influence of the rate of interest on investment is not very great. The movements of the rate of interest in the capital market (i.e., the bond yield) show, moreover, hardly any cyclical component, which fact reduces further the influence of the rate of interest in the cyclical movements.

Let us consider first the modifications that have to be applied to our models to take account of fluctuations in the short-term rate of interest. We have to follow the same procedure as in the treatment of prices: a new line should be introduced for each new variable that is added to the model. Of the formation of the short-term rate of interest, it may be said that it (like other prices) is determined in the short run by the suppliers of short-term credits, that is, mainly the banking organization, usually under the guidance of the central bank.

We consider for our purpose the banking system as a whole, as it were, the combined balance sheet of the central bank and the other banks. The main assets of the banking system are then gold and foreign-exchange holdings and credits (loans, advances, investments, security holdings), and the main liabilities constitute together the money supply (central bank notes and deposits in the other banks). What are the considerations which guide central banks in setting their rates of discount, rates we may consider as representative of the rate of interest for short-term credits?

Various legal or conventional reserve requirements make it necessary for the banking system to hold a minimum of gold cover for the total money supply. Most central banks are required to maintain gold to at least a certain percentage of their sight liabilities. This establishes a relation between gold holdings and currency circulation plus the balances of other banks with the central bank. The latter balances, in turn, may be fixed by minimum reserve requirements, as in the United States, or by conventional reserve ratios, as in the United Kingdom. It follows that the short-term rate of interest is determined primarily by the relative movements of (*a*) the gold stock and (*b*) the quantity of money.

In order to complete the business-cycle mechanism, we shall have to analyze again the direct causes of changes in these two variables.

With respect to the demand for money we may refer to the different motives for holding cash to which Keynes in particular has drawn attention. The most important motive, which is predominant especially in normal times, is the transactions motive, reflecting the necessity to finance transactions. On that account the volume of money would fluctuate with the value of turnover, reflected in our models by the variable total expenditure. Larger expenditure would require a larger quantity of money and would hence lead to a tendency of the rate of interest to increase. There may, further, be the hoarding motive, when the use of money is considered to be not profitable or when an extra cash reserve is desired for unexpected events. To some extent this reflects a comparison of the rate of interest which could be made if the money were invested with the preference for holding liquid assets; hence the demand for money is, in part, dependent on the various rates of interest. Finally, demand may in part be determined by movements of prices, movements in share prices, and many incidental events, particularly political events. All these factors would apply both to the demand for money exercised by private persons and to that exercised by businesses.

The gold stock is an important determining factor with respect to the supply of money in countries adhering to the gold standard. Fluctuations in gold stocks for a single country are quite different from fluctuations for all countries combined. For all countries combined the gold stock shows a very smooth pattern, as annual gold production is only a very small proportion of the available stock. More abrupt changes are possible only to the extent that gold privately held or gold used in ornaments may find its way into the holdings of the central banks (as happens occasionally in countries like India). On the whole, these changes are not very intimately connected with the cycle.

Changes in the gold stocks of individual countries reflect mainly changes in the balance of payments positions of these countries. The balance of payments position of a country depends on many factors. To arrive at net changes in gold, one would have to take account of the balance on trade account, the balance on invisible items, and long-term and short-term capital movements. One of the important factors determining the trade balance is the difference in the economic position between the country under consideration and the countries with which it trades; this balance need not therefore be closely correlated with the business cycle itself. Differences in the cyclical position that may be incidental in character determine this balance. In the course of the last fifty years, for instance, Germany has shown a considerable change in the pattern of fluctuations of her trade balance over the cycle. While before 1914 Germany's exports tended to increase during the depression, no such tendency was visible in the interwar period. Similar considerations apply to invisible items and to capital movements. Such movements in particular are often the result of incidental events, such as the creation of a large new enterprise, the opening-up of a new area, political and psychological factors, etc. As a result of all this, movements in the gold stock are much nearer to being random disturbances than a systematic factor subject to cyclical changes.

In summary, then, movements in the short-term rate of interest are determined primarily by total expenditures as a demand factor and the gold stock as a supply factor; in addition, speculative and other incidental demand factors may play a role. The introduction of the short-term rate of interest in our model, therefore, means primarily that fluctuations in the gold stock are given a role in the determination of the cyclical pattern. To the extent that the level of expenditure makes itself felt through the rate of interest, the expansion of our model simply means the introduction of a restraining factor. A high level of expenditure will, after a certain period, for instance, after one quarter, lead to an increase in the short-term rate of interest, and this will make expenditure in the next quarter slightly lower than it would otherwise have been. Hence, the factor 0.9 in Example III would become slightly lower.

It should perhaps be mentioned that some authors attribute a psychological significance of much greater consequence than the economic influence we have indicated to an increase of the discount rate of the central bank above a certain maximum, for instance, above 6 per cent. They would believe that the transgression of such a critical point would lead to a general restraint in expenditure.

e) Share yield and share prices

After the analysis of the effect of the short-term rate of interest on the cyclical pattern, we should now deal similarly with share prices. We mentioned before that the yield on shares may be considered as a rate of interest and as such will be a factor determining the level of investment. A high share yield will be reflected, *ceteris paribus*, in a low level of new investment. Since the share yield is the ratio of the percentage dividend and the share price, both these factors will require to be incorporated in our model. We will have to deal with share prices in any case, because we have seen[20] that share prices directly affect the volume of speculative income; an increase in share prices creates speculative profits which are usually treated as income.

There is a direct relationship between dividends and profits. For most countries a rather strict relationship can be observed —the higher the profit percentage, the higher the percentage of dividends. There is, however, no proportionality: the dividend rate fluctuates with less intensity, and it never becomes negative. We have treated before the relationship between the profit rate on the one hand, and total income and the cumulated series of investments, on the other hand.[21] As a first approximation we may state that the dividend rate shows fluctuations parallel with those of national income but somewhat lagged because dividends paid out usually correspond to profits some time earlier. In European countries this lag is greater than in the United States. We may estimate it for Europe at approximately ten months. The rate of profit in a certain calendar year centered around July 1 will determine the rate of dividend around May 1 of the next year. In the United States it is found that dividends depend not only on the rate of profit but also rather clearly on the level of surplus, the latter representing the cumulation of undistributed profits.

We now come to the formation of share prices. Different aspects of the market for shares may best be treated in a series of successive approximations. As a first approximation we assume that all buyers and sellers of shares are investors, that is to say,

20. Cf. p. 194, *supra*.

21. Cf. p. 203, *supra*.

they desire to hold shares only because of the income they yield. We assume further a stationary society so that both dividends and the long-term rate of interest remain constant. Under these assumptions, share prices will be proportional to the dividend rate and inversely proportional to the long-term rate of interest. They are in fact equal to the ratio of these two magnitudes. If the dividend rate is 8 per cent and the long-term rate of interest is 4 per cent, share quotations will be 200 per cent of par.

A first complication is introduced if the situation is no longer assumed to be stationary, but both dividends and the rate of interest change. The yields will then be determined by the expected dividends. If in a certain year an extremely high dividend has been paid, shareholders will not assume that this dividend will be maintained but rather that future dividends will be lower. Statistical observation indicates that on the average share prices follow approximately the following rules:

a) The dividend rate considered as normal is reflected in share prices according to the normal level as indicated in the preceding paragraph.

b) The dividend expectation deviates from that average by roughly half the actual distance between the current dividend rate and the average rate. In other words, shareholders expect that when the current dividend is higher than normal the average dividend in the future will also be higher than normal but only by half as much. Normal share prices occur at a dividend rate of approximately 4 per cent. This yield appears to be determined by experience over the past decades. When the actual dividend rate is 10 per cent, the expectation for the future appears to be about 7 per cent, and the share-price index will reflect this yield. Thus, if the long-term rate of interest is 4 per cent, the price will be 175 per cent of par, or 1.75 times as high as it would have been at a dividend rate of 4 per cent.

Hence fluctuations in the share level will be determined primarily by fluctuations in dividends, and these depend in their turn on fluctuations in profits. Profits reflect the business cycle somewhat earlier than wages, since the latter have a certain lag with respect to other series. Total national income, that is to say, the sum of profits (including all nonlabor income) and wages, lags therefore somewhat with respect to profits. This explains why share prices lead somewhat with respect to national income and also with respect to general indices of activity and prices.

Obviously, prices for individual shares may deviate from the above rule. The dividend expectations for individual shares will be determined by certain known facts, such as plans of the corporation, tax plans of the government, etc. In abnormal times, further strong deviations may occur with respect to all shares, owing to general expectations with respect to the economy as a whole. We have referred earlier to the low relative level of share prices during the inflation in Germany.[22]

Share prices will deviate from the standard indicated above when there is a pronounced speculative boom on the stock exchange. We refer here to a situation in which the public at large participates in speculation. This will occur only in countries in which there is a general desire for speculation and even then only after share prices have been rising for a considerable time. A further necessary condition may be that there is a certain availability of savings for which no good investment opportunity is available. The United States is clearly the country in which these conditions are best satisfied. A certain tendency toward speculation may also be observed in England, France, and Belgium, rather less in the Netherlands; in Germany it appears to be very small. In the United States, savings were available in particular in 1928 and 1929, when incomes were very high and the amounts required for investment were smaller than those provided by savings. Thus, the speculative boom in 1928–29 could assume dimensions which had been entirely unknown before. The boom was reflected not only in increases in share prices but also in the prices paid for a New York Stock Exchange seat. Figure 49 shows both magnitudes, the latter since 1870.

When the public at large starts to participate on a large scale in stock-exchange speculation, a new factor in the formation of share prices is added. This large body of speculators will be

22. Cf. p. 44, *supra.*

guided by stock-exchange profits made some time earlier. That is to say, the increase of share prices itself, for instance, from the first to the second quarter, will become a factor in the determination of the demand for shares in the third quarter and thereby of the share price in that quarter. This will introduce a new characteristic, which was also present in Example III, in which income in the third quarter was in part determined by the increase of income from the first to the second quarter.

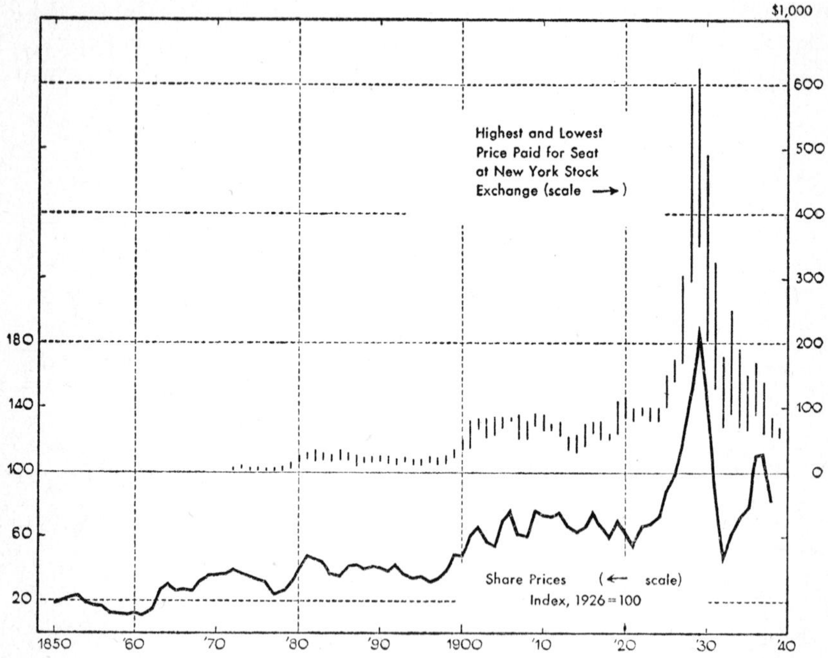

FIG. 49.—Price paid for a Stock Exchange seat in New York (in thousands of dollars) and index number of share prices at the New York Stock Exchange (1926 = 100).

Which way will the forces that operate in the share market affect the cyclical pattern? The most striking and, for recent cyclical history, the most important example is provided by the Stock Exchange boom in the United States in 1929, to which we have referred. Speculative tendencies on the part of the public pushed share prices up above their intrinsic value, which we may define now as the value shares would have had on the basis of their dividends, taking account of the expected lower future dividend rate as in normal periods. Hence share yields became extremely low, thus providing an additional stimulus for investment. During the period when share prices increased, speculative incomes were also very high; hence total consumption expenditure was also stimulated. Both these movements could not continue; a fall in incomes was probable as soon as share prices ceased to increase. The moment at which the two stimulating factors disappeared was in part determined by random exogenous events which contributed to the end of the Stock Exchange boom in October, 1929. In this connection, reference has been made by some authors to the second large crop after that of 1928 and to the increase of the discount rate above the critical level. To explain the upward turning point, however, it is by no means necessary to seek the assistance of such an extraneous event. We have seen in Example III that the turning point can also occur as a necessary phase in the movements of a model of the sort treated there—and the formation of share prices in periods of acute speculation approaches that model.

SUMMARY: SUCCESSION OF THE DIFFERENT PHASES OF THE CYCLE

In order to summarize our analysis of the cyclical mechanism, we shall now provide a short description of the most important reactions in the order in which they occur. One should realize, however, that such a description has a great scientific danger. It suggests rather than proves. A really exact explanation of cyclical movements can be given only along the lines of our models I–IV, expanded as far as necessary in the ways indicated in the pages just preceding. Since it appeared that the occurrence or nonoccurrence of turning points depends on the intensity of certain reactions and not simply on qualitative considerations, a purely qualitative description cannot be considered as a proof. But we shall give it, nevertheless, because it may make for livelier exposition and thus contribute to a better understanding.

A second danger in this description should be mentioned, that of generalization. It is not implied that every cycle develops according to exactly the same scheme. Often the intervention of disturbances is so important that they completely change the entire picture; there are also systematic differences between cycles, to which we shall refer below.

We start our description in the depression period, characterized by a low level of production, low prices and incomes, unemployment, and large liquidity of business. This low level has, after a certain period, led to a certain consolidation which makes it possible for entrepreneurs to pay attention to certain more favorable developments. These will develop gradually and more or less automatically. Inventories have been reduced; there is a certain need for the replacement of the means of production; labor productivity increases under the pressure of the depression. Speculative incomes, which had been negative as long as commodity and share prices fell, become zero. The rate of profit becomes higher by the reduction of capital at a constant level of profits: the natural rate of interest increases. On the other hand, the discount rate and the wage rate are low. These factors lead to a resumption of expenditure, both for investment and consumption: recovery starts. Sometimes an exogenous factor may provide an impulse; but in any case the preparedness to respond to favorable impulses has been increased by the factors we enumerated.

Once the recovery has started, it has a tendency to reinforce itself. The process of recovery is cumulative. Larger expenditures lead to increases in income, hence higher profits, and these in turn will lead to larger expenditure. Higher demand will raise prices. The increase in prices creates speculative incomes and so will the increase in share prices as a result of increased profits. As prices rise, the wage rate will increase too, but with a certain lag. The increasing tendency to invest will lead to an increasing demand for credits, after use has been made first of the liquid means which were at the disposal of the economy. Initially, financing will be done with short-term credits and lead to an increase in the short-term rate of interest. As profits increase, short-term credits will be consolidated. As production increases, stocks will be brought to a higher level too. Gradually the boom phase of the cycle is approached, with high production, high prices, high incomes, and little unemployment. Sometimes an absolute peak is reached in the sense that production cannot be expanded further, either because total productive capacity is in use, at least in certain industries, or because the credit system cannot stand any further expansion and banks start to ration credit, or, finally, because no further labor is available in certain industries. But even without such ceilings or bottlenecks, certain less favorable tendencies will develop. The rate of profit is affected unfavorably by the increase in total capital; speculative incomes decline as the rate of increase in prices and share prices falls. The need to replace means of production slackens; labor productivity declines. Production may remain for a certain time at a high level because it lags behind orders, but the entire economy becomes more vulnerable. As Kaldor has put it, the equilibrium of the economy is now stable with respect to upward shocks but unstable with respect to downward shocks.

As a result of such systematic factors, possibly reinforced by random factors, screened as it were (if Kaldor is correct) in the unfavorable sense that only the downward factors make themselves felt, the tide turns. If the boom has had a very speculative character, the turning point may be very sharp and may lead rapidly to a lower level. Once the downward process has started, it, too, has a tendency to be cumulative. The reduction in profits will lead to a fall in investment, to a further decline in incomes, and hence to a general decline in expenditure. This chain of events will repeat itself. Reduced demand for commodities will make prices fall; this will lead to negative speculative incomes. Such negative speculative incomes will also occur as a result of a fall in share prices. These declines may be reinforced by forced sales of those who cannot obtain credits to bridge temporary deficits. There is a temporary illiquidity which, in earlier crisis periods, has often led to a financial crisis of serious consequences. Gradually, however, the phenomena to which we referred in the beginning of our summary will make themselves felt and the whole cycle is completed.

OVERSAVING VS. OVERINVESTMENT

We must now turn to a question which has played an important role in discussions of the cyclical problem. Can an upper turning point be prevented by saving more or by consuming more? Some writers maintain that the recovery ends because of a lack of savings; investments cannot be financed and will therefore have to be reduced. Other writers, on the other hand, have held the opinion that a larger volume of consumption was necessary to maintain recovery. The proper answer to the question depends on the assumptions of the different theories—often tacit assumptions. In order to test the applicability of the theories, it is necessary to verify the realism of the assumptions made.

The most essential point in connection with the maintenance of a high level of activity is whether total expenditure for consumption and investment combined will be increased or decreased. A second point is whether increased or decreased amounts will correspond also to increased or decreased quantities. If a certain industry is fully employed, then a greater total amount spent on its products will lead only to an increase in prices, not to an increase in production. Much depends, therefore, on whether one assumes the existence of full employment in one or both of the two industries, the industry producing investment goods and the industry producing consumption goods. After these preliminary remarks we may try a direct answer to the question.

Total expenditure consists of expenditure of income plus the expenditure of amounts obtained through credits. The latter are mainly investment expenditures. A shift by consumers in favor of consumption expenditure, accompanied by an equally large reduction of savings, will tend to increase total expenditure as long as the creation of credit is not completely inelastic. The entrepreneurs who desire to make investment expenditure will, if they have less savings at their disposal, compensate in any case part of this reduction by an increased demand for credit. The increase in consumption expenditure is matched, therefore, by a smaller reduction in investment expenditure. Hence there is an increase in total demand. Only if (1) the creation of credit were entirely inelastic would the total demand of expenditure, as a limiting case, remain the same; in that case it would as a first approximation be indifferent whether consumption expenditure or savings increased. And if then, further, (2) consumption goods industries were fully occupied and (3) the investment industries were not fully employed, an increase in consumption might reduce the total volume of production and an increase in saving might increase it. It would also be possible that the total volume of production would decline if condition (2) were fulfilled, even though total expenditure and consumption expenditure increased, that is to say, if assumption (1) were not fulfilled.

These three assumptions which have to be satisfied in order that (*a*) an increase in consumption expenditure will lead to a crisis and (*b*) an increase in savings would prevent that crisis have indeed been made, explicitly or implicitly, by the first group of writers referred to, among whom Hayek should be mentioned in particular. The first assumption is in accordance with reality with respect to many a period of very tight credit, especially before 1914. Even then, however, the second and third assumptions were rarely fulfilled. And since 1914 the first assumption has not been fulfilled either.

Since it would appear to be better from the cyclical point of view to have larger consumption rather than larger saving, what point, if any, is there in saving? The answer is that here too there are limits. An increase of consumption expenditure will lead, as we have seen, to an increase in total expenditure because of the expansion of credits. When the point of full employment of the total economy is reached, any further increase in consumption expenditure will only lead to increases in prices and no longer to an expansion of production. That would be the limit of a desirable expansion of consumption.

ECONOMIC STRUCTURE AND CYCLICAL PATTERNS

We observed in chapter vii that cyclical movements do not follow the same pattern in every country. We shall endeavor now to seek an explanation of the differences between cycles in different countries and to see in particular to what extent these differences can be explained on the basis of differences between the countries in their economic structure.

It is clear that active economic intercourse between various countries will tend to even out any differences between their cyclical patterns and in this way set a limit to the magnitude of such differences. This was the normal situation in the nineteenth and early twentieth centuries. In such circumstances, cyclical fluctuations in all countries tended to run parallel; in fact, economic conditions in small countries with a relatively large foreign trade were almost completely determined by the conditions prevailing in the larger countries.

The tendency toward parallel development operates first of all through prices, which tend to move up and down jointly in all countries as a result of international competition. This applies in particular to the prices of goods and services which have a world market, such as the relatively light raw materials and the services of capital. It applies much less to goods and services with a restricted mobility, such as relatively heavy commodities (iron), commodities which cannot be moved (dwellings), and labor. Even without the existence of specific restrictions, international competition with respect to such commodities and services can operate only in an indirect fashion, via their products or through competing commodities or services.

The tendency toward parallelism exercises itself also through the quantities in international trade. A depression in country A will make itself felt by a reduction in the quantity it will import from country B; country B may also be affected, as the yield of its investments in country A declines. Both factors would show up in the balance of payments of country B which would develop in an unfavorable direction, with consequent pressure on the currency of country B. If this country were to try to stay aloof from the depression in surrounding countries and to maintain its wage level and price level, its exports would decline even more and its imports would tend to increase. It is clear, therefore, that there must be a strong pressure on country B to follow the cyclical pattern of other countries.

Despite these tendencies toward parallelism, differences in the cyclical pattern can well occur. There may, first, be differences in amplitude. If country X produces relatively more commodities that are subject to large fluctuations in demand and country Y more commodities with a smaller fluctuation in demand, country Y will be less affected by a depression than will country X. The differences indicated may be due to the fact that the production of country X is concentrated heavily on capital goods, luxury items, or raw materials; as we have seen, the amplitude of the cyclical fluctuations in the sale of these commodities is greater than for other commodities.

Second, differences in phase are possible. A country will undergo cyclical fluctuations relatively later than other countries if it produces mainly types of commodities that are relatively slow in feeling changes in business conditions. But since the lags involved are usually small, no large differences are possible on this account.

Differences in period are not likely to occur. If they did, they would soon lead to differences in the actual cyclical position which would tend to be evened out by the operation of the factors mentioned above. Differences in period become more likely, however, as the connection between the various countries becomes less intense and particularly if the period of the cycle in one country is a multiple of that of the cycle in other countries. The difference in the period of the cycle between the United States and Europe fulfils these two conditions. Owing to its size, the United States is much less influenced by international economic conditions than are most European countries. The period of three and one-half years which appears to characterize the United States economy is just about one-half the period of the cycles in European countries. The two cyclical patterns have continued to exist side by side for a considerable time, with every other recession in the United States coinciding with one in Europe.

It goes without saying that much greater differences in the cyclical pattern become a possibility as soon as international competition is severely limited. This occurs, unintentionally, in periods of disturbed exchanges; and it is the specific object of such policies as import quotas, import duties, and exchange control measures. The most extreme examples of such policies were seen in the U.S.S.R. after 1918 and in Germany after 1933. In both countries the entire economy became at the same moment controlled in a high degree, as a result of which business cycles were practically eliminated.

If countries are completely separated from each other, each will show the cyclical pattern reflecting its own economic structure. If the separation is incomplete, it is no longer true that the structure of each country determines the cyclical pattern of that country. In part, the pattern will reflect the structure of the countries with which it trades. The more intimate the trade connections are, the less will be the difference between the cyclical patterns in the different countries.

In successive periods of time, changes in the cyclical pattern may be expected even within one country, as a result of changes in the economic structure of that country over time.

Which are the structural characteristics that are particularly responsible for differences in cyclical patterns? In order to answer this question, we have to refer to our explanation of the cycle and to see which structural coefficients were of particular importance in determining the shape of cyclical movements. As we have seen, the formation and use of income and hence the magnitudes which determined these processes were of dominating significance, namely: (1) the marginal propensity to consume and a coefficient which, on the basis of analogy, may be called the "marginal propensity to invest"; (2) the lag between income and consumption; (3) the tendency toward speculation, determining the magnitude of speculative incomes; and (4) the lifetime of capital goods (to the extent that the echo principle is of importance). In addition to these major coefficients, a number of others are also of considerable importance, and some of them, such as the elasticity of the supply of goods and of factors of production, may be of primary significance in particular phases of the business cycle.

Differences in cyclical patterns should therefore be expected particularly where there are striking differences between the structural characteristics mentioned. Most pronounced in this connection is, no doubt, the difference between free and controlled economies in the marginal propensity to invest, "controlled economy" to be interpreted in a wide sense so as to include economies in which the state would engage in a public works policy in a depression to compensate the decline in private investment. The most pronounced differences in cyclical patterns existed, accordingly, between the U.S.S.R. and Germany, on the one hand, and most other countries, on the other hand.

It may well be possible that the short period of the American cycle (the Kitchin) is due to the shortness of the lags between income and expenditure in the United States.[23]

It is almost certain that the lifetime of machinery has been reduced from the nineteenth to the twentieth centuries. The reduction in the period of the cycle in the course of the nineteenth century has sometimes been ascribed to this cause. It is to be noted, however, that the tendency toward reduction in the period is not clearly observable after 1914.

There are no clear indications of differences in the marginal propensity to consume, either between countries or between the early nineteenth century and the present time. No conclusions can therefore be drawn as to any possible effect of this crucial coefficient on differences in cyclical patterns.

When there is full employment of productive resources and of the credit resources of a country, the elasticity of supply of both mineral materials and capital is very small. This situation may materially affect the shape of cyclical movements. Conditions of full employment occurred more frequently before 1914 than after that time, at least in countries with free economies. Whether this change has been accompanied by a different cyclical pattern can be determined only after a more detailed analysis of the effects of temporary reductions in elasticity of the type indicated. Since, even before 1914, full utilization of resources occurred for brief intervals of the cycle only, it is not probable that the total period of the cycle or the rate of damping would have been materially affected by it. The shape of the cyclical peak and the relative importance of price and quantity movements in the cycle did, however, depend on it: in the cycles referred to, prices of mineral raw materials and the rate of interest showed very sharp peaks. But such peaks were by no means characteristic of all pre-1914 cycles.

23. Cf. p. 188, *supra*.

Finally, certain general reasons may be advanced to make it plausible that no great change in cyclical patterns occurred in the course of the past century. In the first place, two very fundamental characteristics of the economy have remained unchanged: the use of money and the profit motive. Furthermore, the distribution of the national income among the factors of production has not changed much, which would make it appear plausible that the marginal propensity to consume had remained approximately unchanged. Third, the period of one year has remained the natural unit of time in many respects. Certain typical lags in the formation and use of income and in the periodic appraisal of business conditions have thus remained unchanged. However this may be, the absence of adequate statistical material with respect to the nineteenth century makes it particularly difficult to analyze the effects of possible changes in factors such as those mentioned here.

CHAPTER FOURTEEN

CYCLICAL MOVEMENTS IN INDIVIDUAL MARKETS

INTRODUCTION

WE HAVE indicated in chapter viii that prices and quantities in a number of individual markets show cyclical fluctuations which have periods different from those of the general business cycle. Sometimes these fluctuations are clear only for either prices or quantities. We shall now turn to an explanation of these special cycles. They are not of great importance for the explanation of the general business cycle; it will appear, however, that they have great scientific significance. Because they occur in a more limited field, they can be studied more accurately and the relationship of the various variables is simpler. Study of these cycles will reveal certain basic types of movements that show certain dynamic characteristics in their simplest form. Such a study is therefore of great importance for a good understanding of economic dynamics, quite apart from the relative weight of the commodities involved in the economy. This study will also permit a greater attention for details than is usually possible in studies of general cyclical problems.

THE HOG MARKET

As a first approximation the explanation of the individual cycles in the hog market may be presented as follows. If for one reason or another there is an unusually large supply of hogs, the price will be unusually low; otherwise consumers will not be prepared to consume a larger than normal quantity of pork. This low price will have an unfavorable effect on supplies; but this influence will not be felt immediately; the "production" of pigs requires a certain period. The natural process, consisting of a gestation period of four months and, in most countries, a fattening period of a year would in itself lead to a lag of sixteen months; to this should be added a period of a "psychic lag" on the part of the farmer who requires a certain time to appreciate a certain market situation. Various authors, therefore, assume a total lag of a year and six months to a year and nine months. Hence a year and a half, or somewhat more, after a low level of prices there will be a relatively low supply of hogs. This will lead to a high level of prices almost without a lag. This high level of prices will, again in a year and a half or somewhat later, lead to a high supply of hogs. Hence there is a tendency to a lasting cycle. Characteristic of this mechanism is that prices and quantities show opposite movements, with low prices corresponding to a typical situation of "overproduction." The model of the hog market is the simplest model of alternating over- and underproduction of commodities of which the volume of production can be controlled. A necessary condition for the occurrence of overproduction, that is to say, a larger production than the suppliers would themselves be prepared to offer in the long run, is a lag between price and the corresponding supply. If there were no lag, suppliers would always be able to regulate supply in accordance with the price. This necessary lag is the only dynamic characteristic of our model.

It will be noted that we deal here again with a very simple case of endogenous fluctuations but of a type different from that given in Example III. This model is still much simpler and is particularly suitable as a methodical starting point for the study of endogenous fluctuations. It has the advantage that the effect of the different data on the character of the movement can easily be seen. Thus it is clear that the period will be double the lag between a change in prices and a change in the quantity supplied. To illustrate a number of other characteristics of the model, we use a graphical representation which is closely related to the demand and supply curves (Fig. 50). The line *AB* is the ordinary demand curve for pork. The line *CD* may be compared with the supply curve; but it should be understood in this sense that it indicates for every price p, the quantity x which will be supplied after a year and a half, that is to say, after the assumed lag. It is assumed that the quantity supplied does not depend on the current price. There will probably always be some effect of the current price, but in the particular case of the hog market this effect appears to be extremely weak and may be disregarded. Hence the instantaneous supply curve would be a vertical, or nearly vertical, line. Since the quantity supplied depends on the price a year and a half earlier, this line would, however, be subject to constant shifts. It is therefore simpler in this case to work with a supply curve as indicated by the line *CD*. There

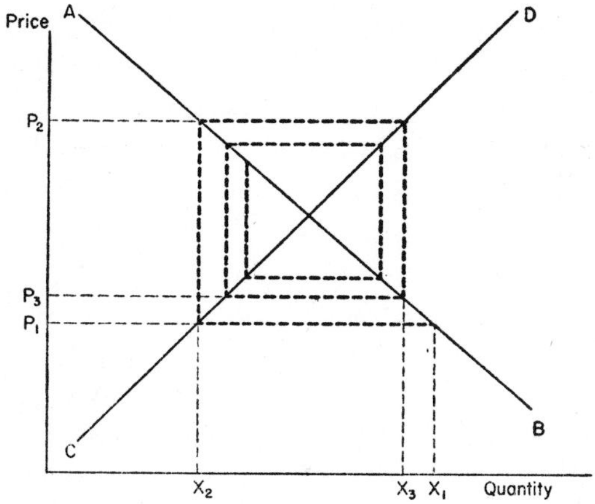

FIG. 50.—The cobweb theorem: diagram to determine the movement of prices and quantities if supply reacts to price with a certain lag.

would seem to be no objection to calling *CD* a supply curve even though this means some expansion of the concept of a supply curve. We might also call it a quasi-supply curve.

If we measure time in units equal to the lag, the quantity supplied at time 1 will be equal to x_1 (as shown in the diagram) which, on the basis of the demand curve, will lead to price p_1 at the same time. This price p_1 will after one lag period lead to a quantity supplied x_2, which can be found by using the line *CD*. The quantity x_2 will lead to a price p_2, etc. The entire further development of x and p can be read from the diagram, and it will readily be seen that a fluctuating movement will occur. Strictly speaking, our considerations apply only to individual periods of time which are not connected and are at distances of approximately a year and a half. However, if one knows all these points, the intermediate positions may be "filled out" in a similar way, so as to give a picture of the full development.

This development over time has been called the "cobweb theorem" because of the shape of Figure 50. The same diagram will also assist us in understanding the character of the movement on the basis of the slopes of the lines AB and CD. (1) If both lines have the same absolute slope with a contrary sign, there will be a purely periodic movement. (2) If the slope of the quasi-supply curve is greater than that of the demand curve, that is to say, if supply is less elastic than demand, there will be a damped periodic movement. (3) If the slope of the quasi-supply curve is less than that of the demand curve, there will be an antidamped movement. In the first and third cases, the equilibrium position in which the price and the quantity are determined by the co-ordinates of the point of intersection will not be attained.

This fact is also of principal significance since it indicates that any qualitative reasoning which tends to prove an approximation to an equilibrium position can have only very limited validity. It should further be clear that the movement is set off only if and when a certain disturbance from equilibrium occurs. If initially there had been a position in accord with the point of intersection of the demand and supply curves, no movement would have occurred. The larger the initial disturbance, the greater the amplitude of the movement.

When the slope of the quasi-supply curve is less than that of the demand curve, the amplitude of the resulting antidamped movement cannot, of course, increase without limit, as would result from an automatic application of the cobweb diagram. At a certain point the limit of the area is reached in which the approximations used, for instance, the straight-line demand and supply curve, remain valid. Beyond that point, the theorem should not be applied without the necessary adjustments.

As we have indicated, the preceding model reflects only the essence of the mechanism determining the prices and quantities in the hog market. A number of other factors which we have neglected so far are of a certain importance in a second approximation.

On the demand side we have neglected the influence of changes in incomes and prices of competing commodities. Among the latter, beef is the most important. Demand may therefore increase not only by a decline in the price of pork but also by an increase in income or by an increase in the price of beef. These influences are on the whole less pronounced than those of the pork price, since the latter shows wider fluctuations. But during the depression from 1929 to 1932, the effect on pork consumption of falling income was also of considerable importance. A country with large pork exports may also be affected by measures of commercial policy abroad. Both causes did in fact in a number of countries break the regularity of the hog cycle in the depression.[1]

On the supply side, there is also an influence of the cost of production, in particular of the price of corn. Corn prices, however, fluctuate much less than hog prices and are therefore of secondary significance.

A more fundamental point is whether the plans of farmers are not determined by the expected future price rather than by the current price. In principle this should be so. But the question is how these price expectations are determined. It would be wrong to assume that the cobweb theorem necessarily implies that the expected price is equal to the current price. The theorem is compatible with much more general hypotheses. If one were to assume, for instance, that the expected price would be halfway between the current price and the equilibrium price, the same theorem would apply. This in itself, however, would double the degree of damping. And one would have to assume a slope of the quasi-supply curve twice as steep with respect to the price axis to arrive at a movement of prices and quantities equal to that found earlier.

A number of other complications, to which reference has been

1. The opinion of Joseph Schumpeter (*Business Cycles* [New York and London, 1939], II, 430) that the entire hog cycle may be attributed to fluctuations in income is in any case incorrect for Europe, since incomes there do not fluctuate with a three-and-one-half-year period.

made in recent English and German publications, should be mentioned. In England, hogs are fattened during a shorter period, from four to eight months. This should reduce the lag by eight to four months. Yet the English cycle is not shorter than that in other countries where hogs are fattened for a longer period. An explanation of this phenomenon may perhaps be found in the influence of the international competition which determines in part the hog-price level in England.

The supply of hogs may also in part be determined by prices ruling much longer ago, since it depends also on the number of sows available, and this number is in part determined by a much earlier price situation; a sow normally produces five or six litters of pigs. The consequences of this fact have not yet been fully studied. Data necessary for such a study have only quite recently been collected in a regular fashion. But recently the hog market has been subject to many regulations which have affected the pattern of the movements.[2]

A more accurate study of the details of the hog cycle can also be made if a distinction is made between two phases of the production cycle which are often exercised in different farms: the production of pigs—for which there is a separate market—and the subsequent fattening. It would lead us too far to go into these details of the analysis. In this connection we refer to the literature.

THE COFFEE MARKET

After our exposition concerning the hog market, we can be brief in an explanation of the fluctuations in prices and quantities in the coffee market. On the whole, they show the same characteristics. Here, too, the fluctuation of prices is opposite to that of quantities (after elimination of the trend movement from the latter). Here, too, one may state that the demand side responds with a very small lag while there is a considerable lag in the adaptation of supply.

It takes seven years before a coffee tree yields coffee beans. If, therefore, the price situation is favorable and leads to increased

2. Wagemann has pointed out (*Narrenspiegel der Statistik* [Hamburg, 1942], p. 266) that the supply of hogs in Germany continued to fluctuate even after prices had been fixed. An analysis of this phenomenon has not yet been made.

plantings, it will be at least seven years before increased production comes to the market; usually it will take somewhat longer because a certain time elapses before the initiative to additional planting is taken. One may expect, therefore, fluctuations with a period of approximately double this period, and they do in fact occur. These fluctuations will be particularly strong as a high price level may perpetuate itself for seven years before any reaction appears in the market. During those seven years quite considerable plantings will be made.

As in the hog market, disturbances occur, among which differences in yield of the coffee trees should be mentioned especially. When there is an abundant yield, there will be a tendency toward a lower price that may interrupt the normal course of the cycle.

Since 1907, moreover, the coffee market has not been one of free competition. The government of Brazil, a country whose fate depends heavily on coffee, has oftentimes intervened in the market, taking considerable stocks out of the market and actually destroying them in order to influence prices. As a result, the tendencies mentioned have been much less clearly visible in recent decades. The coffee market is nevertheless of historic and theoretical interest; the long period of the production process is also a factor of significance in the regulation of the market which cannot be disregarded with impunity.

THE TWO-YEAR CYCLE OF AGRICULTURAL PRODUCTS

The explanation of a tendency toward a two-year cycle in prices and production of agricultural products would also be found in the length of the production process, together with the fact that production here is not continuous but discontinuous. Let us assume, for instance, that, by a random cause such as extremely favorable weather, the crop of sugar beets should be very large. As soon as the crop figures are known, this will lead to a relatively low price. This price will last for the major part of the crop year, until the new crop comes in prospect. The low price will still prevail at the time when the new sowings are made. At this low price the production of beets may be relatively unprofitable; hence the area sowed with sugar beets will be relatively low and hence, normally, the succeeding crop will also be low. As a consequence of this the price in the next year will tend to be high. In the succeeding year this high price will lead to a larger area sowed and so generally to a larger crop. This will lead to a tendency to a zigzag movement which has often been observed.

This movement, however, can be disturbed to a very considerable extent by many factors. The most important disturbing factor is the fluctuation in crop yields. In the second year, as we have seen, the area sowed will be low. If, however, in this year the yield per acre is unusually large, it may be that the crop as a whole will not be small but average. This would interrupt the normal zigzag movement. Similarly, a large area sowed may be accompanied by a very low yield.

Other disturbing factors are the prices of products the farmer may grow instead of beets. Changes in these prices will affect the decision as to the area to be sowed with beets. The same applies to changes in the cost of production.

There may also be factors operating on the demand side, which would produce deviations from the mechanism indicated above. A strong cyclical recovery will push sugar prices up even when the crops are particularly abundant. This influence will be least pronounced in the case of agricultural products that satisfy very pressing needs, such as wheat and potatoes, but it is quite clearly observable in the case of sugar beets and cotton.

Furthermore, if one considers the market in individual countries, disturbances may originate in the crop movements in other countries, and they are not always parallel. There is, finally, a small systematic deviation from the simple pattern sketched above, on account of the fact that farmers are guided not only by the price at the moment of sowing but also, though in a much weaker degree, by the price of the preceding year. From investigations made by Donner it would further appear that farmers have a tendency to offset a change in the area sowed during one year by a change in the opposite direction during the next year. This fact in itself, without any other considerations, would be enough to explain a zigzag movement; but this would then not be a movement that could be explained on the basis of economic considerations.

THE AMERICAN MARKET OF RESIDENTIAL CONSTRUCTION

As in the other cases, the actual pattern in the residential market in the United States is the result of causes that constitute the nucleus of the mechanism and of other factors which may more or less accurately be described as disturbances. For a good understanding, therefore, we first treat this nucleus, purposely abstracting from a number of factors to be discussed later.

Here, too, the time period of production has a role of importance. The building of a house will usually take one-half year to a year. Hence, a favorable situation for building houses will not immediately lead to a corresponding supply of dwellings. Two further complications should be added. In the first place, a house is a durable commodity. The total supply of dwellings or of "dwelling services" is therefore a result not only of the building process in the period immediately preceding but also of building activity in all preceding periods. As an approximation, one may say that all dwellings constructed earlier contribute to the supply of dwelling space; the number of houses of earlier centuries that have been demolished is in most cases quite small in comparison to the supply of houses that are still useful. For some cities with particular characteristics this may not be quite true; a somewhat more complicated relation will have to be devised for them.

A further special characteristic of the housing market is the inertia of price, that is, of rents. As a result, partially of long contracts concluded when houses are rented, partially also of the compartmentalization and the imperfection of the housing market, there is a great lag between the movements in the demand and supply factors and the corresponding movements of rents.

The essence of the model which may explain fluctuations in American residential construction is the following. The level of rents is determined mainly by the number of houses available a number of years before. This number develops at such unequal rates that in comparison to the relatively smooth increase of the population there is sometimes a deficiency, sometimes an excess, of considerable magnitude. We shall explain this fluctuating growth in a moment. As a result of it, rents also fluctuate strongly. The level of rents and the positive or negative excess of dwellings will determine the volume of building activity. The additions to the stock of houses are a reflection, therefore, of the deficiency, but with a considerable lag: in addition to the lag of reaction in rents, there is the further lag between rents and the decisions to build, to which, finally, the period of construction of the house should be added. This may add up to a total lag of nearly four years. The additions to the stock of houses have a tendency to decrease the deficiency to the extent that they are in excess of the number of families who desire a dwelling. We have here the mathematically interesting figure that the decrease of a certain series (namely, the deficiency) is proportional to the value of the same series four years earlier. The consequence of this relation may be illustrated most conveniently by a numerical example; it should be borne in mind again that such an example does not constitute a proof.

Assume that the shortage in the first four years of a given period increases from 0 at the beginning of the first year to 4 at the beginning of the fourth year. Assume that the different reactions are such that the reduction in this deficiency (as a consequence of building activity) is equal to 0.4 times the shortage four years earlier. In order to compute further the changes in the deficiency, we have to compute its decrease in year 5. This will be 0.4 times the deficiency during year 1, which was 0.5. The reduction in year 5 is then $0.4 \times 0.5 = 0.2$. Similarly in years 6, 7, and 8, respectively, $0.4 \times 1.5 = 0.6$; $0.4 \times 2.5 = 1.0$; and $0.4 \times 3.5 = 1.4$. Continuing this simple scheme, we easily find the accompanying figures.

It will be seen that a complete cycle is run in a period of approximately sixteen years. The example has been chosen in such a way that it reflects the situation in the American market for residential construction. The difference in principle from the special cycles discussed earlier is that here the period of the cycle equals four times the lag (of four years) which is the dynamic characteristic in this example which determines the wave movement. It may be shown mathematically that the ratio of period to lag will not always be 4; when the waves are undamped, however, it will be exactly 4. If the number 0.4 indicating the amount of reduction of the shortage in response to the shortage existing four years earlier (more concretely, the intensity by which the building industry responds to a shortage, whether through rents or not) should be replaced by another number, one could obtain damped or antidamped cyclical movements. The reader may easily experiment with various numbers.

EXAMPLE V

Year	1	2	3	4	5	6	7	8	9
Deficiency at beginning	0	1	2	3	4	3.8	3.2	2.2	0.8
Average deficiency	0.5	1.5	2.5	3.5	3.9	3.5	2.7	1.5	0
Reduction	......	......	......	......	0.2	0.6	1.0	1.4	1.6

Year	10	11	12	13	14	15	16	17	18
Deficiency at beginning	−0.8	−2.2	−3.3	−3.9	−3.9	−3.3	−2.2	−0.8	0.8
Average deficiency	−1.5	−2.8	−3.6	−3.9	−3.6	−2.8	−1.5	0	......
Reduction	1.4	1.1	0.6	0	−0.6	−1.1	−1.4	−1.6	−1.4

The essential difference from the case of the hog market—the simplest case of an alternation of overproduction and underproduction—lies in the long lifetime of houses, as a consequence of which production cannot be identified with total supply. In the case of the housing market, production is equal to the increase in supply over the preceding year.

A number of disturbing factors have so far been disregarded. Some of them are actually dominating in the market of residential construction in countries such as the Netherlands. The prominent role played by the shortage or excess of dwellings in the United States in the dynamics of the market of residential construction should be attributed to the large size these shortages can assume and to the sharp responses of rents and residential construction to these shortages. In part, these strong reactions were determined by the almost complete absence of government intervention in residential construction (at least until 1933). Thus, in 1918 residential construction stopped almost completely. In our terminology we might say that the war acted as a strong exogenous disturbance which gave a new impetus to the mechanism of fluctuations.

We may now devote some attention to the factors so far left out of consideration. The demand for dwellings depends, apart from rents, also on the level of income and the number of families. In general, the latter series will show a regular and almost monotonic movement which will not give rise to any unexpected changes in demand. Incomes will fluctuate with the business cycle, and it might therefore be expected that rents would move accordingly. As we noted, however, a very considerable lag should be taken into consideration in this connection.

On the supply side, that is to say, the supply of newly built houses, there is the influence of building costs in addition to that of the level of rents. High building costs will depress the level of building. This factor would therefore exercise an influence in the direction of a movement counter to that of the general cycle, also with a certain lag. Furthermore, the incentive to build depends not only on the profits that can be made on rental construction; a large part of construction is for owner use. Therefore, a certain effect is felt of the amount of savings available and also perhaps of unexpected increases in income. On both types of building there is, further, an important influence of the regular availability of credit. In times of uncertainty residential construction is often greatly hampered. We do not refer in this connection to the normal effect of the rate of interest which may be considered as part of construction costs; we refer rather to an influence which shows a pattern clearly different from that of fluctuations in the rate of interest. Thus, for instance, residential construction in the Netherlands in 1907, 1932, and 1935 was suddenly very low. In the United States, residential construction was low in years when a large number of mortgages were foreclosed. In the United States, however, the credit position was closely related to the state of the housing market, a high foreclosure rate coinciding with a large excess of dwellings. But this does not apply as a general rule in all countries.

Owing to these special factors, the actual pattern of the market of residential construction is obviously different from the simple model we have traced; many irregularities will be found to exist. It would appear, further, that the undisturbed movement in this case is damped but has been kept going by new disturbances. There is, in any case, a tendency toward a systematic movement which should be understood in the way indicated.

CYCLES IN THE IMPORT OF RAW MATERIALS

At the end of chapter viii we have drawn attention to cycles in the volume of imports of raw materials. It would appear that they should be considered as a consequence of the acceleration principle in inventories. This principle, as we have seen,[3] is due to the tendency to keep stocks proportionate with sales. Here, too, a certain lag will occur. On the basis of a number of statistical data, it would appear that the stock at the end of the year would be proportional to, or at least correlated with, the turnover during the year. For convenience we may assume that stocks are equal to one-fourth of the yearly turnover. Let us assume now a chain of succeeding enterprises, for instance, import, wholesale, production. The volume of factory sales is indicated by series *A* in Example VI below. Let there be one ini-

EXAMPLE VI

Year	1		2		3		4		5		6		7		8		9
A. Factory sales	64		64		64		64		128		128		128		128		128
B. Factory stocks		16		16		16		16		32		32		32		32	
C. Increase in *B*	0		0		0		0		+16		0		0		0		0
D. Wholesale sales $=A+C$	64		64		64		64		144		128		128		128		128
E. Wholesale stocks		16		16		16		16		36		32		32		32	
F. Increase in *E*	0		0		0		0		+20		−4		0		0		0
G. Importers' sales $=D+F$	64		64		64		64		164		124		128		128		128
H. Importers' stocks		16		16		16		16		41		31		32		32	
I. Increase in *H*	0		0		0		0		+25		−10		+1		0		0
J. Import $=G+I$	64		64		64		64		189		114		129		128		128
K. Excess imports $=J-A$	0		0		0		0		+61		−14		+1		0		0

3. Cf. p. 165, *supra*.

tial change between years 4 and 5. Then factory stocks would be as shown by series *B*. Since they refer to the end of the year, they have been entered between the other figures. Series *C*, indicating the increase in stocks, follows from the preceding series. The sum of *A* and *C* would give the purchases by producers or the sale of the trader (*D*). Continuing the computation in a similar way, we finally arrive at the imports, as in line *J*. It will be noticed that this line, in comparison to line *A*, shows a tendency to a zigzag movement with a period of two years. This is shown by line **K** representing excess imports, or *J–A*. If sales indicated in line *A* were to change not once but repeatedly, the difference indicated by **K** would show each time a tendency toward a zigzag movement very much in accordance with the observations shown in Figure 39.

CHAPTER FIFTEEN

EXOGENOUS MOVEMENTS

THE processes of movements treated in the preceding chapters are all endogenous or primarily endogenous in character. This applies to the process of general, or trend, development, in particular to the extent that it is determined by capital accumulation; it applies also to the processes of inflation and of business cycles. This type of movement has in general received much more attention from economists than have the processes which are primarily exogenous in character. Among the latter, we may mention some aspects of the general long-run development (the effects of increases in population and of increases, or decreases, of natural resources), all seasonal and similar movements, a number of the random movements (for instance, those which result from changes in crops), and some sudden changes of economic structure. All these movements are approximately exogenous; approximately, because for a strictly exogenous movement to occur, it would be necessary, as we have seen in chapter ix, that all adaptations of the economic variables take place without any time lag. It is possible to extend the field of exogenous movements arbitrarily, by concentrating the study on sufficiently small parts of the economy. The smaller the part, the larger is the number of influences which come from the outside; and if the reactions of the economic variables in the small segment of the economy under consideration are rapid, the movements may appropriately be described as exogenous.

The method usually applied in the study of exogenous movements is that of comparative statistics. This method indicates in principle the new equilibrium which will be established, in the segment of the economy under consideration, for every change in the data. If the equilibrium establishes itself rapidly, the particular segment will indeed pass through a number of successive different positions of equilibrium; the method of economic statics will therefore be adequate to describe and explain these various positions.

The method of comparative statics will be most satisfactory when the changes in the data are slow and all in one direction. In those situations, the possibility of the adaptation of the economic variables to the data is greatest. Strictly speaking, the laws of economic statics are applicable only if the new position of the data satisfies these two conditions: (1) it is known also for the future and (2) it will be always the same in the future. Economic statics is less permissible when (*a*) the position of the data in the future is unknown and/or (*b*) the position of the data in the future is known but does not remain the same.

In the first case, there will be different assumptions concerning the future position of the data each with its own probability; this introduces the concept of risk. This situation occurs, for instance, in markets of agricultural products as a consequence of changes in crop yields. We shall demonstrate with a simple example the type of deviations from those expected on the basis of economic statics that will occur in the explanation of movements in these markets.

Let us assume that there has been an unusually large cotton crop. If one were to explain the phenomena which follow—low prices, a larger quantity sold, etc.—on the basis of comparative statics, it would be necessary to assume that in the future the cotton crop would be in every year as large as in this one year. The amount of the reduction in price could then be read from the demand curve for cotton; the price would have to be at such a level that a quantity equal to this single large crop could be sold every year. The quantity sold would increase by the full increase of the crop.

This assumption, however, would be quite unrealistic. It should be replaced by a different assumption, namely, that after this large crop a number of crops of unknown size will occur in the future, with an equal probability of excessively large and excessively small crops and with the greatest probability of an average crop. The assumptions of economic statics are now no longer applicable; in particular the price, the quantity supplied, and the quantity demanded will now no longer remain unchanged over time. Demand and supply relationships will have to be made considerably more complicated, for the quantity supplied and demanded will now depend not only on the current price but also on the expected future prices. If, in a case like this, one desires to study the deviations between the results of statics and dynamics, it is a good practice to study first the simplest possible case which has the minimum of new features. In this particular case, that is possible without going far from reality.

We assume now that on the demand side the influence of future prices may be disregarded; the demand curve for economic statics continues therefore as valid. On the supply side, on the other hand, we assume that the prices of the current and the next crop years enter into consideration but not the prices of years further ahead. We might express this by saying that the suppliers have a "horizon" of two years. With respect to the price expectations of the suppliers we may now distinguish three cases: (1) they expect higher prices for the next year, (2) they expect lower prices for the next year, and (3) they expect the same prices for both the current and the next years.

In the first case, suppliers would reserve their entire supply for the following year and supply nothing in the current year; in the second case, they would supply everything in the current year and supply nothing in the next year; whereas in the third case, it would be indifferent to them in which year they offered their supply. It will be noted that we have disregarded the costs of storage connected with the retention of part of the supplies; it would not be difficult to take these costs into consideration but, in order to keep the case as simple as possible, we leave them for the moment out of account.

Expectations (1) and (2) are illogical because of the consequences to which they would lead. If all supplies were kept for the succeeding year, prices would rise very strongly and would be higher this year than next, in contrast to the assumption itself. Similar considerations apply to case (2). Therefore, if we make the further assumption that the expectations should be compatible with economic common sense, only the third possibility concerning the expectations remains. If we assume a static demand curve, this assumption is compatible with economic common sense only if the quantity supplied is equally distributed over the two years. In this case, therefore, not the entire extra crop will be supplied in the first year, but half the surplus in excess of a normal crop will be kept for the succeeding year.

In the next year, as soon as the crop is known, the suppliers will again establish a supply plan for the two-year period which has then started. In this plan, the supply for the first year of the period, that is, the second year of the previous planning period, may be different from what would have been anticipated the year before. Again, however, half the total supply expected for the two-year period will be offered in that year, and the other half will be reserved for the third year. The total expected supply for the two-year period will be equal to the actual crop in the second year, plus the surplus carried over from the first year, plus the expected, normal crop of the third year.

Hence, as a consequence of an unusually large crop there will be an increase in supply not equal to the surplus above normal but equal to half the surplus above normal. If one had assumed that suppliers looked ahead not two years but three, one would have found that only one-third of the surplus would be supplied and that the remaining two-thirds would be added to stocks.

There is thus a clear difference between the results of comparative statics and those of the first simple approximations of dynamics. These first approximations make it possible to describe the actual events in the market much better than would be possible with the aid of statics alone. It is not difficult to proceed to a second and to further approximations, for instance, by taking account of the cost of storage or of the effects of an unusually small crop. It would lead us too far, however, to go into further details here.

Case (*b*) mentioned above, where the position of the data in the future is known but does not remain the same, is applicable in particular to seasonal movements. To the extent that one limits the discussion to normal seasonal movements, it may actually be stated that these can be anticipated. Economic subjects plan their actions in response to these known seasons, and this will lead to systematic deviations from what would be expected on the basis of economic statics. These movements can be understood with the assistance of approximately the same theoretical methods as those employed in the preceding paragraphs. The only difference is that in this case the expectations are not uncertain and hence that no account has to be taken of a probability distribution of the expected values.

If, for instance, the demand for coal declines during the summer, mines will not have to reduce their production by the full decline since they know that demand will again be higher during the next winter. In part, therefore, they will produce for stock and thus bridge over the dull season.

The large supply of eggs in the spring that in earlier years was marketed almost entirely—as a consequence, the price used to fall very sharply—will now in part be preserved since the technical means are available, because it is practically certain that the supply in the fall will be very much lower.

The effect on the price of such a seasonal excess supply, therefore, will be entirely different from the effect of a permanently increased supply as a consequence of a larger number of hens or of lower prices of chicken feed. The latter cases may be treated with the help of static demand curves; the former case of seasonal supply cannot be treated in that way.

For most fresh vegetables and fruits, however, the situation of comparative statics is still very closely approximated, because the preservation of fruits and vegetables is much less extended than that of eggs.

It follows from the above examples that the field of application of comparative statics is much more limited than one might think at first. The adaptation of economic variables sometimes occurs rapidly but not completely in those cases where the new value of the data is not considered as permanent. In those situations, economic variables show fluctuations parallel with those of the data but not with the intensity that would be expected on the basis of comparative statics.

CHAPTER SIXTEEN

THEORETICAL POSTSCRIPT

HAVING treated, in the preceding chapters, the different forms of economic movements in a concrete way, we may usefully review the theoretical methods employed. This will give us an opportunity to provide a more definite answer to a number of problems which we have solved so far only in a preliminary way.

Time after time we have found that the economic variables —prices, quantities sold, incomes, stocks—did not adapt themselves immediately to changes in the data. For slow and unilateral changes in data the assumption of immediate adaptation constituted sometimes a reasonably accurate approximation, but it did not for rapid changes in the data. Hence, although the changes in the economic variables depend on changes in the data, they do not depend on them in the simple way often postulated by comparative statics. To understand the changes in the economic variables, consideration has to be given to two factors: changes in the data and the reactions of the economy to such changes. These reactions are such that one single change in the data may lead to a movement of economic variables over a long period of time, in the same way as one single push may cause a swing to move back and forth for a long time.

In actual life, moreover, the data change continuously. The economic system is continuously subject to shocks. These shocks are so many and so manifold that with the exception of a few very large individual shocks they may legitimately be considered as a series of random numbers. Certain categories of shocks, such as the fluctuations in crop yields, actually satisfy this condition with a high degree of approximation. It has sometimes been concluded from this that economic fluctuations, particularly cyclical fluctuations, are nothing but a purely arbitrary and random succession of changes. A series of numbers drawn at random, for instance, the results of a game of chance, it is said, would also indicate increases and decreases. Hence all attempts to find laws of business cycles would be futile, just as it would be futile to look for laws in the successive results of a game of chance. We have referred in this connection to the quasi-period of three years in the figures for crop yields which might provide an explanation of the short cycles with a period of approximately three years in the United States.

This way of looking at cycles is not correct, however. Only if the economic variables adapted themselves immediately to the data would a random fluctuation in the data lead also to random fluctuation of the economic variables. But the fact that the economic variables adapt themselves only slowly leads to a somewhat different and more complicated situation. The effect of a shock at time 1 will be felt in the position of a certain economic variable at a large number of succeeding time units. Conversely, the position at a certain time, for instance, time 10, depends on the shocks which occurred at a series of time units, 10, 9, 8, 7, 6, etc. In order to compute the deviation of a certain economic variable at a certain moment of time on the basis of these different shocks (in the way of our simple examples in chap. xiii), it would be necessary to multiply each of these shocks with different coefficients in order to add up their influences. Some of these influences might be negative. The magnitude of the weighting coefficients to be used would depend on the structure of the economic model, i.e., on certain data which would be considered constant, first among them certain coefficients of elasticity. One might say, therefore, that every economic variable may be considered as a weighted average of all preceding shocks, with the weights determined by the structure of the economy under consideration. But this implies at the same time that the nature of the cyclical movements depends as much on the structure as on the random shocks. Hence every study of the "laws of business cycles" must take account of the effect of the economic structure on the nature of cyclical movements. The knowledge of these laws forms the basis for changes in the structure by appropriate reforms which would make cyclical fluctuations less harmful.

From what has been said it follows also that the way in which random and systematic components in economic movements are woven together is not so simple as is sometimes implied in certain statistical practices. In particular, there is no question of an addition of a systematic and a random component in the cyclical movement, at least not on the basis of our theoretical model. A systematic movement occurs when, after one initial shock, the system is left to itself without further shocks. In certain simple cases the system will then describe, for instance, a sine curve. As long as no further shocks occur, there will be no further random component. But if further shocks do occur, one cannot say that they should be added to the systematic movement which existed at first; for the prior systematic movement is interrupted as soon as one new shock occurs, and a new systematic movement is started which will last until another new shock occurs. The actual movement is, therefore, the succession of parts of various systematic movements.

If the shocks occur in rapid succession, so that there is a new shock in every new time unit, this description does not lose its validity, but it does lose much of its usefulness. In such situations it is preferable to use the description given before (which is always valid, even when the number of shocks is limited), that the position at every unit of time is a weighted average of all shocks in the past. The movement of the economic variable under consideration can then be considered as the sum of a number of random components but not as one random component. No systematic component needs to be added; the systematic influence of the economic structure is expressed in the weights which enter into the weighted average. Hence, in the cyclical movement, the separation between a systematic and a random component is a problem of an entirely different nature from what is usually assumed in statistical practice.

This practice would be applicable in cases in which there is a systematic basic movement, for instance a trend, a seasonal component, and an undisturbed cyclical component, to which at each unit of time is added a random deviation that has its consequences at that unit of time but not later. To take the hog cycle as an example, this would mean that if the price were high by some random cause, no increase in supply would follow from this a year and a half later. This situation might be imagined if the farmers, knowing that the high price was due to a random cause, would not count on its continuation. This reaction is possible, of course, but it is likely to occur only for relatively small random deviations of short duration; in statistical practice this treatment would therefore be legitimate for small random fluctuations. For cyclical movements, and in particular for the influences on the economy of changes in crops, this treatment would seem less legitimate, and no attempt to separate random and systematic movements should therefore be made.

The movements which we have studied in our models were all systematic, endogenous movements that would occur if no further random changes in the data took place after an initial disturbance of the equilibrium. These movements will therefore at best indicate the tendencies shown by reality. Knowledge and analysis of these movements is nonetheless of much significance, in particular if one wants to study the consequences of various forms of business-cycle policy or—going one step further—if one wants to select the most suitable measures of business-cycle policy. In business-cycle policy it will rarely be possible to insulate the economy from random disturbances, but it is possible to change the structure of the economy in such a way that its responses to these disturbances will be much less serious. If, as a result of economic policy, the endogenous movements are heavily damped, the economic variables will deviate much less from their normal values than before; any tendency toward a boom or depression will be nipped in the bud, and a certain degree of stabilization will have been achieved in that way.

The simplest type of endogenous movements will have only one component, for instance, one exponential movement or one periodic movement. As soon as one makes the structure of the economy in the model more complicated, in a closer approximation to reality, movements with more components will occur; they will occur as the effect of one and the same system of relations between the various economic variables. To some extent this was already shown in Example IV (the theory of Kalecki), in which we took account of the process of accumulation which had been disregarded in the simpler Example III. If in certain relations one were to incorporate further characteristics of significance for long-term movements, a movement with more components would clearly appear. It would then not be possible to state that the different components were due to different "causes" (except perhaps as a very rough approximation).[1]

A separation of trend movement and cyclical movement is therefore acceptable only as an approximation and not in principle. This may appear as a theoretical nicety, but it is more than that. It is a question of paramount importance also in the study of business-cycle policy. We mentioned that the objective of such a policy should be to make the damping of the cyclical component as large as possible. However, if the cyclical component and the trend component follow from the same economic structure, will not any change in the structure change the trend component also, possibly in such a way that the damage to the economy is greater than the advantage obtained from the stabilization of the business cycle? This problem raises serious questions for study in connection with the theory of business-cycle policy. They do not fall within the scope of this book, and we must therefore limit ourselves to a simple indication of the problem.

We are now in a position to give a better answer to the three questions raised on page 60 concerning the nature of cyclical movements. On the basis of our interpretation of the causes of economic fluctuations, this nature may be indicated as follows.

1. The cyclical movement is in part a really cyclical phenomenon, in part a random succession of increases and decreases. Sometimes the turning point may be advanced by exogenous causes, such as an unfavorable crop or some political event. But there are also endogenous factors, which come from

1. For instance, as we indicated in chap. x, the elimination from our models of theories that are of importance only for short-term movements will yield only the trend movement as the movement of the model. The relations disregarded may be, for instance, those of the small lags, the effect of variables that change quite rapidly, such as crop fluctuations, and inventory fluctuations. A more detailed treatment of the questions raised in this connection is unfortunately not possible in the limits of this book.

the preceding period of recovery and boom and which lead to the turning point. The recovery may have been started by a new invention or the opening-up of new markets; but it may also be the result of causes flowing from the depression: the depletion of stocks, increases in labor productivity, increases in profitability as a result of the arrest of the price decline of commodities and shares. Often exogenous and endogenous forces will co-operate.

2. It follows that successive cycles are not entirely separate. They would be separate if endogenous forces were of significance, for instance, only at the upper turning point but not at the lower turning point. If that were the case, then the recovery and boom would lead to a crisis, but the latter and the succeeding depression would not lead to the next recovery. But we have indicated that there are also endogenous forces that will lead to a succeeding recovery. These forces are weaker than the endogenous forces that lead to the end of a boom; at least, this is normally assumed.

3. Our explanation of the cyclical movement did not consist of a separate explanation of its four different phases. It appeared that the cumulative upward and downward movements, together with the turning points, could be explained from one system of economic relations, as in our Examples III and IV. It is therefore not necessary to provide separate theories for these four phases. But it is nevertheless possible, for there are also certain systems of relations possible, as given in our Examples I and II, which can explain only unilateral movements. Should statistical evidence make it plausible that reality could better be described by such unilateral relationships, then it would be necessary to provide a separate explanation of the turning points, either in random exogenous factors or, more systematically, in changes of elasticities at the approximation of the position of full employment. In both cases one could consider that there were special causes of the turning points. Statistical analysis has so far not indicated that this type of explanation is necessary, and in any case the systematic change of elasticities when a situation of full employment is approached can better be incorporated in the theory from the beginning. If

one does this, there is again one theory for the three successive phases of recovery, boom, and crisis. Therefore, we preferred the approach which explains the entire process from one single theory; but this does, of course, not exclude the role of random disturbances in reality.

In the preceding chapters we have referred repeatedly to "equilibrium values" of economic variables, without further specification. We are now in a better position to give an accurate description of this term than would have been possible at an earlier stage. The concept originates in economic statics. Under the assumptions of economic statics, a stationary position is possible, that is to say, a position that will continue forever, once it has come into being. In economic statics such a stationary position is also called an equilibrium position. It is by no means certain that such an equilibrium position is under all circumstances possible in reality. It is in fact quite improbable that such would be the case. Let us assume for a moment that an equilibrium position would be possible. Every change in the data would change this equilibrium position. To the extent that the data themselves fluctuate around a certain average, as may be the case for crop yields, one could indicate as the equilibrium position that position which corresponded to the average value of these data. But with respect to a unilateral movement of the data, such as the growth of the population, this treatment is not possible. Here one might consider the concept of a moving equilibrium. One might speak of an equilibrium development as distinguished from an equilibrium position. But it is also quite possible that even with constant data of the values no equilibrium position is possible, for a constant equilibrium would imply the constancy of all variables. This would imply, for instance, that the stock of capital goods would remain constant, and thus the phenomenon of net investment would be excluded. Hence an equilibrium position cannot exist in an economy in which the average level of investment is above zero. In such an economy an equilibrium development can exist if this concept is properly defined. We have seen above that the movements which an economic system may describe, as long as there are no new and rapid changes of the data, may consist of a number of components, including both unilateral and periodic movements. These different components may have different relative amplitudes. In that respect, too, there are very many possibilities of movements for one and the same model. Which of these movements the model will adopt in reality depends on the initial change of the data by which the movement is set in motion. A trend component may be accompanied by weak or by strong cyclical components. We may now define as the equilibrium development that component of the possible movements which has the weakest periodic component, that is to say in practice, the trend movement. When an economy follows its trend curve for a certain period, there is no risk of a decline resulting from a cyclical movement as long as no new change in the data occurs. In that respect, therefore, there is an analogy with the equilibrium position in simpler systems, namely, the tendency toward the maintenance of a certain movement. Therefore, we describe as the equilibrium value of a certain economic variable that value which this variable would assume if the system were to describe a movement without periodic components.

In the simple models of economic statics a distinction is made between models with stable and those with unstable equilibria. Similarly in the more complicated models, the equilibrium development of some may be more stable, that of others less stable. The criterion for stability is found in the movements of the system after a change in those data that can be changed. Some systems will respond by a very sharp cyclical movement, others by a very heavily damped cyclical movement which will quickly work off the initial disturbance of equilibrium. Everything depends here on the structure of the different systems. And as we have said before in this connection, the objective of the theory of business-cycle policy is to indicate in which way the structure of a system has to be adjusted in order to obtain an equilibrium development that is as stable as possible. As has been mentioned, it is conceivable that stability can be obtained only at the expense of a slower rate of progress. In that case, a criterion for a choice between these two possibilities would have to be found. But this falls outside the scope of our book.

PART THREE

BUSINESS-CYCLE POLICY

CHAPTER SEVENTEEN

INTRODUCTION

PART III will be devoted to a discussion of the ways in which economic movements may be influenced, in other words to a discussion of economic policy. We define "economic policy" as the activity of the government in the economic field. We use the term, therefore, in a somewhat more limited sense than it is sometimes used; in particular, we do not include a discussion of the economic policy of individuals, enterprises, labor unions, etc. Thus, we shall not deal with any measures of business-cycle policy that may be adopted by individual enterprises. With respect to the economic behavior of the individual subjects, we shall in general assume that no differentiation can be made between political and nonpolitical motives. In the activity of the government, on the other hand, a distinction can be made between its normal objectives and the corrections of the consequences of individual economic activities which it wants to make. Such corrections may be necessary because (1) the government may sometimes be able to achieve what individuals cannot achieve; (2) the government may enforce a certain behavior on individuals or groups of individuals who do not know what is best for them; and (3) the government may give particular attention to the interests of the economically weak.

The ultimate objective of economic policy is the same, therefore, as that of economic activity in general but is directed toward the welfare of the community, that is, the population as a whole; the interests of the different groups are weighted against each other, and the government endeavors to achieve the general objective in a better way than the activities of the individual economic subjects could achieve it. The objective may be defined as the maximum possible welfare for the population as a whole. This concept, which cannot be discussed in full detail here, has many different aspects or components; it is a many-dimensional magnitude. For practical purposes, these aspects may be grouped into a few global aspects, the most important of which are (*a*) a maximum total production, (*b*) a satisfactory distribution of total production over the different commodities, (*c*) a satisfactory distribution of total production over the different persons, and (*d*) a satisfactory distribution of production over time.

One might indicate (*c*) and (*d*) as economic justice and economic stability, respectively. We shall give prominence in our discussions to aspects (*a*) and (*d*) because they touch most directly on the movement of the main economic variables. One of the most important elements of economic justice under (*c*), full employment, practically coincides with the first objective of a maximum volume of production.

With respect to the distribution of production over time, the following observations are pertinent. The ultimate purpose of all economic policy should be, as we have said, a situation of a maximum satisfaction of the community. It is a debatable question how the concept of maximum satisfaction of the community should be linked to that of the satisfaction of individual persons (an important problem which falls outside the scope of our treatment); but it can hardly be doubted that the satisfaction of the great majority of people would be larger if the total supply of goods and services they enjoy during the period of a cycle were distributed more equally over time. A simple example: the total satisfaction of an income of ten each year is greater than the total satisfaction of a fluctuating income which is eleven one year and nine the next. The increase in satisfaction when income goes from ten to eleven will be smaller than the decrease in satisfaction when income declines from ten to nine. For this reason a change from a stable income of ten to an alternating income of nine and eleven means a loss in total satisfaction. Only extremely adventurous natures might find in the mere fact of change a satisfaction that would outweigh the loss mentioned.

Against this argument that a stable income is preferable to a fluctuating income with the same average, the proposition has been advanced that in a stabilized economy progress would be less rapid: each boom, it is said, stimulates new inventions which lead to a rate of progress greater than that which would prevail in a society without business cycles. The weak point in this proposition is that no attention is given to the setbacks resulting from a depression. It would seem more reasonable, therefore, to take the position that the rate of progress would be as large in a stabilized society as in one which is subject to cyclical fluctuations; it is true that some new inventions may not be applied, but those are likely to be the ones which in our present society would ultimately prove to be unprofitable. We would believe, therefore, that the maintenance of the business cycle could hardly be defended on these grounds. For this reason we assume in what follows that stabilization should be considered a desirable objective of economic policy.

OBJECTIVES, CRITERIA, AND INSTRUMENTS

These few words may have served to indicate the general direction of the ultimate objective of economic policy. As the more immediate objective of each part of that policy or of each single form of economic policy, one may indicate the change which each form is to achieve in the level or the movement of certain specific economic variables, e.g., reduction of the level of unemployment or reduction in the fluctuations of employment. According to whether the objective of a certain element of economic policy is a change in the average level, in the trend movement, or in the cyclical movement of a certain variable, we may distinguish structural policy (in the more limited sense of the word), trend policy, and cycle policy. Structural policy in the broader sense of the word may also be used to include both the structural policy in the narrower sense and the trend policy.

A distinction should be made between the objective and the criterion of economic policy. We consider as the criterion of economic policy that variable by which the execution of economic policy is guided. If, in executing a policy of public works, the policy is continued until unemployment has reached a certain level, then the level of unemployment is the criterion of the policy followed. Criterion and objective may coincide, especially if the objective is a relatively narrow one. They coincide in the case just mentioned. But the criterion may also be different from the objective; for instance, it may be more symptomatic in character. A monetary policy that has as its objective the stabilization of the business cycle may use as its criterion a certain price-index number. Generally speaking, it is desirable that criterion and objective coincide, but this is not always possible. If, as for instance in our first example, one were to consider stabilization of employment as the objective, but available unemployment statistics were incomplete and referred, say, to union members only, then it might be necessary to use these limited unemployment statistics as the criterion.

In order to define a particular form of economic policy completely, it is not sufficient to indicate the criterion; a quantitative indication of the policy to be undertaken will also be required. In other words, it is necessary to indicate with what intensity one intends to respond to a certain deviation of the actual from the desired value of the criterion. Suppose that the criterion chosen is the volume of unemployment, which it is desired to stabilize at 5 per cent, if necessary by the execution of public works. This policy is fully defined only if one indicates at the same time to what extent public works will be undertaken in a particular month at the beginning of which unemployment might, for instance, be at 6 per cent. All too frequently, economic policy is discussed without such exact indications. It need hardly be said that this does not promote the clarity of the discussion. Much, indeed, depends on whether the government responds weakly or with great intensity to a certain deviation of the criterion.

Using another expression, one might also describe a certain specific form of economic policy as a change in one of the relations (indicating a certain reaction) of the economic structure of the economy.

Next to the criterion of economic policy, we want to mention the instrument of that policy. We define the instrument as that variable which is manipulated in order to achieve the objective. In the execution of public works we consider these works as the instrument; in credit policy the volume of credit is the instrument; etc.

It will prove to be convenient in our further treatment to distinguish the different forms of economic policy from a number of other points of view, admitting at once that the exact lines of demarcation between the various categories are not always clear or simple and may require a fuller description. We shall give these descriptions later, as far as necessary.

A first distinction may be made between direct and indirect policies. We define as direct policies all those which use as their instrument the volume of production, consumption, any part of production or consumption, or an intermediate stage between production and consumption; we consider as indirect policies all those which use other instruments. In the category of indirect policies we include in particular all forms of economic policy which change one or more of the prices (in the broadest sense of that word) and thereby the incentive to produce and thus affect indirectly the volume of production. In a more theoretical sense of the word, direct policies are those which employ quantities as the instrument, rather than prices, and in particular stream and flow quantities rather than stock quantities.[1]

A second distinction is that between global and detailed policies. Detailed policies are those which require a large administrative apparatus controlling the behavior of individual enterprises. Price policy, performed by government intervention in the market as a supplier or demander, would be a global policy; but a price policy performed by the exercise of control over individual suppliers or demanders would be a detailed policy. The execution of public works is a global policy, the control of investment plans of individual enterprises a detailed policy. Clearly, a global policy is preferable to a detailed policy if the former can achieve the objective set.

A third distinction is that between incidental and systematic policies. This distinction is of importance particularly with respect to forms of economic policy that are calculated to affect the cyclical movements of economic variables. A systematic policy is a policy that leads to systematic changes in the movements, for instance, to an increase in the rate of damping of a wave movement or to the total elimination of cyclical fluctua-

1. Cf. p. 31, *supra*.

tions. We would consider as an incidental policy, on the other hand, measures against unemployment taken during a short crisis period and abandoned shortly thereafter. All sorts of measures of a transitional character also constitute incidental policies. The result of a systematic policy may be described as a permanent change in a certain relation, for instance, in a demand or supply relation in a certain market. If, for instance, the government were to accept the execution of public works as a definite policy in any depression period, followed by its withdrawal from the market in boom periods, then the demand for certain types of investment goods would depend on fluctuations in national income in a different way than before. Similarly, the institution of a legal floor under farm prices would make the movement of farm prices different from what it would have been otherwise. In these cases there is a permanent systematic change in a certain relation which is quite different from occasional government intervention by the exercise of some additional demand for certain commodities.

MEASUREMENT OF EFFECTS

In order to determine the effects of a certain economic policy, it would be necessary, in principle, to compare the development of the economy in question under this policy with the development which would have taken place without the policy. This implies, first of all, that one cannot simply observe what has happened after the introduction of the policy and attribute it entirely to the policy. Thus, it would be inaccurate to say that the recovery in production in the United States after the introduction of the New Deal was the result of the New Deal; an appraisal of the policy would require a comparison of the recovery observed with what would have happened without the New Deal policy. Second, our statement implies that one should observe the level of economic activity not only at one moment but the whole movement during a certain period. This is of importance in particular whenever a certain policy would lead initially to a reduction of production but at a later stage to a more rapid growth of production. This might be plausible, for instance, with respect to the Russian economic policy of forced investment. Generally speaking, an increase in savings may have this effect. And it will be necessary to take into account the effects in all sectors of the economy, not only those effects which are obvious but also those which are not so readily seen. The well-known example of import duties may be quoted in this connection: the beneficial effect on the industries which are directly protected is usually easy to observe; but one should take into account also the effects on the export industries which, each perhaps in a slight degree only, but all together to a considerable extent, would be subject to the unfavorable influence of reduced imports leading via the balance of payments to reduced exports.

In practice, it is often far from easy to determine the effects of a certain economic policy because it is usually extremely difficult to state what would have happened without this policy. Sometimes, however, it is possible to have a definite opinion concerning this hypothetical development. It may happen, for instance, that measures of economic policy have not been taken in another country which is in a similar position to the country under consideration; by comparison of the economic development in the two countries certain conclusions may be drawn. Thus, in the period 1924–26 Denmark and Norway appreciated their currencies greatly, while Sweden and the Netherlands did not follow this policy. The currency of Belgium was depreciated in 1935 but not those of the Netherlands and France.[2]

Second, it is sometimes possible to draw conclusions concerning the effect of certain forms of economic policy when similar situations have occurred in the history of the country itself. Thus it might be possible to compare events in or after the first and the second world wars. Or one might make a comparison of what has happened in successive depressions or in successive ascending or descending branches of the "long waves" or in corresponding seasons.

Finally, it may actually be possible to calculate what would have happened without certain measures of economic policy. In order to do this, it will be necessary to know accurately and quantitatively the way in which the economic mechanism (or, if one prefers, the economic organism) operates. In other words,

2. See p. 86, *supra*.

all coefficients (elasticities, etc.) have to be known. Thus, for instance, in order to compute the effects of the restriction measures in the international tin market, one would want to know how production would respond to prices, costs, and productive capacity "in normal times," that is to say, without a restriction policy; this would permit an estimate of the volume of production without these restrictions. It would further be necessary to know how demand depends on the international business cycle, the price, and, possibly, certain other factors, as well as on the development of stocks under the influence of prices and other factors, in order to compute the hypothetical development of prices and stocks. It may sometimes be possible to come to a conclusion as to the effect of a certain economic policy, along these lines. The method indicated, scientifically the most desirable one, has been applied to the example just quoted[3] and also to the measurement of the effects of the agricultural policy of the American government after 1933.[4]

Only after ascertaining the effects of various economic policies will it be possible to formulate a comparative judgment regarding these policies and hence to decide which are the more desirable.

In the chapters that follow we shall discuss only those elements of economic policy which aim at changing the movements of economic variables. Accordingly, we shall primarily discuss business-cycle policy and trend policy. As has been said, we shall not deal with the policies of the individual enterprise or (with a few important exceptions closely related to our subject) with structural policy in the more limited sense of the word, policy whose objective is to change the equilibrium level.

Before we start the discussion of the various types of measures of economic policy, it will be necessary to elaborate somewhat further the objectives of economic policy (chap. xviii).

We shall divide our discussions of cycle policy further into a treatment of indirect policies (chaps. xix and xx) and one of di-

3. M. J. Schut, *Tinrestrictie en Tinprijs* (Haarlem, 1940).

4. U.S. Department of Agriculture, *Agricultural Adjustment 1937–38* (Washington, D.C., 1939), chap. v; Geoffrey S. Shepherd, *Agricultural Price Control* (Ames, Iowa), 1945.

rect policies (chaps. xxi and xxii). As to the indirect policies, we devote an entire chapter to the most important among them, namely, tax policies (chap. xix). Other forms of indirect policy (interest policy, wage policy, price and exchange-rate policy) are discussed in chapter xx. Among the direct policies, the expenditure policies of the government are again dealt with in a separate chapter because of their eminent importance (chap. xxi).

With respect to each form of economic policy we first give a description and justification and then analyze the effects of the policy. This analysis is followed by a discussion of practical experience with that policy, in so far as such experience is available and has been studied. In our final chapter (chap. xxiii) we shall endeavor to draw some general conclusions.

CHAPTER EIGHTEEN

OBJECTIVES OF TREND POLICY AND BUSINESS-CYCLE POLICY

IN ORDER to describe the objectives of trend policy and business-cycle policy, we shall start out by sketching the general economic development which, in our view, should be considered as the ideal result of these policies. Some divergence of opinion is possible, of course, with respect to what might be considered the ideal development; it is inevitable that opinions here are somewhat subjectively colored. We shall have an opportunity to compare our opinion with that of others on the most important controversies in this field.

We sketch, first, the ideal development for a country without foreign trade, that is to say, either for the world as a whole or, by approximation, for a large area which is nearly autarchic. We shall indicate only the broad outlines of the economy, paying no attention to details. The main aspects of the economy are determined by the following magnitudes: (1) the volume of production, (2) the level of prices, (3) the quantity of money, (4) the distribution of income among broad groups of the population, (5) the distribution of income among consumption and investment, and (6) the extent of the government's participation in the economy, that is, the level of taxation and the level of the government debt.

THE VOLUME OF PRODUCTION

The volume of production should be as large as possible and should be achieved by the use of all productive factors (labor, capital, and nature) which are prepared to offer their services. Involuntary unemployment of the factors of production, in particular of labor, should be avoided as far as possible. In addition, the number of working hours should approximate as nearly as possible the desires of the majority of those working. In selecting the number of working hours, workers should have before them this alternative: either longer working hours and a correspondingly higher wage or shorter hours and a correspondingly lower wage. If the alternative is put in this way, the working day selected will probably not deviate much from eight hours. If productivity increases further in the future, a further reduction in working hours is likely to be preferred.

Will there be a sufficient quantity of capital goods and of nature for the employment of all those who are prepared to work? With respect to the long-run development this question answers itself. An equilibrium is possible for any quantity of each of the factors of production; this equilibrium will be found by the price mechanism. In a country that is rich in capital, the rate of interest will be low; hence each enterprise will invest a relatively large amount of capital per worker. In a country that is poor in capital, a high rate of interest will produce a correspondingly economical use of capital. Similar considerations apply to the use of land. The distribution of activity over the different branches of industry will also be influenced by the price of capital and the price of land.

The objectives set out imply that we cannot accept as objectives of economic policy (*a*) the fluctuations as shown by the business cycle or (*b*) stabilization of the volume of production and employment at a level lower than that corresponding to full employment. One may consider stabilization at a level of (approximately) full employment as an objective of business-cycle policy by itself or as an objective of a combination of business-cycle and trend policy. Many of those who consider the stabilization of fluctuations around the average level of a cycle as the objective of business-cycle policy in the narrow sense would at the same time advocate a structural policy that would raise this level as a whole. We shall have to analyze further whether these two objectives are compatible; we think that they are; and it is then clear that stabilization at the high level is preferable to stabilization at an average level. Throughout, it should be realized that stabilization does not imply a development over time which is horizontal but rather one which shows a trend movement depending on various factors which we have discussed.

THE LEVEL OF PRICES

If at a given moment it were possible to start with a completely clean slate, without any link with the past, the level of prices would be indifferent; as is well known, a simultaneous increase of all prices in the same proportion would entail no change in the volume or in the composition of production. However, if prices are bound to the past, as is the case in reality, the level of prices is not indifferent. Great changes in either direction are then undesirable, among other things because they lead to large profits for some, large losses for others. They would, moreover, promote speculative activity.

The primary requirement with respect to the relation between prices is, speaking generally, the existence of such a relation between the prices of the products and those of the factors of production that the marginal enterprise just breaks even. This means, in approximate terms, that the level of wages should be equal to the marginal productivity of labor and means similar requirements for the other factors of production.

Considerations of a similar nature apply to the prices of individual commodities. They should be at such a level that they guarantee equilibrium between the quantity supplied and the quantity demanded; but since we discuss primarily the main outlines of the economy, we shall not deal with this question here. For the great majority of commodities, this equilibrium will be established rather easily and automatically if cyclical movements are eliminated. Only for a few commodities with a long period of production or a long lifetime need this objective be pursued separately (see chaps. viii and xiv).

With respect to the movements of the general level of prices, sharp movements in either direction are, as we have stated, undesirable. They lead to speculative profits or losses which in the long run have always most undesirable consequences. Smooth and slow movements are therefore required. Since a slow decline of prices would lead to some, even though small, book losses on commodity stocks and hence would exercise a restraining influence on economic activity, a slow increase or stability would probably be most desirable for the economy.

THE QUANTITY OF MONEY

The most desirable quantity of money is determined by the most desirable quantity of cash of each household and business enterprise. If, in the absence of sharp price movements or of threats of other disturbances in the economy, no special cash reserves are desired, the most desirable amount of cash for each economic unit will be proportional to the volume of payments it has to make during the period for which the cash should serve. Thus, for the economy as a whole, the most desirable amount of money will be proportional to the total value of turnover or to the total value of national income provided that (*a*) there are no changes in the payments plan during each payment period and (*b*) there is no change in the relative proportion of the various types of households.

A more detailed analysis would produce a number of other conditions, but we may limit ourselves here to the most important ones. Some examples may be given with respect to the two points mentioned. The payments plan of a worker's family, for instance, may be defined by the time and the magnitude of payments made by that family. Usually these payments are characterized by great regularity, e.g., the grocer is paid on Saturday, the landlord on Monday, the baker daily, etc. Generally speaking, each week a new amount of income will be received, most of which will be spent during that week. The average cash of a worker's family would therefore represent a small proportion of its yearly income. For a white-collar worker who is paid once or twice a month, the ratio of cash to income would be larger. If, therefore, the number of white-collar workers were to increase sharply compared to the number of manual workers, the average ratio of cash to annual income would also be changed considerably. But shifts of this nature, to which we referred under (*b*), usually occur only slowly.

In business, too, payment habits change only slowly. They might change not only in the periods of payment for wages, salaries, deliveries of raw materials, etc., but also by vertical integration of enterprises. All these changes occur only gradually. It may therefore be stated that the most desirable quantity of money is approximately proportional to the dollar value of total turnover, that is, approximately proportional to the product of an index of prices and the volume of production. In a stabilized economy, therefore, it would have to increase slowly.

THE DISTRIBUTION OF INCOME

With respect to the distribution of income, there are primarily social objectives relating to the personal distribution, such as the realization of a more equal distribution and perhaps the limitation of nonlabor income. These questions touch our subject only laterally and we may leave them out of account.

Apart from the effect of the distribution of income on its use, to which we shall refer in the next section, the functional distribution is a matter of great importance. If the ideal economic development is to take place under a system of free enterprise, it will be necessary, as we have noted, that wage rates shall be such that the marginal firm can still exist. In other words, the wage rate should not exceed the marginal productivity of labor. We shall come back later to these and similar equilibrium conditions.

We return to more direct questions of how economic movements should be influenced when we consider how the wage rate and the rate of interest should vary over time. The equality of the wage rate and the marginal productivity of labor would imply that the wage rate should move proportionately to the level of prices and the marginal productivity of labor.[1]

THE USE OF INCOME

With respect to the distribution of the national income over consumption and investment, two objectives should be put forward:

a) Fluctuations in these two magnitudes should be avoided as much as possible; this is the business-cycle objective. If total production and the level of prices are approximately stabilized,

1. If the production function is an exponential function, as Douglas believes, the marginal productivity of labor would be proportional to the average productivity of labor.

the distribution of income over consumption and saving will also be stable since, as we have noted, there is a pronounced regularity in the use of income for large groups of the population. Stability in income will contribute to stability in new investment; but it will not in itself stabilize reinvestment; here the echo principle may still make itself felt. It might be necessary, therefore, to limit the fluctuations in reinvestment separately.

b) It is desirable that all savings be used in investment because otherwise there would be a prolonged, structural depression accompanied by continuous hoarding. The volume of investment depends in part on technical possibilities; it is conceivable that in a country which is at the peak of technical development, the number of investment possibilities is limited. In a country which is not at the peak, there will probably always be technical possibilities. If investment possibilities are limited, it would make no sense to maintain savings at a level in excess of these possibilities. It may then be necessary to apply corrections to the use of national income and to direct a larger proportion toward consumption.

If technical possibilities do not impose limitations, a choice is possible between allocation of a smaller proportion of national income to consumption, thus permitting a faster annual rate of growth of productive capacity, and allocation of a larger part of national income to consumption with a correspondingly slower growth of the volume of capital. The choice between these two possibilities will be affected by the relative appreciation of present and future welfare; in the past, this choice has been so affected primarily by the opinions of individual persons concerning their personal welfare rather than by the community's views of the total welfare of the community. A concrete and numerical choice in this matter would be particularly difficult to make.

GOVERNMENT

The most desirable size of the government economy, in comparison to the rest of the economy, depends on a number of factors not all of which belong in the field of trend policy and business-cycle policy. We may mention technical considerations with regard to certain needs that can best be satisfied by the community, strategic considerations that may require a larger influence of the government on the economy than would be warranted on purely economic grounds, etc. In view of such considerations, no objective can be set in this field solely on the basis of the trend and cyclical aspects of economic policy.

But the magnitude of the government's share in the economy also has a direct bearing on business-cycle and trend policy. Thus, if it is desired to manipulate government expenditure as a means of business-cycle policy, such expenditure must have a certain minimum size to constitute an instrument of sufficient influence. If it is further believed that incomes should be subjected to heavy taxation in order to restrict savings, a certain minimum size of the government economy is again implied. Activities of the government on a scale which prevailed in the nineteenth century, when less than 10 per cent of the national income was paid in taxes, would provide an insufficient point of application for trend or business-cycle policy. During World War II, on the other hand, the extent of government activities was larger than was necessary for active business-cycle policy. For the future, an optimum should be found somewhere between these two extremes; it would appear that the 1938 situation was not far removed from this optimum for most European countries.

In addition to the question of desirability, that of possibility should also be considered. The possibility of collecting taxes depends on the wealth of the country, its taxation system, the tax rates, etc. It is probable that there is a limit to the total yield of taxation which lies far below total national income because taxation itself can exercise an unfavorable influence on economic activity. There is no doubt a point beyond which any increase in taxation would reduce national income. Experience would indicate that it is possible in peacetime to set aside at least one-fourth of the national income for governmental purposes; in wartime, a larger proportion can be taken, although this requires means other than taxation. The ratio of taxes to national income in the United States in 1929, 1938, and 1947 is set out in Table 15.

OPEN ECONOMY

We may now consider the objectives of trend policy and business-cycle policy for a country that depends to a significant extent on trade with other countries. Such a country has much less freedom in the choice of its economic development than do countries with a closed economy. One might go so far as to say that a country which depends to a large extent on foreign trade need not and cannot have a cyclical policy of its own. If the world cycle is stabilized, the cycle in a country with an open

TABLE 15

THE RATIO OF TAXES TO NATIONAL INCOME

	1929	1938	1947
BILLIONS OF DOLLARS			
1. National income	87.4	67.4	202.5
2. Taxation:			
a) Federal	3.7	4.8	38.8
b) State and local	7.3	8.3	13.1
Total	11.0	13.1	51.9
PER CENT			
3. Taxation as per cent of national income	12.6	19.4	25.6

economy will also be stabilized; and if the world cycle is not stabilized, a small country with an open economy will not succeed in stabilizing its own business cycle anyway. Similar observations might be made with respect to the trend: the speed of development, it might be said, is also entirely determined by the rate of growth of the world economy.

But these fatalistic views are exaggerated and therefore dangerous. They are dangerous in particular because almost all countries in the world depend heavily on international trade, and each country might therefore push onto others the responsibility for an undesirable cyclical or trend movement. In this way a better international economic policy could never be achieved.

The variables which for a country with an open economy are indeed practically given are the prices of imported commodities in terms of foreign currency, the prices of export commodities in terms of foreign currency (for countries exporting world staples), and the world demand curve for the country's exports. An autonomous economic policy for such a country would still leave the following possibilities to regulate its own cycle: (*a*) the manipulation of the rate of exchange, thus adjusting the price level in national currency of international commodities and regulating the supply price in foreign currency of nonstaple international commodities, and (*b*) the regulation of domestic demand for commodities, which may provide a compensation for possible fluctuations in a foreign demand.

The policy under (*a*) in particular might be applied in a depression by depreciation, which would soften the internal fall of prices and stimulate exports; and the policy under (*b*) might be applied through the government's increasing its demand in a period of depression. In periods of boom the opposite policy should then be followed. In addition to exchange policy, the direct regulation of imports might also be applied. In this way, a country with a large foreign trade can yet follow a business-cycle policy of its own. The objectives of this policy would in principle be the same as those of countries with a closed economy; but it is now less certain that these objectives can be entirely realized. A good example of such an independent antidepression policy is that followed by Sweden from 1931 to 1935.

Similar considerations apply to trend policies. By exchange-rate policies and the stimulation of savings, it is possible to some extent to set a rate of development in one country which is independent of that in other countries. An important example of this is the development in Japan after 1931.

In small countries, however, the necessity to maintain a certain equilibrium in the balance of payments brings in another inevitable objective of their business-cycle and trend policy. This necessity will be the more rigid as the country concerned has less international reserves; if such reserves are completely absent (as they were in Germany after 1934), the country must balance its current international payments. But when a country disposes of certain gold and foreign-exchange reserves, it can permit itself an import surplus in periods of depression and can thus achieve a greater degree of cyclical stability. It would then be necessary to restore the reserves in boom periods, in order to make possible the application of the same policy in a succeeding depression.

Limitations similar to those with respect to cyclical policies apply with respect to the trend development of an open economy. Thus, in particular, the trend of prices can hardly differ from that in the rest of the world unless the economy would accept continuous appreciation or, more likely and more serious, continuous depreciation of its currency. The rate of growth of exports, and thereby that of imports, is also limited by conditions abroad. More independence is possible with respect to the percentage of national income saved, especially if the government is prepared to intervene in the capital market. Without such intervention, there will be a further link through the international capital market, and the rate of interest will fluctuate with rates abroad; even the level of taxation cannot be too divergent from that in other countries, at least not higher, because of the possibilities of capital flight. Only a country with very rigorous exchange controls, such as Germany after 1933, could disregard these difficulties.

MONETARY EQUILIBRIUM

The objective of business-cycle policy is often formulated as "monetary equilibrium," which is sometimes defined in this way, that all business and private households together would in each time period spend as much as they receive. In other words, for the economy as a whole there would be no hoarding, either negative or positive; the flow of income would not be interrupted or increased. Such a situation is also sometimes referred to as one in which there are no disturbances of equilibrium coming "from the side of money," in particular no disturbances due to "incomplete exchanges."

An incomplete exchange transaction is one in which commodities are exchanged for money but money is not again exchanged for commodities. Such transactions would have no place in the theoretical model of an economy without money, such as that assumed by Walras, in which the only form of exchange is that of one commodity against another commodity. It is sometimes said that the objective of business-cycle policy should be the approximation of a situation which is reflected by equations like those of Walras.

This objective, however, should be taken with some grains of salt. There is, first, no objection to that deviation from "monetary equilibrium" which consists in a gradual increase of the quantity of money. To the contrary, it is desirable that the circulation of money should increase as the value of turnover increases. These increases should be gradual; as indicated above, the increase should be in the order of a few per cent a year, in accordance with the increases of the population and of productivity.

Second, the desire to approximate the situation expressed by the system of equations of Walras is in many respects impossible of fulfilment, as this system does not reflect many technical and institutional facts that are of great importance in reality, such as the definite lifetime of many commodities, the length of the period of production, and many other similar facts. It may be admitted, however, that in general the deviations from the equilibrium situation due to monetary factors are among the most important and that for this reason the objective of monetary equilibrium can be accepted as a first approximation.

Are the objectives set out in the preceding sections attainable? The first condition for this is that they do not contain logical or technical inconsistencies. A logical inconsistency would be present if we had assumed, for instance, that total income would have to be larger than the sum of all individual incomes. Other and more important possibilities of logical inconsistencies are conceivable. No such inconsistencies are present, however, in our objectives. A technical inconsistency might be present if we had assumed a relation between production and employment that was not compatible with the production function. But that type of inconsistency, too, we have avoided.

More conditions than these have to be fulfilled to render possible a development without a cyclical component. As we have seen in chapter xvi, the movements in the economy are the result of (*a*) changes in the data (disturbances) and (*b*) reactions of the economic mechanism to such disturbances.

Many of these disturbances, such as fluctuations in crop yields, wars, other calamities, or strikes, cannot be avoided. Hence, a complete stabilization of the business cycle is impossible. But much depends on whether the economy tends to develop these inevitable initial movements into large deviations from equilibrium by cumulative reactions or whether the response of the economy is an immediate tendency to reapproach the equilibrium situation. Depending on the nature of the relations among the economic variables (which reflect these reactions), the result may be either a movement of slight damping and a long period and therefore of a large amplitude or a heavily damped movement with a short period; in the latter case, disturbances will soon spend their force and do little harm. We have discussed the relationship between the "elementary relations" and the form of economic movements in chapter xiii, particularly in developing our examples, and we shall have to make use now of the knowledge gained at that stage.

In order to achieve a more stable development, it will be necessary to adjust one or more of the relations among the various economic variables. For instance, investment will have to react differently to fluctuations in national income, or the wage rate will have to react differently to changes in employment, prices, etc. As a limiting case this change of reactions may mean that one of the variables is entirely stabilized. Specific forms of economic policy usually consist in the change of one relationship, sometimes in the stabilization of one variable. It cannot be said in advance whether this will yield stabilization of the entire economy. A definite answer could be given only on the basis of a computation in the manner developed in chapter xiii, a computation which is generally difficult, especially when the system of relations is complicated. In simpler systems limited to the most important relationships, as in Example I, it may be possible to arrive at a conclusion by qualitative reasoning alone, provided that the reactions that have not been changed by economic policy, i.e., those that have been left free, do not run counter to the attempts toward stabilization.

In the chapters that follow we shall analyze first the effect on economic movements of individual forms of economic policy. In a final chapter (chap. xxiii) we shall take up the question as to what extent a combination of these individual forms of economic policy is desirable in order to achieve the best approximation to the objectives set.

CHAPTER NINETEEN

INDIRECT POLICIES. I. TAX POLICIES

CLASSIFICATION OF TAXES

IN THIS chapter on tax policy we want to discuss all basic decisions which determine the total system of taxation. These decisions include, first, the choice of the type of taxes, then, the rate structure with possible fluctuations in rates, and, for certain types of taxes, the degree of progression. We start the systematic description of tax policy and its consequences with a classification of taxes according to economic considerations. On this basis, taxes may be classified as follows:

1. Direct taxes
   - i. Income taxes
     - *a*) On total income
     - *b*) On certain forms of income (wage tax, profits tax)
   - ii. Capital taxes
     - *a*) Recurrent capital taxes
     - *b*) Death duties
2. Indirect taxes
   - i. General (turnover taxes)
   - ii. Specific
     - *a*) Excises
     - *b*) Customs duties
     - *c*) Social security payments

This classification does not include all existing and conceivable taxes; the few taxes, however, that cannot be incorporated in this scheme are usually unimportant and may be left out of consideration here.

Each of these taxes has a rate; most indirect taxes are fully determined by the rate because they are proportional. Direct taxes, on the other hand, are usually not determined by one single rate; there usually is a whole series of rates with a certain progression. Finally, tax rates and progression may be variable over time; this element will also have to be known in order that the tax system be determined.

Before discussing the effects of the institution, increase, or decrease of any one of these taxes separately and before expressing a judgment with respect to them, we want to make certain general observations concerning these effects.

The immediate consequences of any tax consist, obviously, in taking away certain amounts in one spot of the economy and adding these same amounts in one or more other spots. It follows, therefore, that the use of receipts of a tax determines in part its effects. With respect to the use of the sum total of tax receipts we assume in this discussion, except in the beginning, that it is given in advance and is not changed; the tax receipts are spent in given amounts for salaries of officials, expenditure on supplies, interest payments, unemployment expenditure, etc. We shall therefore consider only such changes in the tax system as leave the total yield of all taxes unaffected; we shall always consider the replacement of one tax by another.

In principle, every such change would affect the equilibrium position of the economy, that is to say, it would affect all variables entering into this equilibrium position.[1] The increase of a certain excise duty means not only an increase in the yield of that tax but also, in principle, a change in the basis of the tax, namely, the price of the article taxed, and this change will lead not only to direct but also to certain indirect effects. In order to obtain an entirely accurate knowledge of the effect of such changes, it would be necessary to determine the new equilibrium position. Although not very much can be said a priori concerning the results, it may be stated that in the great majority of cases the indirect consequences are smaller than the direct ones, so that a change in taxes which affects a certain category of economic subjects unfavorably in its direct effects is likely also to affect that group unfavorably in its total effects.

If the economy is not in static equilibrium but performs cyclical movements, these movements will also be affected by the tax system. In principle the change in the cyclical pattern would also have to be known before a final judgment on any tax

1. Cf. chap. xvii.

change is possible; in practice, however, rough approximations will often be both necessary and satisfactory here.

DIRECT AND INDIRECT TAXES

We shall turn now to tax policy and its effects, and, in order to do that, we shall successively open for discussion the various decisions which have to be taken to determine the entire tax system of a country. As a first decision we take that of the total amount of taxes. We have discussed this question above when dealing with the extent of the government's operations in the economy; it is a more general question which is not suitable for treatment in this chapter. We may therefore move on to the next decision. That is the decision of the distribution of taxes between direct taxes and indirect taxes. As indicated, we shall discuss this decision in the form of an increase in direct taxes accompanied by an equally large decrease in indirect taxes. It will readily become clear that the effects of a shift of this nature depend much more on other characteristics of these types of taxes than on the mere fact that they are direct or indirect.

Let us assume, first, for a country without foreign trade, a choice between two taxes, namely, a proportional direct tax on income and a proportional indirect tax with the same yield imposed on all uses of income. Both these taxes would be somewhat unusual, the direct tax in that it would be proportional, that is, without progression, and the indirect tax in that it would bear not only on all expenditure but also on savings. It will readily be seen that the effect of these two taxes would be the same. The direct tax would constitute a proportional reduction of all incomes, the indirect tax an equally large proportional increase of all prices; in real terms nothing would have been changed in the relation between incomes and prices.

Replacement of an indirect tax on all uses of income by a direct tax on all incomes would also have no effect even if the country did have foreign trade, if the indirect tax had been accompanied by an import duty of the same amount on all imported commodities and an export subsidy of the same amount on all export commodities, and both were then abolished at the same time as the indirect tax.

These conclusions are changed when, as is usually the case,

the indirect tax is in one respect or another a partial tax. A first example of this is that the indirect tax is not levied on savings. The increase of a direct tax which is to correspond to a decrease of an indirect tax can in this case be smaller percentage-wise than the decrease in the indirect tax. This will lead to relatively larger consumption and a reduction of savings. In other words, the segment of the economy that was not subject to the indirect tax will be unfavorably affected; the reverse would apply if the indirect tax were increased—in that case the sectors which were subject to this tax would be unfavorably affected.

Similar considerations apply when there are no compensating import duties and export bounties or when they exist for certain commodities only; in that case, indirect taxes affect the domestic segment of the economy unfavorably, compared to the foreign segment. A reduction of indirect taxes will then improve the position of the domestic sector.

The most important differences between indirect and direct taxes, however, is usually that the latter have a much more progressive character than the former, so that much higher percentages are levied of high incomes than of low incomes. Indirect taxes, on the other hand, are on the whole regressive rather than progressive in character, except in so far as first necessities are exempted. The replacement of an indirect tax by a direct tax with the same yield will therefore usually mean heavier taxation of higher incomes and the payments made out of these incomes, including savings, and a reduction of the burden on lower incomes.

As a consequence, a greater proportion of national income will be consumed and a smaller proportion saved. It is not certain in advance whether this fact in itself will change total national income and, if so, in what direction. If all savings are necessary for investment, the smaller amount saved may, in the long run, lead to a reduction of the amount of capital compared to what it would otherwise have been. In that case, national income will fall. If, on the other hand, not all savings are necessary for investment, there would be no such effect, and, owing to the greater consumption demand, the volume of production would in fact be above what it would have been otherwise. There is, further, an indirect influence of an increase in direct taxation on total national income. The higher direct tax may affect the incentive of the earners of higher incomes (usually the entrepreneurial group of the economy) and may therefore restrain their activity.

It will be clear from this that the effect of the shift on the level and the general trend of production cannot be stated in general. It would be necessary to have much more knowledge of the relations to which we referred, in particular of the effect of high direct taxes on the entrepreneurial activity and of the amount of savings that can be invested. It is usually assumed that the level of production will be somewhat unfavorably affected, but for rich countries the opposite may be true. Especially in poor countries, the rate of growth of production is likely to be affected unfavorably. More positive conclusions can be drawn with respect to the influence that an increase of direct taxes combined with a reduction of indirect taxes would have on the cyclical fluctuations of production, although here, too, no final conclusions can be drawn. The higher taxation of high incomes will exercise a more restraining effect in a boom than in a depression because in a boom a much larger amount is represented by high incomes than in a depression; and, since in the depression a part of the savings will not be used anyway, there will be little, if any, restraining effect at that time. Only the stimulating effect of the reduction in indirect taxes will then be operative. Hence, such a change in tax policy would lead to a certain stabilization of cyclical fluctuations. This in itself may favorably affect the level and the rate of increase of production because of the reduced uncertainty and the lesser tendency toward hoarding that may result.

The change in the tax system referred to will affect not only the trend and cyclical movement but also the economic structure in the more limited sense of the word; thus, an increase of direct taxes combined with a corresponding decrease in indirect taxes would lead to greater economic justice.[2]

In order to arrive at a final opinion with respect to the change discussed, it would be necessary to know more about the effects

2. Cf. p. 264, *supra*.

on the level and the trend movement, with respect to which the two unsolved problems raised above are of much importance. Our preliminary impression would be that a further increase of progression would have a favorable effect. Since progression cannot increase much more for the very high incomes, the taxation of the middle incomes could most appropriately be increased.

GENERAL AND SPECIFIC TAXES

The next step in the determination of the tax system is that of the distribution of indirect taxes over general taxes and specific taxes. The general principle of this distinction has already been discussed in the preceding section, in connection with the point that even the most general indirect tax, the turnover tax, is not entirely general. An increase of indirect taxation in a certain segment of the economy, with a corresponding simultaneous reduction of a more general indirect tax—a relative increase therefore of the degree of taxation on that particular segment—must always make production in that field of the economy more difficult. A relative increase of the excise duty on tobacco will reduce the activity in the tobacco industry with respect to activity in general; a relative increase of wage costs compared to other costs, e.g., by an increase in social security payments, will mean a reduction of employment in comparison to the use of capital, etc. An exception to this rule might be found only in some cases of increased taxation of so-called "inferior commodities," the demand for which can increase as prices rise. A change in relative indirect taxation, therefore, constitutes a means by which less desirable types of production can be restrained or other, useful, types of production can be promoted. Thus, employment may be increased by a reduction of social security payments and a corresponding increase in other taxes that are not proportional to wages or by an actual employment bonus. Domestic production may be favored compared to imports by making it relatively cheap, i.e., by levying import duties rather than a general turnover tax. Again, it will not be clear a priori in such cases whether total production will be increased or decreased.

The effect on total turnover depends on second-order effects of these changes. The meaning of this term may be clarified with the help of an example. We assume an increase in the excise duty on tobacco, combined with a corresponding reduction in the general turnover tax. The resulting increase in the price of tobacco products and the decrease in the price of all other commodities will lead to a decreased demand for tobacco and an increased demand for all other commodities. As far as production as a whole is concerned, there is, therefore, a certain tendency toward compensation. If the elasticities of demand and supply for both categories of commodities were the same, there would be no change in total demand. Such changes in total demand as do occur are therefore the effect of the differences between these elasticities. One speaks of second-order effects in particular when these differences are rather small.

Since the effect on total turnover is a second-order effect, this type of change in taxation will usually not be advocated on the basis of considerations of general economic policy. On this account, these changes are of relatively less importance for our present purposes. Since, moreover, the effects of each concrete change of this category can be determined only if one knows the specific conditions and the actual numerical values of the elasticities involved, we shall not pursue further the discussion of this type of changes.

INCOME TAXES AND CAPITAL TAXES

A further decision is to be made between the distribution of direct taxes over income taxes and capital taxes. A capital tax which is so low that it can be satisfied out of the income from that capital is in fact the equivalent of a tax on unearned income. A shift from income tax to capital tax will, therefore, affect, on the one hand, capital formation and, on the other, the use of labor.

With respect to the former point, there is a difference of opinion as to the effect of a reduction of unearned income. On the one hand, such a reduction may be expected to affect capital formation unfavorably, because the same amount of saving will now yield a smaller result. On the other hand, this smaller yield may stimulate the incentive to save in order to achieve the same total income as before. Pending a further investigation of these questions, it may be assumed provisionally that the effect of this shift on capital formation would be small.[3]

It is usually assumed that a relative decrease of taxation on pure labor income will stimulate activity. However, the opposite effect may also occur. To the extent that one can neglect the opposite tendency, a moderate shift in the direction assumed would therefore be favorable with respect to activity.

If a shift in the direction of capital taxes were so pronounced that these taxes could no longer be paid from the income, liquidation of capital would take place. In that case, the effect on private capital formation would become pronouncedly unfavorable. Unless the government were to allocate the yield of this tax to capital formation, total capital formation would also be endangered, and the net result would be unfavorable, except in situations where the need for capital was saturated. As income taxes are almost always highly progressive and bear therefore most heavily on high incomes (which, on the average, contain also the highest amount of unearned income), a shift of the nature discussed will not constitute an important shift in the total taxation of the different income groups. The use of income will, therefore, as a first approximation, not be much affected, and the influence from a cyclical point of view will probably also be small.

In the light of the above, a trend effect will be noticeable (and in an unfavorable sense) if (*a*) the capital tax becomes very high, (*b*) its yield is not applied to official capital formation, and (*c*) all savings can be used for investment because the country concerned is not in a situation of a capital satiation.

An important form of income taxation is the tax on corporate profits. This tax may be levied either on total profits or on distributed profits or on undistributed profits. A special tax on distributed profits would tend to promote corporate savings which may be a long-run advantage for a country where capital is short: it would speed up the trend of capacity. In countries where capital is abundant and where corporate savings are less necessary, the cyclical aspect of this type of tax will be more

3. Cf. the discussion of the effects of the rate of interest on saving, above, p. 190.

important. This aspect would be unfavorable: the tax would promote investment in a boom and promote hoarding in a depression. Hence, from the cyclical point of view this tax should be rejected. An extra tax on undistributed profits has the opposite effect and may be recommended for countries with abundant capital because of its anticyclical effects.

Every tax on corporate profits, whatever its details (unless the progression were based on the rate of profit), has always the disadvantage that it cannot be really progressive. There is no reason to assume that the shares of large corporations are in the hands of persons with higher incomes than are those of the shares of smaller corporations. The opposite may well be true. Therefore, higher taxation of the profits of large corporations than of those of small corporations constitutes an intervention in the degree of concentration of corporations, and it is by no means certain whether this serves any social purpose. If it is intended to tax the large shareholders more heavily, other means can be employed.

The broad determination of the amount of the different types of taxes indicated in the preceding paragraphs implies at the same time the determination of the average rate of these taxes. Given, for instance, the total national income and the total desired yield of the income tax, the average rate is determined. Similar considerations apply to other taxes. The degree of progression, however, is not yet determined. It may still be changed without affecting total yield; more can be levied from the higher incomes and correspondingly less from the lower incomes. We do not need to discuss separately the effects of a change in progression, as we have discussed this question already when we compared indirect and direct taxes.

FLUCTUATIONS IN RATE OVER TIME

The determination of the average rate still leaves open a possible variation of the rate over time. The most important choice which is open here is the following: Should rates remain unchanged during the period of a cycle, or should they be adjusted anticyclically, or cocyclically? In the past the unconscious reaction of tax rates with respect to business cycles has almost always been that of an anticyclical variation. In bad times taxes were increased; in good times they were lowered. The interest of the government's finances was considered the primary consideration: in the depression a budget deficit had to be avoided at all costs, and in good times no need was felt to create a surplus. It was believed that the objective of a balanced budget also served the economy as a whole; it would promote confidence in the government's credit and, in that way, promote the stability of the monetary system as a whole.

Gradually the view has gained ground that the interests of the economy as a whole are also harmed by this policy—in a way which at first had not been realized so clearly—and this the more the larger the share of the government in the total economy; for this policy implied the imposition of heavier taxes in times of depression, thus stimulating the depressive forces, and the promotion of the expansionist forces in the boom by tax reduction. The government failed to use for purposes of monetary equilibrium the large amounts over which it had control. If part of the high tax yields of the boom were taken out of circulation and these same amounts were used in the depression to exercise additional demand for commodities and services, monetary equilibrium would have been promoted. Gradually, then, the opinion has made headway that the anticyclical movement of tax rates is not desirable and that it would be preferable either to change rates with the cycle, increasing them in the boom and lowering them in the depression, or to keep rates constant during a cycle.

By either policy, the yields of taxes in the boom will be higher than in the depression; the difference will be greater when rates are changed in accordance with the cycle. Although this greater fluctuation in tax yields is no doubt beneficial from a business-cycle point of view, the frequent change of rates, on the other hand, is a disadvantage for business. Stability of rates provides an element of stability in business planning and is hence beneficial to total activity. It will exercise a favorable effect on the level of production and its trend movement. It is further possible even at stable rates to affect the fluctuations in yield: the higher the degree of progression, the greater will be the difference between boom yields and depression yields. In the light of these considerations, it would appear to us that much is to be said for constant rates through the cycle.

With respect to the experience of tax policy, much less can be said with certainty than might have been expected. There is, of course, an abundance of data with respect to the tax policies in most countries. But studies that analyze systematically the effects of different tax policies, in particular with respect to the more general problems are as infrequent as they might have been useful. There are various reasons for this.

In the first place, the statistical and other material on tax policies is extremely detailed; a large preliminary study is therefore necessary to make this material intelligible and to put it in a form which makes it comparable for different countries and different periods. Some notable results have been achieved in this respect; we may mention in particular an important report published in Sweden, concerning the burden of taxation in a number of countries before and after the first World War.[4] The League of Nations Secretariat has also published important material concerning the level of import duties in a number of countries before and after World War I.[5]

Second, the effect of the general characteristics of tax policy, such as the total level, the distribution over indirect and direct taxes, etc., depends on the economy as a whole to such an extent that every comparison of results involves necessarily a comparison of the general economic situation of the countries and periods concerned. But the proper description of this general economic situation also requires extensive and comprehensive work of a type not satisfactorily achieved until the past few decades; in this respect, we refer in particular to the studies on national income of various countries.

Furthermore, the differences between countries in their general economic situation depend not only on differences in taxation policy but on many other factors as well. One of these, a

4. E. Lindahl, *Undersökningar rörande det samlade skattetrycket i Sverige och utlandet* (Stockholm: Statens Offentliga Utredningar 1936: 18 Finansdepartementet, 1936).

5. *Memorandum on Tariff Level Indices* (Geneva: League of Nations, World Economic Conference, 1927).

very important one, is the relative availability of capital. The separation of the effects of such factors on the welfare of a country is a problem that has become manageable only very recently and that requires very good statistical data for all the other relevant factors. Data with respect to the capital intensity of production in various countries, however, are not among those which can be said to be particularly good.

These various factors may perhaps explain why so few inductive studies have been made in this field. Most results have been achieved with respect to more specific and partial problems. Studies have been made, for instance, of the effects of increases or decreases of excise duties or import duties for a few commodities and of the influence of the tax changes in the United States after 1933. Generally speaking, it may be said that the direct effects of partial changes in taxation are in accord with theoretical expectations. With respect to the indirect effects, the "shifting of the tax burden," usually very little can be said with certainty; this is due to the fact that for this purpose the elasticities of demand and supply of the markets concerned have to be known, and here again only the very first steps have been made.

SUMMARY

On the basis of an assumed given total yield of all taxes, we have, in the absence of sufficient quantitative studies in this field, successively analyzed in a qualitative way the effects of changes in the distribution over direct and indirect taxes and over the different types of indirect and of direct taxes. We have seen, in this connection, that an increase of specific indirect taxes will almost always lead to reduction of the activity taxed; accordingly, these taxes provide certain instruments of control which, however, do not have great significance with respect to total activity. We have further seen that the four following policies (1) relative increase of direct taxes, (2) relative increase of capital taxes, (3) relative increase of the taxation on undistributed profits, and (4) increase in progression lead to (*a*) greater equality and (*b*) a reduction in savings and an increase in consumption. We may refer to the preceding sections for the qualifications that apply to these statements. The reduction in savings and the corresponding increase in consumption will lead to three sets of consequences: (i) in general, the trend development will become slower as a result of reduced capital formation; only in rich countries with an abundance of capital may this effect be absent; (ii) in rich countries where part of income is hoarded, the volume of production will increase; and (iii) in all cases, the cyclical movement will become more stable.

A scientifically justified choice of changes in the tax system will be possible only when more information is available concerning the magnitude of the reactions indicated. Clearly the effect will then depend further on the size of the changes in rate or in the changes in progression, etc., applied. Our provisional impression is that a higher degree of progression than that existing in this country shortly before the war or corresponding changes in other taxes would have a beneficial effect. It should be accompanied by rates which are stable over time.

Although a certain degree of stabilization of production may be achieved in this way, it is not possible to achieve complete stabilization by tax policy only; despite a high degree of progression, total expenditure in a boom will always remain higher than in a depression; only a further quantitative study can determine by how much.

CHAPTER TWENTY

INDIRECT POLICIES. II. OTHER FORMS

INTEREST POLICY

WE SHALL deal in this chapter with the other indirect forms of business-cycle policy. We shall take up interest policy first. The rate of interest may be affected by the central bank's establishing its rates with the purpose of influencing the volume of credit and thus promoting stabilization of cyclical movements. This policy may be supported by open-market policy. Open-market policy is exercised by the central bank through the purchase or sale from the banking system of treasury bills or long-term government bonds. The purchase of government paper from the commercial banks will increase their balances with the central bank and hence their liquidity. In this way it will tend to reduce the rate of interest. Similarly, the sale of government paper by the central bank to the commercial banks will reduce the reserve position of the latter and hence tend to increase the rate of interest. Finally, interest policy may be performed by a large-scale conversion operation by the state in order to reduce the rate of interest on long-term loans. If this reduction is in excess of that which has occurred in the free capital market and, in particular, if it is accompanied by some degree of pressure, it may indeed be considered as a form of interest policy.

In a discussion of interest policy, a distinction should be made between the psychological influence in particular situations of a sudden change in the discount rates of the central bank and the general economic influence on the level of activity of changes in the rate of interest. An increase in the discount rate, in a period of business-cycle tension, may be interpreted as an emergency sign and hence provoke a sudden crisis. Whether such action promotes stabilization may, perhaps, be questioned.

The effect of gradual changes in the rates of interest is not very great. The greatest effect is felt, of course, with respect to those forms of activity that are financed in part by credits, i.e., investment. A distinction should be made here between investment in inventories and investment in fixed capital. With respect to the former, no influence of the rate of interest can statistically be distinguished; with respect to the latter, some influence can be established. Statistical studies show, however, that only a small part of the actual fluctuations of investment in fixed capital in the past can be attributed to fluctuations in rates of interest.[1] In other words, rates of interest would have to show much more pronounced fluctuations to achieve stabilization of investment. For that reason, only a limited significance can be attributed to interest policy as a policy toward the stabilization of business cycles. This is due in particular to the fact that the rate of interest can never become negative; this puts a serious limitation on the stimulating effects of interest policy in the depression. In order to compensate the losses on new investment, a negative rate of interest would in fact be required.

With respect to the influence of the rate of interest on the stabilization of the business cycle, it may be admitted that any stabilization achieved by fluctuations in the rate of interest will be increased to some extent by the operation of the multiplier. If investments are somewhat more stabilized, the total value of production and hence the total profits will also be more stabilized via the operation of the multiplier. This would lead to a further stabilizing influence on investment.

If fluctuations in the rate of interest were to be used to stabilize investment, they would have to respond more rapidly and should lead investment, rather than lag behind fluctuations in investment, as they now do.

Experience would seem to confirm these views. It has sometimes been held that the interest policy, and in particular the open-market policy, of the Federal Reserve banks in the United States has, to a considerable extent, contributed to the stabili-

1. Cf. chap. xiii.

zation of the cycle after 1920. Figure 51 illustrates the events. During the periods indicated by small vertical lines, the Federal Reserve banks intervened by interest policy or open-market policy. Cross-hatching above the curve of industrial production indicates an increase of the rate of interest or the sale of government bonds; cross-hatching below the curve indicates a reduction of the rate of interest or the purchase of government bonds. In a number of instances, one might read from the diagram that, after cross-hatching above the curve, there was a downward turn of the curve and that, after cross-hatching below the curve, there was an upturn. But further consideration will show that this did by no means occur in all instances: in 1928, for instance, the policy was without effect; similarly in 1930 and 1931 and in subsequent years. Moreover, the period which elapses before anything happens is quite different; this would make it probable that the turning points were, at least in part, due to other factors as well.

An interesting example of business-cycle policy exercised by means of interest policy is the great conversion of government debt in England in 1932. On that occasion, the rate of interest on long-term government bonds was reduced from 5 per cent to $3\frac{1}{2}$ per cent. England after 1932 experienced an important economic recovery which was particularly strong in the building industry. It is by no means certain, however, that the rise in building activity should be attributed primarily to the reduction in the rate of interest, although that reduction was no doubt of importance. Other factors which promoted the expansion of construction, in particular residential construction, were the fall in the cost of living while money wages remained unchanged or increased, the increase in the number of families, and the increase in rents. A statistical explanation of the movements in residential construction, by means of multiple correlation and on the basis of the factors mentioned and fluctuations in building costs, shows that somewhat less than half the recovery in residential building in England may be attributed to the reduction in the rate of interest.[2] It is interesting to note that activity

2. Cf. J. Tinbergen, *Statistical Testing of Business Cycle Theories*, Vol. I: *A Method and Its Application to Investment Activity* (Geneva: League of Nations, 1939), p. 100.

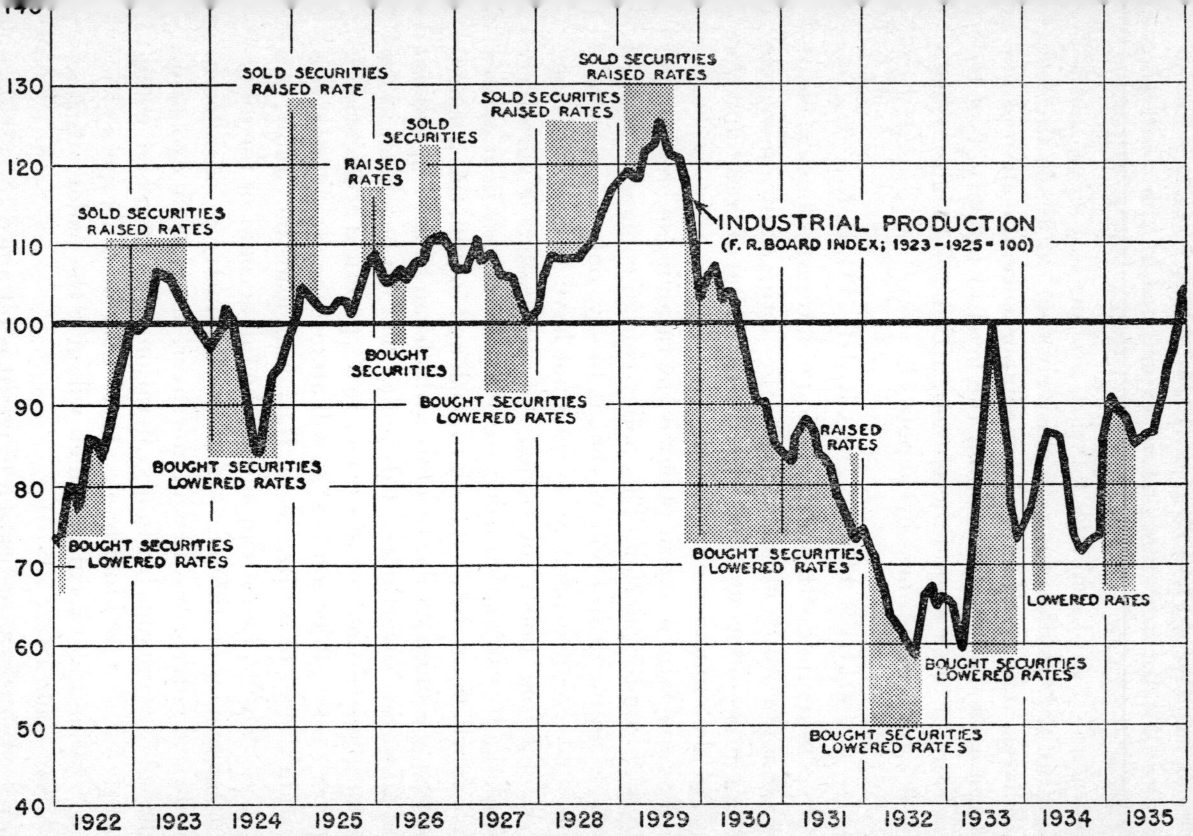

FIG. 51.—Industrial production in the United States and the policy of the Federal Reserve banks. Cross-hatching above the curve indicates an increase of the rate of interest and sale of government paper; cross-hatching below the curve indicates a reduction of the rate of interest and purchase of government paper. The width of the cross-hatchings indicates the period during which the policy was pursued. Source: W. Randolph Burgess, *The Reserve Banks and the Money Market*, (New York and London; Harper & Bros. [1946], p. 249).

did not increase after 1934, although the rate of interest continued to fall considerably from 1934 to 1935.

There is, further, the general experience of the depression years of the thirties, when an extremely low rate of interest in a large number of countries failed to produce any significant recovery. This would prove conclusively that, although the rate of interest may be a factor of some importance, it cannot be one of the main factors determining the level of activity. Not too much importance should therefore be attributed to interest policy as a form of business-cycle policy.

OTHER FORMS OF CREDIT POLICY

In conjunction with our discussion of interest policy, we want to say a few words about various other forms of business-cycle policy which are connected with the extension of credit and the size of the monetary circulation.

A simple form of credit policy is the rationing of credit in periods of rapid expansion. This policy can, of course, be applied only as an incidental policy, that is to say, only when there is too much credit expansion. It does not have as its counterpart a stimulating policy in periods of depression. Figuratively speaking, if systematic business-cycle policies may be indicated as bars which can be used both to push and to pull, this accidental policy is more similar to a rope, which can be used to pull but not to push. Nevertheless, this policy may be beneficial in the boom phase of the business cycle. In its practical application it is open to the objection that it will almost inevitably involve a certain degree of arbitrariness. Rationing leads inevitably to a certain rigidity, and it can never take full account of the different tendencies of different branches of industry or of different individual enterprises. It will, moreover, not restrain expansion which is self-financed. Finally, if rationing is exercised voluntarily by the individual banks, there may be differences of interpretation and execution which will give the policy a further arbitrary character.

A more uniform restriction of credit is obtained by a system of legal reserve percentages. These compulsory reserves exercise a certain restraining influence on credit in periods of high credit tension; this restraint may then be reinforced by an increase in reserve percentages. Most countries do not have such legal coverage percentages, although banks tend to observe certain conventional ratios between cash and deposits. Since in all cases reserve percentages are only of the order of magnitude of 10–20 per cent and lower for time deposits, no strict regulation of the credit system can be achieved by them.

The 100 per cent money plan of Professor Irving Fisher goes much further in the same direction, in that it would require the banks to maintain reserves for 100 per cent of their deposits. This would imply that the regulation of the total money supply, including bank money, would be entirely in the hands of the central bank. Here again, however, it should be observed that the policy works in one direction only. It may limit the expansion of the quantity of money but not its reduction. The 100 per cent plan is no remedy against the destruction of money, which is such an important factor in economic crises.

For these reasons, the regulation of the flow of commodities and services and of the flow of money corresponding to it (the amount of purchases of commodities and services per unit of time) is more important than the regulation of the total stock of money. The regulation of the flows of commodities and services will be discussed primarily when we analyze direct policies. The restriction on the quantity of money in periods of too rapid increase of transactions may in this connection be considered as a useful, occasional restraining factor to limit inflationary tendencies.

Another form of monetary policy which may suitably be discussed at this stage is the commodity standard, advocated by Professor Goudriaan in Holland and by Mr. Benjamin Graham in the United States. The principle of this form of regulation is that the central bank would stand ready to buy and sell at a fixed price packages of warehouse claims for a certain assortment of raw materials. The packages would have a constant composition and would contain claims for the various raw materials roughly in proportion to their significance in world production or world trade. If the average level of prices were to fall below the buying price of the central bank, producers and traders would make up packages of the surplus materials and offer them for sale to the central bank. In this way, production would be maintained approximately at the normal level. If the price level were to increase above the selling price of the bank, it would be advantageous to purchase packages from the central bank and sell them in the free market. In this way, the average price level of raw materials and hence probably also the price level of finished products would be kept approximately constant.

The maintenance of the production of raw materials in periods of depression would provide a stimulating effect at that time. At times of tension, the sale of packages of raw materials by the central bank would be equivalent to an open-market policy in reducing the quantity of money. The raw-material standard would therefore seem to be a more important instrument for the regulation of the business cycle than the other forms of monetary policy discussed so far. It provides automatically both a brake in the boom and a stimulus in the depression; moreover, it would tend to stabilize the price level directly. Nevertheless, its effect is limited in various respects. At times of great scarcity of raw materials, the stock of the central bank might become exhausted before the price level had been stabilized; the restraining influence that the central bank may exercise by the sale of its packages of raw materials may not be adequate. It is possible, on the other hand, that the stimulus in the depression would be inadequate. This stimulus would indeed keep the production of raw materials at an approximately constant level; but it is conceivable that this would not be an adequate stimulus for the production of final goods. It is quite possible that after a number of years of a high level of investment, there would be such a satiation of the entire economy with capital goods that a reduction in demand would be inevitable. This reduction might well last for a number of years, even if the production of raw materials were maintained at a constant level. The demand for other products by the producers of raw materials is in total not very large, since the proportion of total world income they receive is relatively small. Stability of the average level of prices would no doubt be an important factor toward stability of the economy as a whole, but any temporary satiation of the demand for capital goods, as described for instance by the echo principle, might not be much affected by it; nor would it eliminate instability in share prices, another important cause of cyclical fluctuations.

WAGE POLICY

Wage policy may consist either in fixation of the wage rate by the government at a level different from the rate that would have been established in a free market or by influencing the decisions of employers and employees through propaganda or more direct means, such as changes in the rate of unemployment assistance. The cyclical objective of wage policy would always be the stabilization of the level of employment. Three different wage policies may be considered.

1. The first policy advocated would be in the direction of a more pronounced and more rapid cyclical reaction of the wage rate to changes in the cyclical position of business; normally, wages respond both slowly and weakly to changes in the business-cycle position. A greater wage flexibility is advocated in order to achieve an adaptation of wage rates to changes in the profitability of industry. Such a policy would eliminate the rigidity of wages and would thus approximate more nearly the level in an economy without friction. The policy might be achieved by adjustment of wages to the cost of living index or to some index of wholesale prices. Such a policy has been advocated in the depression, on the ground that a greater demand for labor can be achieved only by a reduction in its price; but the policy has also been advocated for a boom period.

2. The opposite policy is advocated by others. They would desire an increase of wage rates in the depression, on the grounds that the depression is due to an inadequate demand for commodities and that an increase in income of the population at large, in particular of the working population, would increase that demand. An increase in hourly wage rates, it is held, would provide the required increase in income.

3. A third, and in a sense intermediate, policy advocates stability of wage rates. This would be accompanied by a gradual

increase in wages in accordance with labor productivity as a structural rather than a cyclical policy. This third policy is advocated on the grounds that by changes in wage rates so little effect can be achieved with respect to employment that the accompanying social friction makes such changes not worth the trouble. This implies, of course, that the fluctuations in employment should be eliminated by policies in other fields.

Discussions concerning wage policy, which have been particularly intensive since 1919, have gradually made clear, first qualitatively and later quantitatively, the relation between the wage rate and the volume of employment. This relation is more complicated than in the normal, partial theory of demand because the wage market is a "large market," that is, a market representing a very considerable part of the total economy and in which the position of the demand and supply curves is not independent of the exchange in the market itself; the simplified assumption of the independence of the demand and supply curves from the results of the exchange, which assumption is applicable to a small market, is therefore not permissible with respect to the labor market.

Because of this complicated structure, there is a large number of causal lines running from the wage rate to the volume of employment. An increase in wage rates, with constant methods of production, will increase the cost of production and hence make unprofitable certain marginal enterprises. On the other hand, the increase in wage rates will increase the income of those workers who were employed and continue to be employed. The demand for commodities exercised by them and their families will increase; this is a favorable factor for employment. The increased demand on the part of labor will be accompanied by a reduced demand on the part of the entrepreneurs. This offsetting factor, however, is relatively smaller, since the marginal propensity to consume of entrepreneurs is relatively small and since any investment entrepreneurs would want to make would usually be made anyway by the use of credit.

In addition to these more static influences, there are certain dynamic influences connected with changes in the wage rate. If the wage rate and hence prices increase, there will be a temporary stimulation of demand; a reduction of wages and prices, on the other hand, may lead to a speculative reduction in demand.

All these factors will make themselves felt in the relatively short run. Certain other factors operate in the somewhat longer run. Thus, in particular, an increase in wages that is considered as more or less permanent will lead to the introduction of labor-saving machinery that may not have been profitable before. The introduction of labor-saving machinery, however, may take a number of years, if it takes place gradually as old machines become obsolete.

It is clear, then, that a change in the wage rate will have both positive and negative influences on the level of employment. The question is how strong each of these influences is and in which direction the balance will be. Only statistical measurements can answer this question. Such measurements, to the extent that they have been made, would indicate that the positive and negative influences neutralize each other to a large extent. In the short run, the total effect may be considered to be slightly negative. Computations which were made for the Netherlands yielded an elasticity of employment with respect to the money wage rate somewhere between 0 and -1. It may be expected that for larger countries the effect would be less. For any small country there is always the relatively important effect via an increase in exports. Since the demand curve for exports will not be affected by changes in wage rates, one of the most important offsetting influences does not come into play as far as exports are concerned. The effect of a change in wage rates on exports is not so large, however, as is usually assumed. For many countries the effect of a reduction in prices of export products on the quantity exported has been found to be expressed by an elasticity in the order of magnitude of 1 or 2.

For a small country the total effect of a change in wage rates on employment is in any case somewhat negative, a lowering of wages leading to an increase in employment, and vice versa. This negative effect will be reinforced by the long-run effects. With respect to business-cycle policy, these further effects may be disregarded. Nevertheless, on the basis of the negative total effect, a policy of wage increases in a depression is not desirable.

In view of the minor magnitude of the effect there is much to be said for a policy of wage stability: the relatively small increase in employment that may be achieved by a severe reduction in wages would not justify the many social frictions which would inevitably accompany such a reduction.

No strong economic objections could be held against a policy that would consist in a variation of the wage rate proportional with the cost of living; one might have social objections against such a policy on account of the friction that would accompany it, but this friction itself would not seem to be altogether inevitable. Stronger social objections would seem to be in order against a policy which would make wages fluctuate with wholesale prices, unless wholesale prices themselves were considerably more stabilized than they now are.

It is clear, in any case, that one cannot expect any wage policy to stabilize employment during a business cycle. Wage policy may at best affect the profit margin per unit of product and hence make production more or less attractive to the entrepreneur; but fluctuations in this margin have only a limited and indirect influence on the volume of production. In other words, there may be a business cycle purely in terms of quantities on which prices and profit margins exercise very little influence. This possibility is also reflected in the fact that our simplest cyclical models (Examples I–IV) did not incorporate the wage rate or the price level but were conceived simply in terms of total income and the total value of output.

The experience of the last twenty years with wage policies would seem to confirm our views. Pronounced cases of wage policy can be found in Germany, the United States, and France.

In Germany all wage rates were reduced by 10 per cent in 1931 by a decree of the Brüning government. In the United States under the New Deal the wage rate was increased suddenly in the spring of 1933 by approximately 20 per cent. In France, too, the Popular Front government of Blum raised the money wage rate a number of times with sudden jumps. These cases are of particular importance in the determination of the short-run effects, because they occurred so suddenly, whereas the other economic variables that affect employment moved much more gradually. Theoretically, one would expect to see a sudden change in employment after a sudden change in the wage rate, the change in employment reflecting the isolated effect of the change in the wage rate. In actual fact, the effects of a sudden change in wages may still be distributed over more than one month; but even if the effect on employment were not entirely abrupt, a quite rapid change in employment would be expected. Yet, in none of these three cases could such a change be observed, and this fact would tend to support the belief that the total effect of changes in wage rates on the level of employment is not great.

A study by Kalecki[3] showed that with respect to France a number of the other factors practically did not change in the period he studied; the negative conclusion on the effectiveness of changes in wage rates would therefore seem to be even better founded with respect to France than with respect to the other two countries.

The relatively skeptical conclusions concerning the effectiveness of wage policy as a form of business-cycle policy would force us to pursue even more actively other forms of business-cycle policy in order to stabilize employment.

PRICE POLICY

We may consider as price policy both the indirect policies affecting prices by means of the monetary circulation and the volume of credit and the more direct forms. The latter consist of (*a*) valorization schemes, that is, purchases and sales of commodities at a fixed price, which we have discussed in connection with monetary policy, and (*b*) price fixation and price control. In this section we shall deal with the latter two policies.

Whereas in the case of valorization the government endeavors to exercise an influence on prices by regulating the quantity supplied or demanded, this is usually not the case when a policy of price fixation is pursued. But some direct intervention in the market may be necessary to make the regulation of prices effective. The fixation of prices may be quite rigid, when the gov-

3. M. Kalecki, "The Blum Experiment," *Economic Journal*, XLVIII (March, 1938), 26–41.

ernment fixes a specific price for each article; or it may be in a more flexible form, when the government issues certain regulations for the calculation of prices on the basis of certain cost components.

The objective of price policy is normally to maintain a given price level or a very gradual movement of prices. With respect to business-cycle policy the level of prices that is stabilized is of less importance than the fact that an attempt is made to stabilize prices.

The level at which prices are stabilized may, however, be of great importance from other points of view; it would, for instance, be undesirable to stabilize prices at a level far from that of free competition. The possibility of monopolistic or semi-monopolistic exploitation of consumers is one of the greatest objections to price fixation. It should further be borne in mind that stabilization of prices does not in itself guarantee a stable volume of output. If the prices of only a few commodities are stabilized, while those of other commodities continue to show cyclical fluctuations, the fluctuations in the output of the commodities whose prices have been stabilized will be reinforced: in the depression their prices will be relatively high, thus reducing demand; in the boom they will be relatively low, thus stimulating demand.

But even if the prices of all commodities were stabilized, this would not in itself be sufficient to eliminate fluctuations in production. We discussed this point when we dealt with the commodity standard which exercises a more direct influence on production, at least on raw-material production. A policy of price stabilization may be credited with the elimination of certain speculative fluctuations in the demand for commodities. Yet other fluctuations may continue to make themselves felt. Cyclical fluctuations in quantities may continue when prices have been stabilized, for instance, as a consequence of the operation of the echo principle, but also for other reasons. The stability of prices that prevailed in the United States from 1923 to 1929 did not prevent the sharp crisis of 1929.

The most important difficulty with respect to price policy is that it can be effective only if the quantities produced are also brought under control. This, however, would lead to one or another form of more direct business-cycle policy, which we shall discuss later (chap. xxii).

EXCHANGE-RATE POLICY

Exchange-rate policy is a particular form of price policy which, however, is logically different from the forms of price policy discussed so far. Exchange-rate policy applies to an individual country and cannot apply, of course, to the economy of the world as a whole. It consists in the manipulation of the rate of exchange, either by the government or by the central bank or by both in conjunction. Formally, this may take either the form of a change in the gold content of the currency unit (Irving Fisher's "Compensated Dollar"), in which case one speaks of "devaluation" if the value of the currency is reduced and of "revaluation" if the value of the currency is increased; or it may take the form of changes in the value of the currency with respect to certain other currencies, without a formal change in the price of gold. In that case the words "depreciation" and "appreciation" are normally used to describe a reduction and an increase, respectively, in the value of the currency under consideration.

The objective of exchange-rate policy is normally not primarily cyclical but rather incidental. Very often depreciation occurs under pressure, as a result of the condition of a country's balance of payments. A policy of appreciation has been followed in a number of cases for not much more than prestige considerations. A more systematic manipulation of the rate of exchange, however, has also been discussed in the last decades. The primary objective was then to combat the depression and increase the level of activity by raising the domestic price level and reinforcing the country's competitive position vis-à-vis other countries. The complement of this policy, namely, an increase of the rate of exchange to put a brake on activity in a boom period, has hardly ever occurred; this policy has been practiced, however, during war or in a postwar world-wide inflation, to protect a country from the rise of prices abroad (Sweden, Canada, New Zealand).

Exchange-rate policy is a form of price policy that operates on all prices of a country. In terms of the national currency, devaluation or depreciation will tend to raise the prices of all exported and imported commodities and hence also of most domestic commodities. The extent to which, and the speed with which, the latter will increase will be very different. As a rule, prices of commodities with a purely national market and which contain little imported materials will increase only slightly. The same will apply to the prices of the domestic factors of production, such as labor and land. Hence, profitability will normally increase, and this will stimulate the volume of output. The prices of export commodities will normally increase somewhat less than the price of foreign currencies, and export products will become cheaper, in terms of foreign currencies, than competing products of other countries. This will stimulate exports, and this stimulus will be transmitted to other industries as the export industries will increase investment and as the workers in export industries, receiving higher incomes, will demand more consumption goods. As a consequence of this, imports will also tend to increase. It is probable, although not quite certain in all cases, that, as a result of these various factors, the balance of payments will improve; but in any case there will be an increase in output, in employment, and in the volume of consumption.

All this applies to one country only. As a first approximation it may be said that the advantages which accrue to the country which depreciates are obtained at the expense of other countries and that the effect of depreciation or, for that matter, of appreciation is negligible with respect to the volume of world output.

Two qualifications should be given, however, with respect to this statement, one unfavorable with respect to the volume of world output and one favorable.

a) Depreciation may be followed by countermeasures on the part of other countries who feel injured by it. Such countermeasures may not only reduce or even nullify the advantages obtained by the country which depreciated first; they may also be in the form of restrictions on international trade which will reduce the welfare of the world as a whole.

b) On the other hand, devaluation of all currencies means an increase in the value of gold. This will tend to increase the value of all gold holdings and hence to improve the reserve position of central banks. This increased liquidity will have a certain expansionary force. The increase in the gold price will also make gold production more profitable, stimulate wage increases in that industry, and generally exercise an expansionary tendency. On account of its expansionary effect via gold holdings and gold production, a successive round of depreciations of various countries may exercise a slightly beneficial effect on the world business cycle.

It is not clear in which direction the balance of these two factors will operate for the world as a whole. But since for the world as a whole other stimuli for the business cycle with much less dubious effects are possible, we should prefer these other measures. If an increase in the world price of gold is desired, this can be achieved by a decision of all countries who are members of the International Monetary Fund, under one of its "Articles of Agreement."[4]

We may start our discussion of the experiences of exchange-rate policy in the past decades by referring to a few cases of appreciation. Guided by prestige considerations, the United Kingdom appreciated the pound sterling in 1925 to its prewar gold value. The view has now fairly generally been accepted that this appreciation caused a long-drawn-out depression in the United Kingdom, which offset the effects of the world-wide recovery from 1925 to 1929. This opinion, however, is not easily verified on the basis of statistics. A much more clear-cut opinion can be formed with respect to the not so well-known cases of Denmark and Norway, which appreciated at about the same time, also on prestige grounds. These appreciations were even stronger than that of England; the rates of exchange of the two currencies were raised by approximately 50 per cent within two years. If one compared the cyclical development in these two

4. Article IV, sec. 7, ". . . the Fund, by a majority of the total voting power, may make uniform proportionate changes in the par values of the currencies of all members, provided each such change is approved by every member which has 10 per cent or more of the total of the quotas."

countries in this relatively quiet period with those of other countries or with those of the world as a whole, it becomes quite clear that industrial production in Denmark and Norway was retarded as a result of this policy.[5]

Against these few cases of appreciation, a large number of depreciations and devaluations occurred, starting in 1929. The general cyclical development of the world at that time was much more complicated; the simple comparisons of the twenties

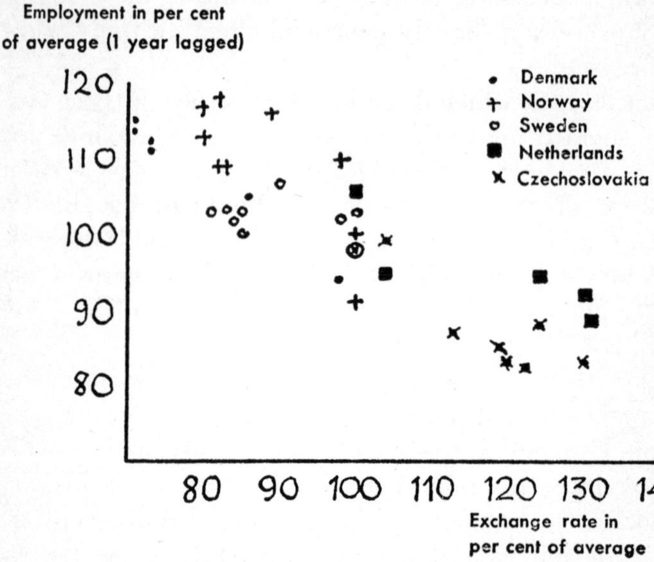

FIG. 52.—The relation between the rate of exchange and the volume of employment for the period after 1929. Both the rate of exchange and the volume of employment for each country are expressed for each year as a percentage of the average for the five countries concerned.

are therefore no longer possible, except perhaps for two of the later depreciations, namely, those of Belgium in 1935 and the Netherlands in 1936. It is in any case remarkable that in both countries employment shows a sudden upsurge very shortly after the depreciation.[6] A more reliable comparison for other countries can perhaps be made as in Figure 52. In this diagram the relative rate of exchange and the relative level of employment are plotted for each country, compared with the average

5. Cf. Fig. 31.

6. Cf. Fig. 32.

for the group of countries considered, with a lag of one year between the relative rate of exchange and the corresponding relative volume of employment. The diagram would provide a way to measure the magnitude of the effect of depreciation. Without a lag, the comparison is less clear and the correspondence between the figures less good.

The experience of individual countries would seem to indicate, therefore, a rather strong beneficial effect of devaluation and an equally large unfavorable effect of appreciation, with respect to employment. It would be much more difficult to isolate

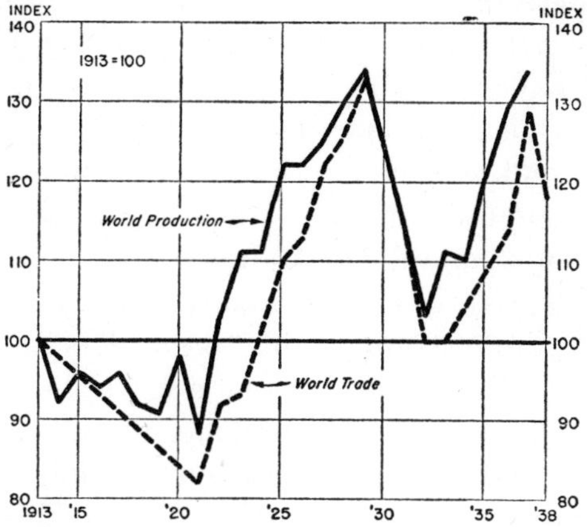

FIG. 53.—The volume of world production and the volume of world trade, 1913–37 (index numbers, 1913 = 100).

the effect on the world cycle of the series of depreciations in the thirties. It might be observed that shortly after the depreciation of sterling (in September, 1931), namely, in the first half of 1932, the world depression became worse. It might be observed also that, again shortly after the depreciation of sterling, namely, from the middle of 1932 on, a recovery in the world economy could be noted. But so many other factors were responsible both for the decline in 1931–32 and for the 1932–33 recovery that an isolation of the effects of the relatively minor factor of depreciation would be impossible.

In this connection, it is interesting to compare the development of the volume of world production and the volume of world trade (Fig. 53). It will be seen that, while the two series increased by the same amount between 1913 and 1929, the volume of trade lagged somewhat since that time compared to the volume of production, even before 1932. Up to 1936 the discrepancy is quite pronounced, but in the boom year of 1937 the volume of trade catches up again with the volume of production.

STOCK-EXCHANGE POLICY

We want to consider in this section all measures of economic policy which have as their objective the formation of prices on the stock exchange, measures whose purpose will generally be to stabilize the prices of shares. A large number of measures may be taken with this same objective, of which some will require much more detailed administration than others. Thus, (1) the increase of margin requirements will be a very global measure. On the other hand, (2) the fixation of maximum quotations is a somewhat more detailed policy, since it will require a system of allocation when demand at the maximum price exceeds the supply. Other measures are (3) taxation of speculative profits, (4) the prohibition of transactions by insiders, and (5) the registration of all share holdings above a certain minimum.

The result of the first measure mentioned, the increase in margin requirements, might be relatively minor. True, it would eliminate part of the speculative demand, and this may be helpful in periods of boom speculation; but even a relatively weak speculative demand may disturb the equilibrium. The institution of maximum quotations is a more effective measure because it would radically eliminate the possibility of making excessive profits on the stock exchange, except in unofficial dealings. Heavy taxation of speculative profits by means of a capital-gains tax would achieve nearly the same result without imposing rigidity on the market, as maximum quotations would do. The prohibition of forward transactions in shares by insiders may eliminate certain speculative movements altogether; it would be hard to estimate what the effect of this would be on the general development of share prices. The registration of shares, if complemented by other means, may lead to an almost complete control of the stock exchange; but this would lead us into the field of direct business-cycle policy. If the obligation to register were in itself to exercise a preventive influence, the effect of this policy on the share market might be important.

The effect of a reduction in speculative profits on the developments of the business cycle may be illustrated by a change in one of our cyclical models, e.g., in Example III. Let us assume that, in contrast to the earlier form of that model, now only half the increase of income between the first and the second quarter will be considered as income in the third quarter.[7] Assuming again the same disturbance of equilibrium in the first quarter, the numerical values then run as shown (all figures in deviations from the average).

EXAMPLE III′

Quarter	0	1	2	3	4	5	6	7	8
Expenditure		0	18	25	26	24	21	17	14
Income	0	20	28	29	27	23	19	15	12
(Increase in income) ÷ 2		10	4	1	−1	−2	−2	−2	−2

Continuing this computation, one will find the following figures for income: 9, 6, 3, 1, −1, −1, 0, 1, etc. It will be seen that the cyclical movement is now heavily damped with a maximum deviation of income of 29, instead of 64 as in Example III.[8]

Some experience of policies to regulate the Stock Exchange, during periods of a relatively normal business cycle, was gained in the United States after 1933, when in particular the policies under 1, 3, and 4 were applied. Despite great liquidity, the movements of the Stock Exchange remained within relatively narrow limits during that period. This, however, may also be attributed to the very moderate economic expansion in the thirties. Certain statistical investigations would lead to the conclusion, however, that the measures to limit speculation did have a noticeable effect.

7. If the speculative income were eliminated altogether, Example III would be replaced by Example I.

8. Cf. Fig. 54.

CONCLUSIONS

The conclusions of this chapter would seem to be that from an international point of view the various forms of indirect policy discussed can have only a very moderate effect. From a national point of view, exchange-rate policy may be most successful, whereas in a country where the speculative tendencies are great, an appropriate stock-exchange policy may be of relatively great importance. Only very moderate results may be expected from interest or wage policy. Credit-rationing may restrain booms, but it cannot be operative in the reverse sense. Among the various forms of monetary policy, the commodity standard offers most attractive possibilities, but it will also not always be effective nor will it, or any other form or price stabilization, necessarily prevent cyclical fluctuations in quantities at constant prices.

These conclusions imply certain assumptions concerning the quantitative extent of the forms of policy discussed. We consider, for instance, an interest policy of a conventional extent, e.g., an increase or decrease of the rate of interest by one half of 1 per cent or, at most, 1 per cent, compared with what it would have been in a free market; a wage policy which would make wages fluctuate, for instance, with the cost of living; changes in the rate of exchange by 10, 20, or 30 per cent. If the policies were to be applied in much stronger doses, the results might be nearly proportionately increased, but in many cases this will not be possible. The effects would also depend on the speed with which the policies are applied.

CHAPTER TWENTY-ONE

DIRECT POLICIES. I. EXPENDITURE POLICIES

WE SHALL now turn to a treatment of the measures of direct economic policy intended to influence trend and cyclical movements. In this chapter and the next we shall discuss measures of policy that affect the volume of output directly. We shall deal first with the expenditure policy of the government, as a very important example of direct policy that is particularly, though not exclusively, concerned with the regulation of business cycles. All other forms of direct policy will be discussed in the next chapter.

The central objective of a policy of government expenditure or, more specifically from a cyclical point of view, of a policy of compensating government expenditure is that the exercise of additional demand for goods and services by the government can compensate undesired movements in the demand by individuals and business. Such a policy would then consist in a large demand in periods of depression and a relatively smaller demand in periods of boom. This is typically a global policy; it would not require any intervention with the actions of private business.

One normally thinks in this connection of a public works policy, such as construction, road-building, canal-building, land improvement, and sometimes residential construction. Sometimes, also, military objects have been used for the same purpose.[1]

Normally, such expenditures are financed by loans; the advantage of this method of financing over financing by taxation in the depression is that it uses money which otherwise would

1. Cf. also p. 331, *infra*.

not have been used. A similar beneficial effect in a depression can be obtained with financing by the creation of credit. This would have to be compensated by the formation of reserves in periods of better conditions; if the policy were initiated during a boom period and reserves were created first, the increase in expenditures in the succeeding depression could be financed, in whole or in part, from these reserves. The policy of compensating expenditure has as its corollary that the budget is not balanced every year. In good years there will be a budget surplus and in depression years, a budget deficit. Over a whole cycle, however, the budget might be balanced; the term "cyclical budget" has been used in this connection.

The objective of this policy is to achieve a stabilization of total demand for goods and services. This objective may not be fully achieved in countries that rely to a large extent on foreign trade, but even there it may be achieved in part; hence incomes too will be relatively more stable. Seen from an incidental point of view, the policy may be considered as a remedy against depression with the objective of raising the volume of employment. In analyzing the effects, a distinction is usually made between (*a*) the direct effects, i.e., the increase of employment on the public works themselves, (*b*) the indirect effects, namely, the effects in the industries which provide the raw materials and capital goods for these public works, and (*c*) the secondary effects. The direct and the indirect effects together are called the "primary effects." The increase in incomes in the public works and in the industries which deliver the raw materials and capital goods for these works will lead to a further demand on the part of those who have received these incomes; this demand in turn will lead to a further increase in income; and so on in successive rounds. The total increase in income in these rounds is called the secondary effect of the public works policy. The advantage of government expenditure as an antidepression policy is that the total effects (the primary and secondary combined) are far in excess of the primary effects; thus it might be said that the government not only obtains the finished public works but also enriches the community with more goods and services.

After this brief exposition of the main motives for a policy of compensating government expenditure, we shall discuss in some more detail the different aspects of this policy, referring to both the protagonists and the antagonists of the policy. The first question to be discussed is whether the objective will actually be achieved.

Compensating government expenditures might succeed in approximately stabilizing the total demand in terms of money for goods and services. This would also stabilize all incomes and hence the total demands, both on the part of entrepreneurs for investment and on the part of families for consumption purposes, for we have seen that both demands depended first of all on the level of national income and on its components (chap. xiii). To some extent, the demand would also depend on the level of prices, but prices, too, will tend to be much more stable if total income is stabilized. Hence, compensating government expenditure or, more precisely, the readiness of the government to engage in compensating expenditure would lead to a stabilization of the "natural" factors determining demand and would hence make itself superfluous.

The policy of compensating government expenditure might be expressed by a great reduction in the marginal propensity to spend, that is to say, in the ratio between an increase in income and the resulting increase in expenditure on consumption and investment goods. In our Example III we assumed this ratio at 0.9. Let us assume now that, as a result of compensating government expenditure, the ratio were reduced to 0.1. This would affect the course of income and expenditure in Example III as shown.

EXAMPLE III″

Quarter	0	1	2	3	4	5	6	7	8
Expenditure		0	2	2	0	−2	−2	−1	2
Income	0	20	22	4	−18	−24	−8	+15	+25
Increase in income		20	2	−18	−22	−6	+16	+23	+10

The further course of income for quarters 9 through 14 would be as follows: 13, −11, −25, −17, 6, 24, etc. It appears then that the cyclical movement would have a much shorter period, namely, six to seven quarters as against five years; and the maximum deviation would also be much reduced.

Figure 54 compares the development of income in Example III (business-cycle movement without policy), Example III′ (business-cycle movement with part of the speculative income eliminated), and Example III″ (business-cycle movement with compensating government expenditure).

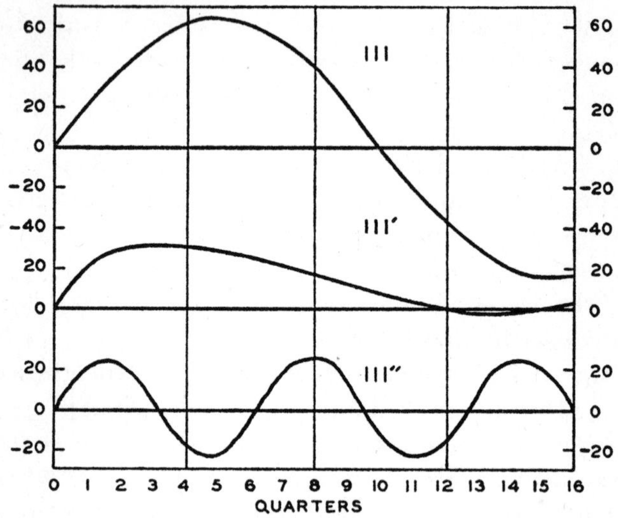

FIG. 54.—Fluctuation in national income: (*a*) without business-cycle policy according to III; (*b*) if speculative incomes are reduced to one-half (III′); (*c*) with compensating government expenditure (III″).

It has sometimes been held that the method of compensating government expenditure is a superficial form of business-cycle policy, since it attacks only symptoms and does not provide the necessary basic corrections A sharp distinction should be made here, however, between the initial application and the application after a certain time. Initially, one may consider this a symptomatic policy; but, as income becomes stabilized, basic corrections do take place: excessive expansion of capital and investment in the wrong direction are prevented. These are the two developments that will occur if profits are unusually high and prices and the rate of interest deviate too far from their normal position; and these situations will be prevented if stability is achieved over a longer period of time. Whether the ultimate objective is achieved depends on whether the policy will actually lead to the effects set out above. Whether incomes will actually be stabilized depends in particular on the three following factors: (1) the time at which the additional expenditures are started, (2) the extent of the expenditures, and (3) the responses of the entrepreneurs which are of particular importance in the second chain of the argument, namely, that a stabilization of income will lead to a stabilization of demand and hence to a continued stabilization of income.

In principle, a policy of additional expenditure may be started at any phase of the cycle, with such a (positive or negative) amount of additional income as would be necessary to achieve the level of expenditure desired; but the least disturbance and the smallest discontinuity will be produced if the policy is initiated at the time that the level desired is very nearly approximated. If we accept the position that the level to be approximated is that of full employment, the proper time to start the policy would be at the end of the boom. Some students believe for various reasons that this would not be possible or indeed desirable. There is considerable difference of opinion on this point. Optimists believe that the execution of a moderate amount of public works immediately after the start of a depression would nip in the bud the depressive tendencies, so that relatively small amounts would suffice. On the other extreme, there is the most pessimistic belief that in the beginning of a depression the effect of increased government expenditure will be quite small, that it will be better to wait until the crisis has nearly run its course, and that expenditure on a large scale will be necessary at that time to achieve any success.

Another of the rather pessimistic opinions is that, although it might be desirable to start compensating public expenditure at an early time, it would usually be technically impossible to do so. We shall come back later to this more technical point of the inevitable lag in government expenditure.

A solution of these controversies depends on two important questions. In the first place, on the question we mentioned as to how the individual entrepreneur responds to an increase in government expenditure; and, second, on what other objective factors determine private expenditure for investment and consumption goods.

In the period between 1933 and 1939, when government expenditure was applied for the first time on a considerable scale as a remedy against depression in the United States, the tendency of business to consider public expenditure as something altogether artificial and as a form of government intervention which was undesirable in itself was quite pronounced. This attitude showed itself in a very hesitating response of business with respect to the actual signs of economic recovery. With such response, the policy was inevitably doomed to failure, independent of its intrinsic merits from an objective point of view. If the entrepreneurs were consistently to disregard all the consequences of the increased public expenditure and respond only to what would have happened without this expenditure, the business cycle in the private sector would remain unchanged and the only beneficial effect would be the primary effect. If the additional government expenditure on public works were offset in whole or in part by a reduction in private investment, for fear of "government competition," the net effect could actually be zero, as the primary effect would also be offset by a negative primary effect reflecting a reduction in private investment. In such a situation, the depressive tendencies might continue, for instance, as a result of the echo effect, and, independent of the level of national income, investment might remain at a low level for some time.

If the entrepreneurs did not respond in this way, a policy of compensating expenditure started immediately after the early signs of a depression would have much more favorable effects. The corresponding higher level of national income would increase the level of expenditure by entrepreneurs for investment; but in the echo principle were operative, some decline in investment expenditure would be inevitable, and in order to maintain total expenditure at a stable level, a continued stream of government expenditure would be required. Therefore, assuming a more positive attitude on the part of entrepreneurs, we would come to a position somewhat between the most optimistic and most pessimistic points of view: a public works policy should be started as soon as possible; it may prove, however, that the immediate compensation of the reduction in national income is not sufficient to prevent a depression completely and that government expenditure will have to be continued for a longer period of time.

With respect to the second point, that of the extent of expenditure, some remarks have already been made. It would not be possible to count on a small amount as adequate, at least not the first time. On the other hand, the amount is in all probability smaller than what is sometimes calculated on the basis of past depressions; for, once a policy of compensating government expenditure has been accepted, depressions will be less pronounced and hence the amount required will be smaller.

We have also already dealt in part with the third point, the reactions of the entrepreneurs: an unreasonable amount of distrust on the part of business would, of course, make any favorable result of the policy impossible. If, however, it were possible to persuade employers that the policy is fundamentally correct and if business learned to make a distinction between this type of government policy, which is sound, and other possible government policies, which are not sound, it may be hoped that in the future the reaction of entrepreneurs will not be so negative as it was in the United States between 1933 and 1939.

As we shall show, the policy is indeed fundamentally sound. It is a sound principle that all productive resources should be used; the policy is financially possible if there is no hoarding and if money is created only in proportion to the trend increase in production. Government policies to compensate private demand, with precedence for the latter in order to approximate as closely as possible the optimum utility in accordance with the preferences of individual consumers, constitute an equally sound principle. Provided it is properly financed, i.e., provided that neither too much money is created nor too much borrowed, the policy of compensating government expenditure is therefore sound in principle. It is interesting to observe in this connection that proper financing depends to a large extent on the very fact of the co-operation and understanding of the entrepreneurs. The two factors influence each other. The more positive the response of entrepreneurs, the less will it be necessary to rely on less appropriate methods of financing; conversely, if entrepreneurs hoard their additional income, the financing methods will be less appropriate.

In summary we may say that the objective of a public expenditure policy can indeed be achieved, provided that (1) entrepreneurs understand that the policy is sound in principle and act accordingly and (2) the government spend adequate amounts to bridge the decline in private expenditure that may occur even if national income is kept at a constant level (in particular decline due to the operation of the echo principle).

To indicate the extent to which the objective is achieved and to measure the results of a public works policy, the concept of the "multiplier" has been introduced. This concept has been used both with respect to income and with respect to employment ("income multiplier" and "employment multiplier"). The multiplier indicates the ratio between the total increase of the variable considered and the primary increase. As indicated, the primary increase of employment or of income is considered to consist of both direct primary employment (and income) and indirect primary employment (and income).

The two simplest cases of a calculation of the multiplier are the following. In the first case (I), the additional government expenditure occurs during one time unit (e.g., year); in all following time units, expenditure falls back to the earlier level. In a second case (II), there is a permanent increase in government expenditure by a constant amount. In both cases, the results will in principle continue over an infinite period of time. In case I, income will be higher in the period of increased government expenditure but also in succeeding periods, in a decreasing series, as a result of the successive rounds of expenditure of the additional primary income. In case II, a new stationary level of income and employment will be reached (under certain simplifying assumptions), and the multiplier will indicate the ratio between the increase in the level of income and the amount of the increased government expenditure.

In case I, the multiplier should be considered as the ratio between the total additional income (or employment) and the additional income (or employment) of the public works in the one period of time; in case II, it is the ratio between the increase in the annual rate of income (compared to the period prior to the execution of the public works) and the increase in the annual rate of income in connection with the public works themselves.

Not only is a multiplier calculated in connection with additional government expenditure. The concept has also been used with respect to investment as a whole, including private investment. This method is closely linked with the concept that private investment is independent of the general economic position and that the fluctuations in income may be understood as the result of these independent fluctuations in investment. Even if one does not accept this position and considers investment to be primarily determined by endogenous factors, the multiplier may still be used in this way. It should be realized, however, that a multiplier derived from empirial observation of the relative fluctuations of national income and investment is not applicable to the calculation of the effects of a certain amount of additional investment, if investment itself is in part caused by endogenous factors, for the empirical fluctuations of investment and income will show, in that case, not only the effect of investment on income but also the effect of income on investment.

The size of the multiplier depends on the reactions of the various consumer and producer units which receive the additional income. Calculations of the multiplier have usually been made on the assumption of a severe depression, so that no additional investment as a result of additional income could be expected. Where private investment is taken as the multiplicand, it is assumed that a certain amount of additional private investment occurs but that the resulting increase in income does not provoke any further private investment. The multiplier is then based exclusively on the effects on consumption. All results of saving are "lost" and are considered as "leakages." Saving is considered identical with hoarding. That part of consumption expenditure which is spent on imports is also considered as a leakage. The effect on exports via the increase in income abroad is usually disregarded, as being of minimal size.

Hence the increased income in the second round, owing to increased expenditure on consumption, will be smaller than in the first round. Again, the third round will be smaller than the second one and, it is usually assumed, in approximately the same ratio. The total increase in income or employment obtained by this method will be a finite amount which will be the larger, the smaller the leakages, that is, the larger the marginal propensity to consume and the smaller the marginal propensity to import. The marginal propensity to consume will be large in a country with a very poor population where practically all additional income will be spent on consumption. The propensity will be much smaller in a country with considerable unemployment compensation; for in that case the expenditure by the government on public works will be offset in part by a reduction of government expenditure on unemployment assistance, and the multiplier (measured with respect to the expenditure on public works) will thus be reduced. The marginal propensity to import is small in large countries, and the multiplier in such countries will on this account be higher.

For countries with relatively large international trade, such as England, Germany, Denmark, the Netherlands, multipliers in the order of magnitude of $1\frac{1}{2}$–2 have been computed. For a country like the United States, with very little international trade, one may come to figures as high as 3 or 4. As has been mentioned, all these computations were based on the assumption that additional government expenditure did not lead to increased private investment. One might make a more optimistic assumption, namely, that as a result of the increase in profits investment will increase also. This has often been the expectation when public works policies were initiated. The expression "pump-priming" reflected that expectation. If additional investment occurs, the multiplier will become higher; it may even become infinitely large if an injection of additional purchasing power at one time should lead to a lasting improvement.

On the other hand, it is also conceivable and actually possible that, as a result of public works policy, private investment and even consumption expenditure is reduced below the level it would have had otherwise. This, as we have mentioned, may occur if there is a certain distrust in the future because of the increased government expenditure in particular and of the fact of state intervention in general. This would reduce the multiplier and might even bring it below unity.

For an empirical determination of the magnitude of the multiplier, one would need to know the development of income and employment that would have occurred without the execution of the additional government expenditure program whose consequences one endeavors to measure. This is by no means a simple assignment. One could in principle know this development, if one knew quantitatively all relations which determine the fluctuations of the economy under consideration. In this case one could, as we have done in our various examples, extrapolate a movement that has started and hence one could determine how this movement would have continued without government intervention. In this way, one could conceivably have measured how large employment in the United States or Germany would have been after 1932 without government intervention. Our present measurements, however, hardly permit us to make such computations. No attempts to compute the multiplier in a concrete case of government policy have been made in this way as far as we are aware.

Those authors who have expressed an opinion on the effectiveness of a government expenditure policy, without making any specific reference to the development which would have occurred without the government's policy, make, nevertheless, an implicit assumption with respect to this difficult question. This applies, for instance, to the computations of Gayer.[2] For each of the years 1933–37 he compared the year-to-year increase in national income with the absolute amount of income-creating expenditure of the government and finds that the latter are about one-half the former. On the assumption that the income velocity of money is about 2 per year, Gayer then concludes that the recovery can be attributed almost completely to the government's expenditure policy. Clearly, the assumption that an additional amount of money A brought into circulation by government expenditure will *forever* continue to produce a rate

2. Arthur D. Gayer, "Fiscal Policies," *American Economic Review*, XXVIII, No. 1 (March, 1938), suppl. 101.

of increase of income of $2A$ per annum implies the very unrealistic assumption of an infinitely large multiplier (provided that enough time is allowed). This assumption leads Mr. Gayer almost certainly to an overestimate of the effect of the government measures and hence to too pessimistic a view with respect to the natural recovery. It is probable that without the intervention of the government a certain recovery would have taken place anyway and that only part of the actual recovery is attributable to government expenditure.

The effect of the additional government expenditure has been analyzed in another way.[3] For the period prior to 1933 the relation between national income and a number of other factors, on the one hand, and expenditure for consumption and private investment, on the other hand, can be established. This relation has then been tested for the period 1933–37. It appeared that at the same level of national income and of the other factors a considerably lower amount was spent for consumption and for private investment than would have been the case prior to 1933. It would appear from this test that private consumption and private investment showed a lesser degree of response than would have been "normal" in the preceding period. This may have been due to the general dislike, on the part of business, of government intervention and to the fact that some of the concrete measures of government policy aroused the specific hostility of business because they were believed to affect profit expectations unfavorably. The vacillations of the government's business policy may also have had an unfavorable effect on investment expenditure. Often one measure was incompatible with another, and it took a number of years before the various forms of business-cycle policy were co-ordinated.

With respect to the cyclical effect of additional government expenditures, the concrete nature of the projects to which the additional demand of the government is directed is of secondary significance. In times of depression it is a matter of prime importance to keep the level of expenditure to that of income; the great social benefit of the works is due to the fact that they

3. In an unpublished study by J. Tinbergen.

enable a large number of persons to continue to make their normal expenditure since their income is maintained.

But, from a more general point of view, the choice of projects is also of great importance. The more these projects contribute to an increase in welfare, the better. It is most desirable that they also make possible a permanent increase in employment. This will occur particularly if the objects of expenditure are capital goods that can be used profitably in the future. But such cases will be rare, because, in those circumstances, the capital goods would normally have been produced by private initiative. Among many projects possible, it will, in any case, be necessary to select those that are most desirable from the point or view of the community as a whole. A certain order of priority will have to be established; here, certain computations to which we will refer below can be helpful.

A great variety of projects is possible, and no dogmatic choice among them can be made. One may first select projects that are normally part of ordinary government expenditure. The continuation at the normal level of ordinary government services should have a high priority. The development of underdeveloped areas, much poorer in capital goods than the countries which suffer unemployment, is also of great importance. From a world point of view, there is great utility in the construction of capital goods for areas like China. Many projects of public works at home may be mentioned in third place. After all these possibilities have been exhausted, there would always be the possibility of producing consumption goods to be made available to low-income groups free of charge. Only if there were good reasons to believe that there was no further need, appropriately measured, for any of these things, could some unemployment be accepted; in that case, however, the unemployment should be distributed more equally over the population and should be accompanied by such measures as an increase in the school age, in paid vacations, etc.

A proper order of these various projects should, as far as possible, be established on the basis of objective calculations. These calculations, of course, can never provide a final answer. Many imponderable factors enter into the decision. Thus, a comparison of the need for a new hospital with the need for a new school or for the expansion of public utilities can never be made simply by measurement; nevertheless, if certain norms are accepted, certain computational elements may enter into this choice. Not everyone, however, will be prepared to accept the same norms. The choice of a proper priority scale in government expenditure is, of course, not a difficulty that is peculiar to the policy of compensating government expenditure. It exists in any case with respect to government expenditure.

Any computation should consist in a comparison of profits and losses. In the projects under consideration these two concepts have to be considered from a social point of view. The question at issue is not the income and cost for the treasury but for the community as a whole; for this purpose both income and cost have to be expressed as well as possible in terms of money.

The yield of the project is the increase in income of all members of the community that results from the creation of the particular project; its cost is the increase in costs to all members of the community. When the project is a capital good, the yield will consist, first of all, in the yield of the output for which it is used. If the products of the capital goods are not actually sold but are given away without charge, it will nevertheless be possible, even though it may not always be simple, to estimate an amount in money for this yield. Thus, the opening of a bridge on which no toll is levied will constitute a decrease in transportation costs for many enterprises and individual persons. Inquiries may show the amount of saving in transportation costs. If consumption goods are delivered free of charge, their price in the free market may be taken as a yardstick, provided that the quantity distributed free is small in comparison to the total production of the goods in question.

Cost will consist in the first place in interest and redemption of the cost of the capital good. As to the labor cost, one should not include the full wages of workers who would otherwise have been unemployed but a smaller amount. The amount included in cost will depend on the point of view. The simplest, but perhaps somewhat too fiscal, point of view would be to take only the difference between the wage and the amount of unemployment assistance that would have been paid otherwise. One may also take as a basis the consideration that the work constitutes for the re-employed workers not a real disutility but perhaps rather a positive enjoyment. If one could assume that the position was just intermediate, the social cost of labor might be put equal to zero. The costs would, further, consist in the operating costs of the capital good. With respect to these costs, similar considerations apply. If the capital employed was previously "unemployed," the interest may also be computed as zero.

An example may indicate how some of the so-called "imponderable" factors may be taken into consideration. In order to estimate the value of the output of a hospital, one might assume that every patient would be charged the price he would just be prepared to pay. It would be possible to get an impression of this magnitude by means of an inquiry.

Apart from these calculations, other data will play a role in the selection of the order in which certain projects will be taken up. The time necessary for their execution is an important element, so are possible technical relations with other projects, the geographical position of the project, the share of direct labor cost in total cost, the possibility of postponing the project in whole or in part or of executing it again in whole or in part at an increased or reduced rate, and, finally, the amount of foreign exchange that would be involved.

In order to enable the responsible authorities to make a rapid selection of the various projects, an inventory of projects should be available that provides a convenient record of these various elements for all possible public works. The choice among these possibilities will then depend on the particular situation in which the projects are undertaken, such as the geographical distribution of unemployment, the location of the different industries, the requirements of the balance of payments, etc.

It is clear that the speed with which the government responds to the beginnings of a depression is of great importance for the success of a policy of compensating expenditure. If the lag were to be very large, for instance, some four years, or half a cycle, the additional government expenditure would occur just at the time when the cycle in the private sector of the economy would have recovered and the effects of the expenditure would be to reinforce rather than to flatten the business cycle. The lag must therefore be brief, although it is not quite necessary that the government's intervention be immediate. Complicated procedures make for a rather considerable lag in most countries; according to Professor J. M. Clark, a period of about a year between the decision to execute a certain work and the start of its actual execution represented the normal speed of procedures.[4] Various ways are open to reduce this lag; a measure of great importance is the advance preparation of plans for public works with periodic minor revisions of these plans. Swedish experience of the years between 1933 and 1938 indicates that much shorter lags are possible; on the average, there was a lapse of only four and a half months before the actual execution of a particular work could be taken in hand. One of the main causes of delay is usually the desirability of having certain works executed by state or local authorities. An important measure to speed up such authorities might be to make the amount of financial assistance from the central government dependent on their speed of action.

One of the most important aspects of a government expenditure policy is the method of financing. While the choice of projects is immaterial from the point of view of business-cycle policy, the method of financing is of prime importance; improper financing may spoil all useful effects of a government expenditure policy. What matters primarily is the net amount of expenditure by which the total demand of the private economy is increased in times of depression and reduced in boom times. If public works in the depression were financed by new taxes which would lead to a restriction of private expenditure, part or all of the additional demand exercised by the government would be destroyed, and the effect would be unfavorable. Financing should, therefore, be done from any one of these three sources: (*a*) reserves previously formed, (*b*) borrowing, or (*c*) the creation of money.

It would be most desirable to finance from reserves previously

4. J. M. Clark, *The Economics of Planning Public Works* (Washington, D.C., 1934), p. 63.

formed; but this requires that such reserves have actually been formed in the preceding boom. If no reserves are available, the choice is between the creation of money and borrowing. There is much to be said for the issuing of government bonds during a depression; we shall refer to this below. But here, too, there are certain limits. As a final means remains the creation of money.

The advantage of the creation of money is that it does not involve the payment of interest. Its great danger lies in the possibility of creating an excessive quantity of money which later on may lead to uncontrollable inflation with its well-known dangerous effects on the economy. Thus, particular care will have to be taken with regard to the scale on which money is created.

The creation of money can in any case be accepted to the extent of the desirable annual increase in the circulation. One will have to bear in mind in this connection that, in the absence of a 100 per cent reserve system, a certain expansion of the note circulation may permit a very much larger expansion of the quantity of bank money. Careful observation and, if necessary, binding regulations with respect to reserve requirements are therefore necessary accompaniments of this policy.

In a period of depression, however, when there is a tendency toward hoarding, the creation of additional money may not in itself be dangerous. At that time there is no risk of inflationary consequences in the creation of additional money. But when there are signs of recovery, full attention should be given to the problem of excess money, and the government should be prepared to take the necessary measures. These may consist in an increase in reserve percentages, a reduction in government activity, and (if there are tendencies of excessive tension in the fields of prices or of production) the fixation of prices and the rationing of credit. It may be hoped, however, that if a policy of compensating government expenditure is successful in greatly reducing the depths of the depression, the recovery will also be much less pronounced and serious measures will rarely, if ever, be necessary. In order to judge the situation, sharp business-cycle observations will be required, paying attention in particular to the quantity of money and its composition, as well as to the various other types of assets and their prices (shares, bonds, real capital goods of all sorts), in order to discover as early as possible any disturbance of equilibrium in the financial sphere. The tendencies toward disequilibrium in the share market could have been observed long before September, 1929!

The preceding paragraphs were concerned primarily with the business-cycle objectives of a policy of government expenditure, i.e., with stimulation in the depression and restraint in the boom. In addition to this, it may be desirable, in a country in which the level of private demand is inadequate, to raise the general level of employment by a policy of government expenditure. In that case, there may be room for a permanent component in the additional government expenditure. How should this component be financed? The financing should be done from resources that can be used permanently without disturbing the equilibrium of the economy. A major part will probably be required to be financed from taxes, levied on income groups with a high marginal propensity to save, since excessive saving is the cause of underemployment. A further source of financing will be the desirable annual increase in the money supply (in proportion to the expansion of production) and, lastly, the acceptable annual increase in the government debt.

It will be clear that there will be no problem of permanent unemployment in an economy in which a gradually increasing amount of real income is continuously spent on consumption or investment, provided that there was full employment initially. These conditions will be realized only if business as a whole makes adequate profits; and this in turn will require a proper relationship between the price level and the wage level. We shall refer to this point in chapter xxiii.

We referred to borrowing as one of the methods of financing. Borrowing in periods of depression is usually considered legitimate, provided that the amounts are repaid in boom periods. This repayment, however, may involve certain dangers; the repayment of considerable amounts in boom periods may lead to excessive investment. Some neutralization of the repayment by increased taxes may therefore be necessary, in order to channel back to the government certain amounts that would otherwise have increased the aggregate demand. To the extent that the yield of these taxes exceeds the level of government expenditure, it may be employed as a business-cycle reserve. This reserve should not, of course, be "invested," in the normal sense of the word, since in that case it would again be added to the circulation. Rather, the reserve should be sterilized or blocked. In a simple exposition it might be said that it should be put in a stock of banknotes; more realistically, it should be kept in a blocked account with the central bank or used to reduce the government's debt with the central bank below the statutory limit.

For various reasons, the method of borrowing is not suitable for application on a very large scale. Every increase in the government debt leads to an increase of the interest burden, and there is, no doubt, a certain optimum of the government debt which should not be exceeded. To the extent that new debt is floated for profitable projects whose yield can finance the interest, there is not much objection to an increase in the debt. Social security funds and institutional investors require, moreover, a certain amount of government debt: the interest provides a stable form of income to these investors. A certain minimum of government bonds should also be held by the banks, to make possible an open-market policy to lower the rate of interest.

The danger of an excessive government debt should not be considered so much in terms of the "interest burden" as with respect to the redistribution of income it involves: certain amounts are taken from the taxpayers by a variety of taxes and are turned over to the holders of government bonds as interest. If it were possible to finance the increased interest payments by means of taxes levied on the owners of government bonds only, and in proportion to their holdings, no difficulties would arise, of course; for every holder the payments would, so to say, go from one pocket into another. Such an arrangement, however, is impossible and undesirable; it would be an inequitable distribution of taxes. It might be possible to distribute the tax over all holders of wealth and thus to eliminate at least one of the most important objections against an increase in the public debt, namely, that it leads to an increase in taxation of producers for the benefit of nonproducers. But since the specific direction of taxes in the ways indicated will be limited, the size of the public debt itself cannot be increased at will.

In a country in which foreign trade plays a large role, a policy of compensating government expenditure involves additional risks, if the world cycle is not stabilized. A considerable increase of government expenditure in times of depression will lead to additional imports. If, owing to the persistence of depressed conditions abroad, exports continue at a low level, it will be necessary to cede gold or foreign exchange or to depreciate the currency. There is always a certain risk in currency depreciation, since it may be interpreted—according to perhaps outdated financial standards—as an indication of weakness either of the government's financial policy or of the currency itself. Depreciation may therefore lead to a withdrawal of foreign capital or to a flight of domestic capital and thus to further depreciation which it may be difficult to control.

The first and most desirable way of eliminating these risks would be the international synchronization of business-cycle policy. If this synchronization is not successful, the country will nevertheless be able to engage, to a considerable extent, in business-cycle policy of its own, if it disposes of an adequate reserve of foreign exchange. If a country has an "international margin," it will be able to allow internal expansion while maintaining its rate of exchange. It may further be possible to keep the balance of trade in equilibrium by special trade agreements. Centralization and bulk purchasing of the raw-material requirements, which follow from the execution of public works and the resulting secondary employment, may be used to bargain for additional export possibilities. Another possibility is to combine a policy of expansionary government expenditure with a policy of import restrictions. Public works may be selected in such a way as to minimize the import component. In the absence of an international margin, it may be necessary, as a final measure, to introduce a very strict regulation of foreign trade and foreign payments, in order to stabilize both the rate of exchange and the domestic price level.

It is somewhat difficult to add to these general considerations a description of the experience of compensating government expenditure. It is true that in the period since 1929, measures have been taken in many countries that were generally in the direction of the policies outlined above; but, as we shall see, many of these measures were tentative and uncertain. The principles and conclusions outlined in this chapter have only gradually crystallized from recent experience; one might say, therefore, that these policies, as such, have not yet actually been put into operation. It should also be added that the experience of the thirties has not yet been subjected to any general and profound analysis.

The policy of government expenditure as an antidepression measure—because this is the form in which the policy was executed—has been applied on a large scale only in the United States and Germany. In England this policy was shunned as a matter of principle. Some smaller countries, such as Belgium and Sweden, have also applied the method, but in a measure which was smaller both absolutely and relatively; in some countries, finally, such as the Netherlands, governments were forced against their will into deficits in the depression and adopted an intentional policy of deficit financing only much later and on a very small scale.

As a matter of fact, those governments which had adopted the policy in principle, like the governments of Belgium and Sweden, have gone less far, quantitatively, than those governments which objected to the policy in principle. Here the figures are a more important guide than the avowed principles.

The projects of expenditure have in general been public works; but there are important local distinctions. In Germany rearmament became soon one of the main objects of expenditure. In the United States special operations such as soil-conservation measures and the Tennessee Valley Authority project may be mentioned in particular. Even for a country like the Netherlands, with a very high percentage of arable land, an adequate supply of public utilities, good streets, sewerage, schools, it was not difficult to establish a long list of projects for which the need could be considered as entirely serious.[5] An interesting experience in the Netherlands was that public works executed by private business with government subsidy (in particular, land improvement) cost the Treasury less than the unemployment assistance of the same workers would have cost; in accordance with the principles developed earlier, the execution of these works was therefore perfectly proper. The same financial results were not obtained in the reclamation of the Zuider Zee, if the value of the land produced is taken at market prices; but the reclamation appears profitable if account is also taken of the opportunity for work that the land offered to people who would otherwise have been unemployed.[6]

Sweden is the country in which the first attempt has been made to make an inventory of suitable public works projects, to be used if and when a new depression would occur.

Public works have generally been financed by loans. Thus, in the United States, the public debt increased greatly during the thirties, owing to the large public works program; and similarly in Germany. In Sweden, where borrowing also occurred, a beginning of debt redemption was made rather quickly. Finland was one of the countries that instituted an official business-cycle reserve. Generally speaking, recovery was too moderate to allow the accumulation of important reserves; in the Anglo-Saxon countries at least, the downturn came as early as 1937, when unemployment had by no means been eliminated. Apparently it had not been possible to move the equilibrium level upward to a point of full employment, at the business-cycle equilibrium. The effects of the oncoming war were also clearly noticeable, so that business-cycle policy became indistinguishable from rearmament policy.

The timing of government expenditure in the years after 1929 was extremely slow. An appeal to continue investing was made to the public utilities in the United States very soon after the crisis, but the extent to which this appeal was heeded was by

5. Cf. the Dutch Labor party's *Plan van de Arbeid* ("Labor Plan") (Amsterdam, 1935).

6. Centraal Bureau voor de Statistiek, "Computation of the Social Value of Land" (in Dutch), *Maandschrift*, XXXVIII (1943), 22.

no means adequate to provide a counterweight to the depressing tendencies. A full realization of the depth of the depression was necessary before the need of extensive public works appeared convincing. No country started its public works program before late in 1932. In Germany the beginning was made at the end of that year, in the United States late in 1933, in Sweden also in 1933, and in Belgium and the Netherlands even later.

With respect to the results achieved, only a few adequate analyses have been made, as we have noted. The results in the United States have no doubt remained below expectations; one of the most important reasons for this has been discussed earlier.[7] In Germany "full employment" was achieved, but the scale of rearmament expenditure was vastly greater than that of public works expenditure in the United States. It is generally assumed that the success of the public works policy in Sweden was considerable, in the sense that a pronounced recovery occurred; but factors other than the public works policy may also have been responsible for this recovery. Among these other factors, the depreciation of the krone, the government support to agriculture, and the favorable tendencies in the demand for Sweden's main export commodities may be mentioned; also, Sweden still had in its industries important possibilities of development, such as did not exist to the same extent in other countries. Some indication of the success of the policy of government expenditure may nevertheless be derived from a comparison with Finland, a country which in many respects was in a position similar to that of Sweden (Fig. 33, p. 87).

The public works policy had no serious balance of payments effects in the cases of Sweden and the United States, as both countries had quite adequate reserves of gold and foreign exchange; both, moreover, had recently improved their competitive position by devaluation. In the United States, in any case, the problem of foreign trade is of such relatively minor importance that the question did not really arise there. Belgium, too, had devalued its currency before engaging on a program of government expenditure. But in Germany the balance of payments

7. Cf. p. 57, *supra*.

problems were extremely serious. Germany did not want to devalue because of the strong inflation fears carried over from the twenties, and it had very small foreign-exchange reserves. For these reasons it had to combine its expansionary financial policy with an extremely strict system of exchange control.

In summary we may state that extremely interesting experience has been gained in many elements of the policy which may be of great use in the future but that a real policy of compensating government expenditure, started in time and understood and appreciated by all groups of the economy, has not yet been applied.

CHAPTER TWENTY-TWO

DIRECT POLICIES. II. OTHER FORMS

IN THIS chapter we shall discuss other forms of policy intended to promote the stability of production by acting on production directly. We do not include in this discussion the business-cycle policy of a completely planned economy; the problems raised by a planned economy are entirely different from the business-cycle problems under discussion and cannot conveniently be incorporated in this study. We shall limit ourselves, therefore, to various forms of the partial regulation of production and among those in particular to measures that have been generally advocated, either because they are directed at a strategic variable in business-cycle policy or because they appear to have particularly favorable possibilities of success. Some of the measures to be mentioned have been advocated on both counts.

INVESTMENT CONTROL

A policy advocated in particular from a strategic business-cycle point of view is the control of investment. This policy would be applied particularly in the boom, in order to prevent unjustified expansion of capital with resulting partial overinvestment. It may be applied by such instruments as construction permits, allocation of raw materials, or allocation of capital goods.

If the regulation of investment is successful, it will have a very considerable influence on activity in general; the fluctuations in investment are of sufficient importance, and the fluctuations in consumption are to a sufficient extent derived, to make stabilization of the former an important instrument in the stabilization of the latter. In a country with much international trade it would be useful to restrict investment in good times as much as possible, in order to free resources for exports, while concentrating investments in depression times. This policy would require priority for investment in the export industries in boom periods.

Restrictions on investment in boom periods may lead to excess liquidity, which in turn may unduly stimulate the prices of shares or lead to an undue expansion of luxury consumption. The policy of investment control should therefore be accompanied either by reduction of this excess purchasing power or by rationing and price control in these other fields.

Investment control may be regulated by various criteria.

a) A rather rough procedure would be to ration, in proportion to the quantities of raw materials or semimanufactured products used in a preceding period.

b) A more refined method would be to allocate on the basis of degree of urgency, which may be judged according to various criteria. With respect to new investment, these criteria might include the expected profits, turnover, or employment; with respect to reinvestment, the age of the capital goods to be replaced, the degree of capacity used of the enterprise, etc.

c) The best criterion would be found by a recalculation, on the basis of certain uniform procedures, of the calculations that guided the individual entrepreneurs in their investment plans; the purpose of this recalculation would be to eliminate all elements of excessively optimistic analysis or prognosis of the business-cycle position. Thus the estimates of prices, costs, and turnover could be reconsidered in a systematic way from a general point of view.

The first criterion introduces a certain amount of rigidity, which is undesirable in general and particularly undesirable in the field of investment; the enterprises or industries that have had large investment activity in a preceding period should not continue to have it in the next period; new industries will require much more investment than old industries, the demand for whose products may be completely satisfied. With respect to the second method, the allocation of a degree of urgency on the basis of divergent criteria implies almost always that the relative importance of these various criteria has to be reconciled by a rather arbitrary choice of statistical "weights"; the measurement of some of the individual characteristics of a qualitative character is, moreover, in itself sometimes rather arbitrary. In order to eliminate these disadvantages, one should start out from the theoretical point of view that the order of importance of investments should depend on their profitability and that a computation of this profitability should give an unambiguous order of priority. However, the difficulty here is that in practice many of these computations are not very certain, much less certain, in fact, than one might think, and that some account has also to be taken of various imponderable factors. It would seem, therefore, that a certain amount of weighting with somewhat arbitrary weights, as well as the use of somewhat arbitrary numbers for some of the imponderable factors, will always be inevitable. The elimination of excessive cyclical elements by the third method will in any case provide an improvement in the selection of projects.

An important objection raised against investment control is that this form of detailed economic policy will require much time and the submission of a large amount of statistical data by many enterprises. The submission of this material will entail considerable friction with entrepreneurs. The judgment of the various projects will, moreover, require a degree of technical knowledge which is often absent in government offices. For these reasons we do not believe a sudden introduction of investment control to be desirable. Rather, investment control should grow more or less by itself. Industry itself will feel the need for it as it plans with an eye to the somewhat more distant future. Progress in this direction can be made in particular by the organization of various industries, with co-operation on the part of the government that should be to the advantage of both. By this process of co-operation, one can move beyond the stage at which government officials with inadequate technical knowledge either make incorrect decisions or are practically eliminated from the decisions. Gradually, the organizations on the part of industry will appreciate the contribution made by officials who have a more general point of view in economic policy than does the individual firm or industry; gradually also, the official agencies will become more expert by experience.

It has sometimes been mentioned as an objection against investment control that certain investments for which there is great need in a period of recovery would not be performed. This objection is fictitious, however, and in fact misses the point at issue. The objection is based on the assumption that the business cycle is something objective which has to be followed. But the very purpose of investment control is to influence the business cycle. Experience in World War II indicates clearly that the adaptability of the economy to investment control is much greater than was assumed before.

The weakness of investment control as a measure of business-cycle policy is that it may be effective in limiting investment in the boom but that it can contribute hardly anything to an expansion of activity in the depression. Its significance with respect to the depression is solely that, by correcting overly optimistic profit calculations in the boom, it may reduce disappointment and, hence, undue pessimism in the depression.

CONTROL OF THE PRODUCTION OF RAW MATERIALS

The second form of direct business-cycle policy to be discussed is the regulation of the production of raw materials. The selection of the production of raw materials to be regulated may be justified with two arguments. First, the production of raw materials is often sufficiently concentrated in large enterprises or in a small number of countries to make the regulation of production technically feasible. This applies in particular to the mineral raw materials, which are of the most importance for cyclical movements. Second, the output of finished articles is linked to the quantities of raw materials available, and a regulation of raw materials may therefore lead to some extent to a regulation of total production.

The great difficulty of this policy is to select the proper criterion for the regulation of the output of individual commodities. A complete stabilization of production at a constant level is, of course, never desirable. Nor, however, could one accept a general rate of increase that would be the same for all raw materials. It is probable that some articles should gradually displace others or, in any case, that the rate of growth for various raw materials should be different. How can one ascertain the proper rate of increase? Clearly not by maintaining constant the individual prices of all raw materials. A stable average price level is desirable, of course, but that does not imply stability of individual prices. The development of the cost of production of one material may be quite different from that of others. If the total demand for goods and services is regulated, the different prices and different rates of output will find their proper level more or less automatically by the reactions of the individual producers; the regulation of each of these individually implies a much greater possibility of mistakes or arbitrary decisions. Even if the total level of output of a given material is determined, there remains the question of the allocation of this total among different producers or different countries. Here again, there is the risk of rigidity, with the corollary of uneconomic production and waste.

Generally speaking, it would not seem impossible to us, with the help of a variety of statistical data, to achieve a reasonable regulation of the production of the various raw materials; but we doubt whether this would mean much as an effective business-cycle policy.

There are other objections to the control of raw materials as a form of business-cycle policy. The value of the output of raw materials is only a relatively small part of total output of all goods and services. The point of application which this policy provides with respect to total production is therefore too limited. There are many ways in which the production of final goods and of services can fluctuate with a constant level of production of raw materials. First, inventories may be used in times of excessive demand and be left to accumulate in periods of depression. Second, the production of articles involving relatively little raw material and much labor can be greatly expanded without any considerable curtailment of production in other directions by the withdrawal of raw materials.

Practical experience with the regulation of the production of raw materials shows, in the first place, that it is technically reasonably feasible, whenever the number of supplying countries is not very great, such as in the case of tin and rubber, or when production is highly cartelized, such as in the case of iron and steel. The criteria used in the past are, however, on the whole not particularly attractive from a general point of view. Understandably, the objective of regulation was generally the producers' interest, which was often the very opposite of the general interest. The regulation of production in practice amounted to restriction in order to obtain the highest possible price. When restriction was replaced by a policy of expansion of production, after the beginning of recovery or in the light of great wartime demand, producers followed the business cycle rather than attempting to regulate it. They could, admittedly, not have influenced the cycle much since the production under their control represented only a small fraction of the total world production of goods and services. The main importance of past control schemes is, therefore, that they have shown that regulation in this field is technically possible. This may be useful in other circumstances, but the usefulness of these policies should not be overestimated.

COMMERCIAL POLICY

A third method of the partial direct control of production is provided by measures of commercial policy, in particular the regulation by quotas of imports and, in some circumstances, exports. The objective of this measure is usually the regulation of activity in an individual country. The policy may be particularly important for the control of the business cycle if the country under consideration is dependent on raw materials for investment goods, for instance, if it imports its timber, iron ore, or raw iron or steel. The Netherlands is a good example of a country of this structure. By a quota system on the imports of these raw materials, it would be possible to influence investment activity and hence activity in general, to a considerable extent. Many of the objections against the regulation of investment, however, apply also to this form of economic policy; in particular the difficulty of selecting proper criteria. There is the further difficulty that the policy may be partly invalidated by the expansion of the domestic production of any available raw materials for investment.

Experience shows the technical possibility of applying quota regulations; but it also shows that they have usually been applied with quite other objectives than business-cycle control. Quota regulations initiated in the depression usually turned into measures of protection for the promotion of domestic manufacturing and were applied, therefore, in particular to manufactured products rather than to raw materials.

CONTROL OF THE CONSTRUCTION INDUSTRY

One industry that is particularly suitable for direct control is the construction industry. Technically, control of this industry permits little evasion, as construction activity can easily be observed. Other arguments in favor of control of this industry are that the period of production is relatively long and that the product of this industry has a very long lifetime. These two elements have a great importance with respect to the cycles in residential construction[1] since both of them reinforce the tendency toward fluctuations. An industry that has these tendencies toward a strong endogenous cycle, which tends to influence general activity, should be particularly desirable as an objective of control. Clearly, the price mechanism is not an adequate instrument to regulate the output of the construction industry; this applies in particular to residential construction.

As an instrument one can use construction permits, available in any case, which may be supplemented by a policy of providing systematic information to the building industry, and the resulting control by the industry itself.

The need for dwellings, which can be computed accurately on the basis of the distribution of the population, its income distribution, and its geographic distribution, provides a suitable criterion for the volume of output of this industry. This does not imply that building in each year should be equal to the increase in the need for dwellings. A certain reserve stock may be built up and maintained, which would guarantee that small deficiencies in production would not immediately lead to difficulties.

1. See p. 241, *supra*.

The production of dwellings may be regulated so as to stabilize either residential construction itself or the general business cycle as much as possible. The second criterion would imply that residential construction would be used partially to compensate fluctuations in other industries by an expansion, for instance, of residential construction in times of depression. We are touching here on the subject dealt with in chapter xxi.

The use of residential construction to stabilize the general business cycle is possible because the need for dwelling changes only gradually and especially because of the long lifetime of buildings; the stock of dwellings is always very large compared to its annual rate of increase, and the latter may therefore be manipulated for business-cycle purposes without any considerable percentage changes in the supply of dwelling services in any one year.

To the extent that an expansion of residential construction in the depression involves certain countries in balance of payments difficulties, a certain adaptation with respect to the raw materials used is often possible; countries short of timber may be able to shift in the direction of stone, brick, cement, and sometimes iron, in order to eliminate excessive use of timber.

CHAPTER TWENTY-THREE

SUMMARY: CHOICE OF AN OPTIMUM POLICY

WE HAVE found in chapters xiii and xvi that the movements of the variables that characterize the economy are determined by a combination of (*a*) certain disturbances of equilibrium resulting from changes in the data and (*b*) the reactions of the economic system. We pointed out in chapter xviii that the changes in the data which occur in this connection, such as changes in crops, political and technical events, etc., are usually inevitable. The harmful effects of these disturbances, each of which in itself is often unimportant, are due much more to the increase of these initial disturbances by the cumulative processes resulting from the responses of the economic system. The movements of the economic variables are determined by successive reactions, each of which is described by a specific economic relation; since each economic variable is determined by such a relation, there are as many relations as there are economic variables. Well-known examples of these relations are the demand relations and supply relations; a particularly simple example of an economic system is that of the hog market; a more realistic but still simple example of the economic system as a whole is given in our Example I, which uses the two relations of the formation of income and the use of income.

Since the economic relations determine the movements which follow from an initial disturbance of equilibrium, it will be clear that a particular objective with respect to these movements can be achieved only by making the relations satisfy certain specific conditions. It will not be possible to leave the relations as they are and yet to achieve a stable movement; for the relations as they are, are responsible for the cyclical movements as we have observed them. It will be necessary, therefore, to change one or more of these relations. It is an important question which relation it will be necessary to change. Is adjustment of one relation enough, or should more than one be adjusted? In which way should they be adjusted?

The forms of elementary business-cycle policy discussed in the four preceding chapters consisted usually in the change of one of the relations of the system. We shall analyze in this chapter which combination of these simple forms of policy is necessary to obtain the best composite business-cycle and trend policy. In other words, we shall have to make a choice and possibly a combination. It is clear that we should prefer that choice which would require the minimum number of changes in relations, yet which would still be adequate to achieve our purpose. The fewer the relations to be changed, the less difficulty will be encountered in introducing the policy. In Professor J. M. Clark's terms, we shall have to select the strategic factors to which to apply changes.

The relations among the various economic variables determine both the character of the fluctuating movements and the equilibrium level around which these fluctuations occur. Usually, the fluctuations are determined by the slopes of the lines that represent these relations in diagrams (or the coefficients in formulas) and by the lags that exist in the relations. The simplest example of the hog cycle shows this very clearly: the characteristics of the fluctuations are determined exclusively by the slopes of the demand and the supply curve and by the lag of supply behind changes in the price. The level around which fluctuations occur depends also on the level of the supply and demand curve. We shall deal in this chapter first with the requirements of stability and later with the requirements of a maximum level.

A distinction may be made between more important and less important relations. We count among the former at least those relations which entered in our Example I and which, so to speak, form the skeleton of the business-cycle mechanism. In the succeeding sections of chapter xiii, we introduced a number of other relations both with respect to commodities and with respect to the financial sphere, which were found to have a certain, but relatively minor, effect with respect to economic movements. The two major relations refer to the formation and the use of income; the two variables which they determine, national income and total expenditure (total demand for goods and services), are the two most important economic variables. These two variables primarily determine each other. For this reason we believe that the regulation of these two variables is of signal importance in the control of the fluctuations of economic developments. Most important is the regulation of the total demand for goods and services, that is to say, the regulation of the use of income; even if the formation of income is left free, no difficulties can arise, since stable total demand will inevitably produce stable income. Stable income, on the other hand, will lead with less certainty to stable demand; demand contains as a separate element the demand for reinvestment which is partially independent of national income, whereas new investment, too, contains a partially independent element. The regulation of the total demand for goods and services can be achieved most directly by compensating government expenditure. For these reasons, we consider this the most important individual form of economic policy.

None of the other individual forms of economic policy would by itself achieve as much stabilization. Thus, the regulation of investment operates primarily as a restraining policy; the same tendency is inherent in the regulation of the production of raw materials which, moreover, has too limited a point of application. The limitations of the various forms of indirect policy are even greater. The effect of a change in the rate of interest on total demand for goods is limited; the same applies to the effect of changes in the wage rate, because of the dual character of this rate as cost and income; a policy of flexible wages involves, moreover, a great deal of friction. Price policy in the form of exchange-rate policy may be quite effective for individual countries but not from a world point of view. Stock-exchange policy may be of consequence in countries where there are strong tendencies toward stock-exchange speculation, since it prevents the formation of speculative incomes and thus operates in the direction of more stable total income.

Any one of these forms of business-cycle policy has in any case some stabilizing influence, and it would be of some advantage to combine one or more of them with the regulation of total demand. In the choice of policy, much will depend on the structure of the country, the state of international co-operation, and the business-cycle position. In a situation where international co-operation is completely absent, a country with much foreign trade will be inclined to resort to exchange-rate policy, complemented perhaps by commercial policy; if there is full international co-operation, measures that will improve conditions in one country at the expense of those in other countries will have to be renounced. When there is a very strong private demand, it may be necessary to add direct control of investment and credit-rationing to a policy of compensating government expenditure. In some industries, such as residential construction, direct regulation may almost always be useful.

In the preceding paragraphs we have discussed the policies required for reduction of fluctuations and indicated that the latter were due to the slopes of the various economic relations and the lags existing in these relations. We have indicated also that the equilibrium level will depend both on the slopes and on the level of these relations. There is thus a set of data which do not affect the fluctuations but which do have an influence on the equilibrium level. Hence it is possible for economic policy to affect the equilibrium level, in addition to operating on fluctuations. It can even be shown that there are as many combinations of these level magnitudes in our relations as there are economic variables whose equilibrium level has to be determined. The equilibrium level of each economic variable can therefore be regulated separately. We shall have to formulate the conditions for the equilibrium levels so that the equilibrium level, or the equilibrium development, of the economy satisfies the objectives set out at the beginning of chapter xvii. Among the various policies, we will again give preference to those which leave free as many relations as possible.

As in the case of fluctuations, we shall consider first the most important relations, namely, again, the formation and use of income. In order not to enter too deeply into mathematical formulations, we shall put the question as follows: What lasting conditions should be satisfied by the formation and the use of income for the equilibrium level of production to coincide with a state of full employment?

The use of income will have to be such that, at the level of income corresponding to full employment, total investment plus total consumption equals national income. It is not possible to say exactly what this condition implies, since the factors determining investment and, to a lesser extent, saving are not known with sufficient certainty. Some of these factors may be mentioned, however. Investment tends to drop when there is a pronounced fall in the profitability of business, when there is an important fall in prices, and when there is uncertainty concerning the future. A surplus of saving will develop also if a country is saturated with investment. Such a situation is conceivable for a country which, compared with other countries, is at the top of technical development; it has often been assumed that this situation occurred in the United States around 1928. Stagnation may occur also if new investment is not profitable because of a disproportion between prices and costs, which is essentially a disproportion between prices and wages. This situation may also lead to the use of part of income in the capital market for the purchase of existing shares, thus pushing up share prices. Some economists have attributed the 1929 Stock Exchange boom to this cause. In order to maintain investment, it will be necessary to take measures to prevent a sharp decline, or too low a level, of the profitability of business, to prevent sharp price falls, and to prevent general business insecurity. Falls in profitability and in prices and, hence, insecurity may be reduced to much smaller proportions by the forms of business-cycle policy discussed in the preceding chapters. There remain, however, these two requirements: (*a*) the need to counteract the consequences of saturation and (*b*) the need of adequate profitability.

We now consider the conditions that apply to the formation of income. In order for income to continue at a level consonant with full employment, the receipts of business on the basis of the total demand for goods and services will need to be adequate to continue business. This implies that marginal enterprises do not operate at a loss or at least not at a loss greater than their fixed costs. This requirement is less rigorous than the requirement that new investment should be profitable; the latter implies not only that no losses are suffered but also that there is a certain profit. We are led back, therefore, to the condition that we had already derived with respect to the use of income, but from this point of view the requirement of profitability of new investment need not apply to marginal enterprises.

The two profitability requirements consist in the last analysis in a condition for the relation between prices and costs, with wages as the most important element in the latter. Essentially, therefore, the condition is one of the distribution of income. The difficulties that may arise here are, therefore, almost entirely in the social field. It is possible for labor to insist on a level of wages that is too high compared to the level of prices, so that (*a*) marginal enterprises would suffer excessively large losses and (*b*) new investment would become insufficiently profitable. This would occur if the transfer of real income to the workers by the increase in wages would make entrepreneurial activity insufficiently attractive in real terms. Hence, investment demand would decline, and perhaps decline more than the increase in consumer demand, as a result of which total demand would be insufficient to absorb total supply at current prices. There would therefore be losses and unemployment because of an inadequate level of investment.

If the wage rate which is consonant with full employment is lower than the wage that is desirable from the point of view of social justice, corrections will have to be found, not in an increase of the wage rate, but in an increase of other income elements of the working class, such as payments for absence due to sickness, free distribution of certain goods and services, etc. —these additions to labor income to be financed by taxes on profits of enterprise or on medium and high incomes. With respect to profit taxes, certain limits will also have to be observed in this respect. It is clear, therefore, that the conditions of full employment are most intimately connected with questions of social justice. An important point to be borne in mind in this connection is that the level of output and therefore the share of all classes in total consumption will be the larger, the nearer full employment is approximated, so that all classes of the community have an interest in full employment's being achieved.[1]

As we have mentioned, however, it may be possible, in countries with a very high level of income, that adequate investment will not come forward at any level of prices and wages whatever. In that situation it will be necessary to equalize income by means of taxation, in order to bring down the level of savings to the given level of investment possibilities.

In addition to these central conditions for full-employment equilibrium, there are other conditions of a more partial nature, relating to the proportions among the various parts of the economy. These conditions will usually be the same as the corresponding propositions of economic statics, such as the condition of the equality of price ratios and marginal utility ratios, the equality of marginal costs and prices, etc. We do not want to go more deeply into this matter. In general, we may say that if the main conditions for stability and full employment are fulfilled, these secondary conditions for the balancing of the parts of the economy with respect to each other may come about automatically by the operation of the free forces of the economy. Certain exceptions, such as residential construction, where the great lag in the process of adjustment and long lifetime of the products of the industry can lead to serious deviations, were mentioned before.

Special mention must also be made of the equilibrium of the balance of payments, in particular for a country heavily dependent on foreign trade. The rate of exchange for the currency should be such as to provide equilibrium among the permanent items in the balance of payments, that is to say, an equilibrium with the exclusion of items that are used to finance a deficit, such as gold payments, short-term credits, or unusually large long-term credits. In this field, again, statistical verification is very well possible.

1. The productivity of labor may be affected unfavorably by a level of employment so high that it leaves insufficient room for regular changes in jobs, etc. "Full employment" should be understood, in this context, as a level of employment which would leave room for such changes.

We may devote a few words to the consequences that might result from business-cycle policy based on a wrong diagnosis and to the measures to be taken to prevent such wrong diagnoses. These questions can best be discussed on the basis of concrete examples. We take as our first example a reduction in employment which is attributed to a cyclical recession but which, in fact, is due to too high a level of wages. Acting on the wrong diagnosis, the government will start to increase public expenditure, thus (we may assume) bringing employment back to the desired level but at the expense of the exhaustion of the foreign reserves of the country and by the creation of additional public debt and money. The proper remedy in this case would be a reduction in wages. Whereas in a real cyclical depression a recovery in private demand for goods and services will occur after a certain time, this recovery will not occur in the present case, except perhaps by chance. Hence the increase in debt and the creation of money will tend to go further and further, entailing the risk of inflation.

In order to prevent such improper policies, a careful analysis of facts will be necessary. In the case under consideration, one should have observed that the decline in activity was greatest, for instance, in the industries in which wages had increased most and particularly in branches with a high proportion of wages to total cost, whereas the characteristic of a cyclical depression is that the decline is greatest in the production of durable goods. In some cases, temporarily disturbing factors such as crop influences may obscure relations of this character; but the better one succeeds in separating influences such as those of fluctuations in crops on the formation of prices and on activity (and this is statistically possible), the shorter will be the period during which one is the victim of the wrong diagnosis. Similar considerations apply in the second case we want to discuss: the case in which a permanent reduction in sales abroad is the cause of a lack of employment, whereas the government believes the lack of employment to be due to a recession in the domestic cycle. The real remedy in this case would be an adaptation of the rate of exchange or, possibly, quota restrictions on imports. Here again, a thorough analysis of the causes of the decline in demand should bring about rapidly the proper understanding of the situation. The importance of such studies will be clear from these examples.

The consequences of a somewhat delayed reaction are less serious, provided that the delay is not more than a few months. It is true that by such delay no counterweight to the depression is given for a few months, but the chances are small that by this fact in itself the depression would assume very serious proportions. To prove this point, it will be necessary to refer again to our examples; with their help we can show that a short increase in the lag of expenditure with respect to income, provided that it is accompanied by a considerable reduction in the marginal propensity to spend as a result of a policy of compensating government expenditure, will lead to movements that are not dangerous in nature.

This may be illustrated by a calculation similar to those we used in our previous models. For this purpose we use again Example III″, assuming, as in that example, that the marginal propensity to spend equals 0.1 but assuming now that the lag between income and expenditure will not be one quarter but two quarters. According to the process with which the reader will by now be familiar, the accompanying figures will then be found.

EXAMPLE III″

Quarter	0	1	2	3	4	5	6	7	8	9
Expenditure			0	2	2	0	−2	−2	0	+1
Income	0	20	20	2	−16	−18	−4	+12	+16	+5
Increase in income		20	0	−18	−18	−2	+14	+16	+4	

The arrows from the income figures to the corresponding expenditure figures are now drawn to reflect a lag of two quarters. It will be noticed that the fluctuations of income are not affected unfavorably but even slightly favorably by this change. But if the lag were increased very much more, the movements would again become entirely different.

The proposition is often advanced that a business-cycle policy, to be successful, must start in one definite phase of the cycle. In its generality we must reject this proposition, if only because of its vagueness. In which phase the policy should be initiated will depend on the type of business-cycle policy and the objective aimed at, and in some cases it will be indifferent at what stage of the cycle the policy is begun.

Possible differences in objective are most important in this connection. We may mention two objectives which are mutually exclusive, namely, stabilization at an average level of activity and stabilization at a peak level of activity. If the first objective were pursued, it might reasonably be thought that the proper

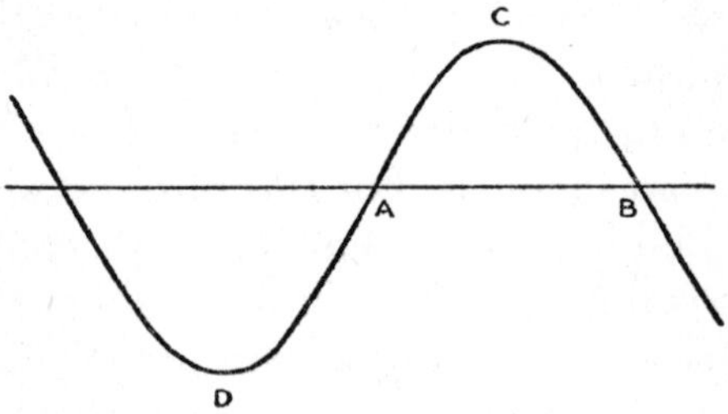

FIG. 55.—Alternative starting points for business-cycle policy

moment to initiate a policy would be when the activity curve is at its normal level. There are two such points in every cycle, namely, in Figure 55, points *A* and *B*—*A* in the recovery and *B* in the recession. Let us assume that the policy is started in *A* by restrictionist measures of such a character that production will follow the equilibrium line *AB* from there on out. This would achieve the objective with respect to production. But production cannot be considered independently of the other economic variables. At the time when production is at its normal level, certain other variables, such as the wage rate and the rate of interest, or the size of productive capacity, will not be at their normal levels. Certain further adjustments will therefore have to occur before the normal situation applies to all variables. These adaptations may in certain circumstances take the form of fluctuations, although probably minor fluctuations, if production itself is stabilized. Such fluctuations would indicate, nevertheless, that the business-cycle objective had not been immediately achieved, although this would not in itself be a very serious objection.

If it were desired to have an adaptation to the equilibrium development with the minimum of fluctuations, business-cycle policy should start before point *A*. The question, however, is how much before this point. This question can be answered only if one knows with sufficient accuracy the mechanism of cyclical movements, as we discussed that in our examples in chapter xiii. Only on the basis of a knowledge of this mechanism is it possible to decide whether adaptation will involve fluctuations or not. We cannot go too deeply into this question here. It will be clear to the reader, however, that the magnitude of the lags in the mechanism is a matter of fundamental importance in this connection. To take a very simple example: if it were desired to control the hog cycle by a regulation of the number of hogs to be fattened, the supply of marketable hogs and thereby the price would not be affected until more than half a year after the start of that policy.

Those who argue that, in order to obtain a gradual adaptation of production to the equilibrium level, the policy should necessarily start as early as the depression (that is to say, in point *D*) appear to assume a mechanism with very long lags. This point of view is somewhat akin to that of Hayek, who attributes investment maturing near point *C*, which involves an unduly large amount of capital, to an unusually low rate of interest in point *D*. We believe, however, that such long lags are exceptional and that it would be satisfactory to initiate the policy shortly before point *A*.

We must repeat, however, that the point at which a policy should be started depends on the objective and the nature of the particular policy; it will, moreover, often be more or less indifferent in which phase of the cycle a certain policy is started. It should not be believed that it will generally be possible to achieve the desired equilibrium development immediately. During the business cycle there is no single point that represents an equilibrium situation in all respects; for that reason, any adaptation will require a certain time. This applies also if the objective of business-cycle policy is selected, as we would select it, as the maintenance of a high rather than an average level. It is even more true in that situation that one cannot consider this policy as a continuation of one particular phase of the business cycle. The total volume of output at the peak of the cycle may be most in accordance with out objectives, but its composition and the level of prices are not optimal, and further adaptation will be required to reach a situation that is fully in accordance with the objectives of the policy.

INDEX

PRINTED IN U·S·A